Lecture Notes in Computer Science 8661

Commenced Publication in 1973
Founding and Former Series Editors:
Gerhard Goos, Juris Hartmanis, and Jan van Leeuwen

More information about this series at http://www.springer.com/series/7409

Sören Auer · Volha Bryl
Sebastian Tramp (Eds.)

Linked Open Data – Creating Knowledge Out of Interlinked Data

Results of the LOD2 Project

 Springer

Editors
Sören Auer
Institut für Informatik III
Rheinische Friedrich-Wilhelms-Universität
Bonn
Germany

Sebastian Tramp
University of Leipzig
Leipzig
Germany

Volha Bryl
University of Mannheim
Mannheim
Germany

ISSN 0302-9743
ISBN 978-3-319-09845-6
DOI 10.1007/978-3-319-09846-3

ISSN 1611-3349 (electronic)
ISBN 978-3-319-09846-3 (eBook)

Library of Congress Control Number: 2014945220

LNCS Sublibrary: SL3 – Information Systems and Applications, incl. Internet/Web, and HCI

Springer Cham Heidelberg New York Dordrecht London

Printed on acid-free paper

Springer is part of Springer Science+Business Media (www.springer.com)

Preface

This book presents an overview of the results of the research project 'LOD2 – Creating Knowledge out of Interlinked Data'. LOD2 is a large-scale integrating project co-funded by the European Commission within the FP7 Information and Communication Technologies Work Programme (Grant Agreement No. 257943). Commencing in September 2010, this 4-year project comprised leading Linked Open Data research groups, companies, and service providers from across 11 European countries and South Korea.

Linked Open Data (LOD) is a pragmatic approach for realizing the Semantic Web vision of making the Web a global, distributed, semantics-based information system. The aim of the LOD2 project was to advance the state of the art in research and development in four key areas relevant for Linked Data, namely 1. RDF data management; 2. the extraction, creation, and enrichment of structured RDF data; 3. the interlinking and fusion of Linked Data from different sources; and 4. the authoring, exploration, and visualization of Linked Data. The results the project has attained in these areas are discussed in the technology part of this volume, i.e., chapters 2–6. The project also targeted use cases in the publishing, linked enterprise data, and open government data realms, which are discussed in chapters 7–10 in the second part. The book gives an overview of a diverse number of research, technology, and application advances and refers the reader to further detailed technical information in the project deliverables and original publications. In that regard, the book is targeted at IT professionals, practitioners, and researchers aiming to gain an overview of some key aspects of the emerging field of Linked Data.

During the lifetime of the LOD2 project, Linked Data technology matured significantly. With regard to RDF and Linked Data management, the performance gap compared with relational data management was almost closed. Automatic linking, extraction, mapping, and visualization of RDF data became mainstream technology provided by mature open-source software components. Standards such as the R2RML RDB2RDF mapping language were defined and a vast number of small and large Linked Data resources (including DBpedia, LinkedGeoData, or the 10.000 publicdata. eu datasets) amounting to over 50 Billion triples are now available. The LOD2 project has driven and actively contributed to many of these activities. As a result, Linked Data is now ready to enter the commercial and large-scale application stage, as many commercial products and services (including the ones offered by the industrial LOD2 project partners) demonstrate.

In addition to the LOD2 project partners, who are authors and contributors of the individual chapters of this book, the project was critically accompanied and supported by a number of independent advisers and mentors including Stefano Bertolo (European Commission), Stefano Mazzocchi (Google), Jarred McGinnis (Logomachy), Atanas Kiryakov (Ontotext), SteveHarris (Aistemos), and Márta Nagy-Rothengass (European Commission). Furthermore, a large number of stakeholders engaged with the LOD2 project, for example, through the LOD2 PUBLINK initiatives, the regular LOD2 technology webinars, or the various events organized by the project. We are grateful for their support and feedback, without which the project as well as this book would not have been possible.

July 2014

Sören Auer
Volha Bryl
Sebastian Tramp

Contents

Introduction to LOD2

Sören Auer[(⊠)]

University of Bonn, Bonn, Germany
auer@informatik.uni-bonn.de

Abstract. In this introductory chapter we give a brief overview on the Linked Data concept, the Linked Data lifecycle as well as the LOD2 Stack – an integrated distribution of aligned tools which support the whole life cycle of Linked Data from extraction, authoring/creation via enrichment, interlinking, fusing to maintenance. The stack is designed to be versatile; for all functionality we define clear interfaces, which enable the plugging in of alternative third-party implementations. The architecture of the LOD2 Stack is based on three pillars: (**1**) Software integration and deployment using the Debian packaging system. (**2**) Use of a central SPARQL endpoint and standardized vocabularies for knowledge base access and integration between the different tools of the LOD2 Stack. (**3**) Integration of the LOD2 Stack user interfaces based on REST enabled Web Applications. These three pillars comprise the methodological and technological framework for integrating the very heterogeneous LOD2 Stack components into a consistent framework.

The Semantic Web activity has gained momentum with the widespread publishing of structured data as RDF. The Linked Data paradigm has therefore evolved from a practical research idea into a very promising candidate for addressing one of the biggest challenges in the area of intelligent information management: the exploitation of the Web as a platform for data and information integration as well as for search and querying. Just as we publish unstructured textual information on the Web as HTML pages and search such information by using keyword-based search engines, we are already able to easily publish structured information, reliably interlink this information with other data published on the Web and search the resulting data space by using more expressive querying beyond simple keyword searches. The Linked Data paradigm has evolved as a powerful enabler for the transition of the current document-oriented Web into a Web of interlinked Data and, ultimately, into the Semantic Web. The term Linked Data here refers to a set of best practices for publishing and connecting structured data on the Web. These best practices have been adopted by an increasing number of data providers over the past three years, leading to the creation of a global data space that contains many billions of assertions – the Web of Linked Data (cf. Fig. 1).

In that context LOD2 targets a number of research challenges: improve coherence and quality of data published on the Web, close the performance gap between relational and RDF data management, establish trust on the Linked

© The Author(s)
S. Auer et al. (Eds.): Linked Open Data, LNCS 8661, pp. 1–17, 2014.
DOI: 10.1007/978-3-319-09846-3_1

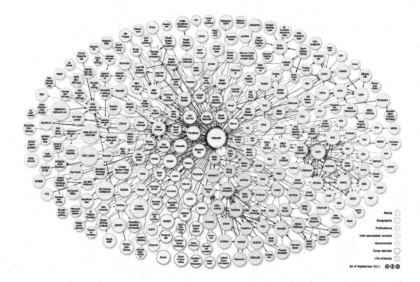

Fig. 1. Overview of some of the main Linked Data knowledge bases and their interlinks available on the Web. (This overview is published regularly at http://lod-cloud.net and generated from the Linked Data packages described at the dataset metadata repository ckan.net.)

Data Web and generally lower the entrance barrier for data publishers and users. The LOD2 project tackles these challenges by developing:

- enterprise-ready tools and methodologies for exposing and managing very large amounts of structured information on the Data Web.
- a testbed and bootstrap network of high-quality multi-domain, multi-lingual ontologies from sources such as Wikipedia and OpenStreetMap.
- algorithms based on machine learning for automatically interlinking and fusing data from the Web.
- adaptive tools for searching, browsing, and authoring of Linked Data.

The LOD2 project integrates and syndicates linked data with large-scale, existing applications and showcases the benefits in the three application scenarios publishing, corporate data intranets and Open Government Data.

The main result of LOD2 is the LOD2 Stack[1] – an integrated distribution of aligned tools which support the whole life cycle of Linked Data from extraction, authoring/creation via enrichment, interlinking, fusing to maintenance. The LOD2 Stack comprises new and substantially extended existing tools from the LOD2 partners and third parties. The major components of the LOD2 Stack are open-source in order to facilitate wide deployment and scale to knowledge bases with billions of triples and large numbers of concurrent users. Through

---

[1] After the end of the project, the stack will be called Linked Data Stack and maintained by other projects, such as GeoKnow and DIACHRON.

an agile, iterative software development approach, we aim at ensuring that the stack fulfills a broad set of user requirements and thus facilitates the transition to a Web of Data. The stack is designed to be versatile; for all functionality we define clear interfaces, which enable the plugging in of alternative third-party implementations. We also plan a stack configurer, which enables potential users to create their own personalized version of the LOD2 Stack, which contains only those functions relevant for their usage scenario. In order to fulfill these requirements, the architecture of the LOD2 Stack is based on three pillars:

- *Software integration and deployment using the Debian packaging system.* The Debian packaging system is one of the most widely used packaging and deployment infrastructures and facilitates packaging and integration as well as maintenance of dependencies between the various LOD2 Stack components. Using the Debian system also allows to facilitate the deployment of the LOD2 Stack on individual servers, cloud or virtualization infrastructures.
- *Use of a central SPARQL endpoint and standardized vocabularies for knowledge base access and integration between different tools.* All components of the LOD2 Stack access this central knowledge base repository and write their findings back to it. In order for other tools to make sense out of the output of a certain component, it is important to define vocabularies for each stage of the Linked Data life-cycle.
- *Integration of the LOD2 Stack user interfaces based on REST enabled Web Applications.* Currently, the user interfaces of the various tools are technologically and methodologically quite heterogeneous. We do not resolve this heterogeneity, since each tool's UI is specifically tailored for a certain purpose. Instead, we develop a common entry point for accessing the LOD2 Stack UI, which then forwards a user to a specific UI component provided by a certain tool in order to complete a certain task.

These three pillars comprise the methodological and technological framework for integrating the very heterogeneous LOD2 Stack components into a consistent framework. This chapter is structured as follows: After briefly introducing the linked data life-cycle in Sect. 1 and the linked data paradigm in Sect. 2, we describe these pillars in more detail (Sect. 3), and conclude in Sect. 4.

1 The Linked Data Life-Cycle

The different stages of the Linked Data life-cycle (depicted in Fig. 2) include:

Storage. RDF Data Management is still more challenging than relational Data Management. We aim to close this performance gap by employing column-store technology, dynamic query optimization, adaptive caching of joins, optimized graph processing and cluster/cloud scalability.

Authoring. LOD2 facilitates the authoring of rich semantic knowledge bases, by leveraging Semantic Wiki technology, the WYSIWYM paradigm (What You See Is What You Mean) and distributed social, semantic collaboration and networking techniques.

Fig. 2. Stages of the Linked Data life-cycle supported by the LOD2 Stack.

Interlinking. Creating and maintaining links in a (semi-)automated fashion is still a major challenge and crucial for establishing coherence and facilitating data integration. We seek linking approaches yielding high precision and recall, which configure themselves automatically or with end-user feedback.

Classification. Linked Data on thé Web is mainly raw instance data. For data integration, fusion, search and many other applications, however, we need this raw instance data to be linked and integrated with upper level ontologies.

Quality. The quality of content on the Data Web varies, as the quality of content on the document web varies. LOD2 develops techniques for assessing quality based on characteristics such as provenance, context, coverage or structure.

Evolution/Repair. Data on the Web is dynamic. We need to facilitate the evolution of data while keeping things stable. Changes and modifications to knowledge bases, vocabularies and ontologies should be transparent and observable. LOD2 also develops methods to spot problems in knowledge bases and to automatically suggest repair strategies.

Search/Browsing/Exploration. For many users, the Data Web is still invisible below the surface. LOD2 develops search, browsing, exploration and visualization techniques for different kinds of Linked Data (i.e. spatial, temporal, statistical), which make the Data Web sensible for real users.

These life-cycle stages, however, should not be tackled in isolation, but by investigating methods which facilitate a mutual fertilization of approaches developed to solve these challenges. Examples for such mutual fertilization between approaches include:

- The detection of mappings on the schema level, for example, will directly affect instance level matching and vice versa.
- Ontology schema mismatches between knowledge bases can be compensated for by learning which concepts of one are equivalent to which concepts of another knowledge base.

- Feedback and input from end users (e.g. regarding instance or schema level mappings) can be taken as training input (i.e. as positive or negative examples) for machine learning techniques in order to perform inductive reasoning on larger knowledge bases, whose results can again be assessed by end users for iterative refinement.
- Semantically enriched knowledge bases improve the detection of inconsistencies and modelling problems, which in turn results in benefits for interlinking, fusion, and classification.
- The querying performance of RDF data management directly affects all other components, and the nature of queries issued by the components affects RDF data management.

As a result of such interdependence, we should pursue the establishment of an improvement cycle for knowledge bases on the Data Web. The improvement of a knowledge base with regard to one aspect (e.g. a new alignment with another interlinking hub) triggers a number of possible further improvements (e.g. additional instance matches).

The challenge is to develop techniques which allow exploitation of these mutual fertilizations in the distributed medium Web of Data. One possibility is that various algorithms make use of shared vocabularies for publishing results of mapping, merging, repair or enrichment steps. After one service published its new findings in one of these commonly understood vocabularies, notification mechanisms (such as *Semantic Pingback* [11]) can notify relevant other services (which subscribed to updates for this particular data domain), or the original data publisher, that new improvement suggestions are available. Given proper management of provenance information, improvement suggestions can later (after acceptance by the publisher) become part of the original dataset.

The use of Linked Data offers a number of significant benefits:

- *Uniformity.* All datasets published as Linked Data share a uniform data model, the RDF statement data model. With this data model all information is represented in facts expressed as triples consisting of a subject, predicate and object. The elements used in subject, predicate or object positions are mainly globally unique identifiers (IRI/URI). Literals, i.e., typed data values, can be used at the object position.
- *De-referencability.* URIs are not just used for identifying entities, but since they can be used in the same way as URLs they also enable locating and retrieving resources describing and representing these entities on the Web.
- *Coherence.* When an RDF triple contains URIs from different namespaces in subject and object position, this triple basically establishes a link between the entity identified by the subject (and described in the source dataset using namespace A) with the entity identified by the object (described in the target dataset using namespace B). Through the typed RDF links, data items are effectively interlinked.
- *Integrability.* Since all Linked Data sources share the RDF data model, which is based on a single mechanism for representing information, it is very easy to attain a syntactic and simple semantic integration of different Linked Data

sets. A higher level semantic integration can be achieved by employing schema and instance matching techniques and expressing found matches again as alignments of RDF vocabularies and ontologies in terms of additional triple facts.

- *Timeliness.* Publishing and updating Linked Data is relatively simple thus facilitating a timely availability. In addition, once a Linked Data source is updated it is straightforward to access and use the updated data source, since time consuming and error prune extraction, transformation and loading is not required.

Table 1. Juxtaposition of the concepts Linked Data, Linked Open Data and Open Data.

Representation\degree of openness	Possibly closed	Open (cf. opendefinition.org)
Structured data model (i.e. XML, CSV, SQL etc.)	**Data**	**Open Data**
RDF data model (published as Linked Data)	**Linked Data** (LD)	**Linked Open Data** (LOD)

The development of research approaches, standards, technology and tools for supporting the Linked Data lifecycle data is one of the main challenges. Developing adequate and pragmatic solutions to these problems can have a substantial impact on science, economy, culture and society in general. The publishing, integration and aggregation of statistical and economic data, for example, can help to obtain a more precise and timely picture of the state of our economy. In the domain of health care and life sciences making sense of the wealth of structured information already available on the Web can help to improve medical information systems and thus make health care more adequate and efficient. For the media and news industry, using structured background information from the Data Web for enriching and repurposing the quality content can facilitate the creation of new publishing products and services. Linked Data technologies can help to increase the flexibility, adaptability and efficiency of information management in organizations, be it companies, governments and public administrations or online communities. For end-users and society in general, the Data Web will help to obtain and integrate required information more efficiently and thus successfully manage the transition towards a knowledge-based economy and an information society (Table 1).

2   The Linked Data Paradigm

We briefly introduce the basic principles of Linked Data (cf. Sect. 2 from [4]). The term Linked Data refers to a set of best practices for publishing and interlinking structured data on the Web. These best practices were introduced by

Tim Berners-Lee in his Web architecture note Linked Data[2] and have become known as the Linked Data principles. These principles are:

- Use URIs as names for things.
- Use HTTP URIs so that people can look up those names.
- When someone looks up a URI, provide useful information, using the standards (RDF, SPARQL).
- Include links to other URIs, so that they can discover more things.

The basic idea of Linked Data is to apply the general architecture of the World Wide Web [6] to the task of sharing structured data on global scale. The Document Web is built on the idea of setting hyperlinks between Web documents that may reside on different Web servers. It is built on a small set of simple standards: Uniform Resource Identifiers (URIs) and their extension Internationalized Resource Identifiers (IRIs) as globally unique identification mechanism [2], the Hypertext Transfer Protocol (HTTP) as universal access mechanism [3], and the Hypertext Markup Language (HTML) as a widely used content format [5]. Linked Data builds directly on Web architecture and applies this architecture to the task of sharing data on global scale.

2.1   Resource Identification with IRIs

To publish data on the Web, the data items in a domain of interest must first be identified. These are the things whose properties and relationships will be described in the data, and may include Web documents as well as real-world entities and abstract concepts. As Linked Data builds directly on Web architecture, the Web architecture term *resource* is used to refer to these *things of interest*, which are in turn identified by HTTP URIs. Linked Data uses only HTTP URIs, avoiding other URI schemes such as URNs [8] and DOIs[3]. The structure of HTTP URIs looks as follows:

[scheme:] [//authority] [path] [?query] [#fragment]

A URI for identifying Shakespeare's 'Othello', for example, could look as follows:

http://de.wikipedia.org/wiki/Othello#id

HTTP URIs provide a simple way to create globally unique names in a decentralized fashion, as every owner of a domain name or delegate of the domain name owner may create new URI references. They serve not just as a name but also as a means of accessing information describing the identified entity.

---

[2] http://www.w3.org/DesignIssues/LinkedData.html
[3] http://www.doi.org/hb.html

2.2 De-referencability

Any HTTP URI should be de-referencable, meaning that HTTP clients can look up the URI using the HTTP protocol and retrieve a description of the resource that is identified by the URI. This applies to URIs that are used to identify classic HTML documents, as well as URIs that are used in the Linked Data context to identify real-world objects and abstract concepts. Descriptions of resources are embodied in the form of Web documents. Descriptions that are intended to be read by humans are often represented as HTML. Descriptions that are intended for consumption by machines are represented as RDF data. Where URIs identify real-world objects, it is essential to not confuse the objects themselves with the Web documents that describe them. It is therefore common practice to use different URIs to identify the real-world object and the document that describes it, in order to be unambiguous. This practice allows separate statements to be made about an object and about a document that describes that object. For example, the creation year of a painting may be rather different to the creation year of an article about this painting. Being able to distinguish the two through use of different URIs is critical to the consistency of the Web of Data.

There are two different strategies to make URIs that identify real-world objects de-referencable [10]. In the *303 URI strategy*, instead of sending the object itself over the network, the server responds to the client with the HTTP response code 303 See Other and the URI of a Web document which describes the real-world object (*303 redirect*). In a second step, the client de-references this new URI and retrieves a Web document describing the real-world object. The *hash URI strategy* builds on the characteristic that URIs may contain a special part that is separated from the base part of the URI by a hash symbol (#), called the fragment identifier. When a client wants to retrieve a hash URI the HTTP protocol requires the fragment part to be stripped off before requesting the URI from the server. This means a URI that includes a hash cannot be retrieved directly, and therefore does not necessarily identify a Web document. This enables such URIs to be used to identify real-world objects and abstract concepts, without creating ambiguity [10].

Both approaches have their advantages and disadvantages [10]: Hash URIs have the advantage of reducing the number of necessary HTTP round-trips, which in turn reduces access latency. The downside of the hash URI approach is that the descriptions of all resources that share the same non-fragment URI part are always returned to the client together, irrespective of whether the client is interested in only one URI or all. If these descriptions consist of a large number of triples, the hash URI approach can lead to large amounts of data being unnecessarily transmitted to the client. 303 URIs, on the other hand, are very flexible because the redirection target can be configured separately for each resource. There could be one describing document for each resource, or one large document for all of them, or any combination in between. It is also possible to change the policy later on.

2.3   RDF Data Model

The RDF data model [7] represents information as sets of statements, which can be visualized as node-and-arc-labeled directed graphs. The data model is designed for the integrated representation of information that originates from multiple sources, is heterogeneously structured, and is represented using different schemata. RDF can be viewed as a *lingua franca*, capable of moderating between other data models that are used on the Web.

In RDF, information is represented in statements, called RDF triples. The three parts of each triple are called its subject, predicate, and object. A triple mimics the basic structure of a simple sentence, such as for example:

```
Burkhard Jung    is the mayor of    Leipzig
  (subject)        (predicate)      (object)
```

The following is the formal definition of RDF triples as it can be found in the W3C RDF standard [7].

Definition 1 (RDF Triple). Assume there are pairwise disjoint infinite sets I, B, and L representing IRIs, blank nodes, and RDF literals, respectively. A triple $(v_1, v_2, v_3) \in (I \cup B) \times I \times (I \cup B \cup L)$ is called an RDF *triple*. In this tuple, v_1 is the *subject*, v_2 the *predicate* and v_3 the *object*. We call $T = I \cup B \cup L$ the set of RDF terms.

The main idea is to use IRIs as identifiers for entities in the subject, predicate and object positions in a triple. Data values can be represented in the object position as literals. Furthermore, the RDF data model also allows in subject and object positions the use of identifiers for unnamed entities (called blank nodes), which are not globally unique and can thus only be referenced locally. However, the use of blank nodes is discouraged in the Linked Data context. Our example fact sentence about Leipzig's mayor would now look as follows:

```
<http://leipzig.de/id>
          <http://example.org/p/hasMayor>
                        <http://Burkhard-Jung.de/id> .
   (subject)         (predicate)           (object)
```

This example shows that IRIs used within a triple can originate from different namespaces thus effectively facilitating the mixing and mashing of different RDF vocabularies and entities from different Linked Data knowledge bases. A triple having identifiers from different knowledge bases at subject and object position can be also viewed as an typed link between the entities identified by subject and object. The predicate then identifies the type of link. If we combine different triples we obtain an RDF graph.

Definition 2 (RDF Graph). A finite set of RDF triples is called RDF graph. The RDF graph itself represents an resource, which is located at a certain location on the Web and thus has an associated IRI, the graph IRI.

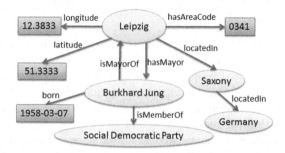

Fig. 3. Example RDF graph describing the city of Leipzig and its mayor.

An example of an RDF graph is depicted in Fig. 3. Each unique subject or object contained in the graph is visualized as a node (i.e. oval for resources and rectangle for literals). Predicates are visualized as labeled arcs connecting the respective nodes. There are a number of synonyms being used for RDF graphs, all meaning essentially the same but stressing different aspects of an RDF graph, such as *RDF document* (file perspective), *knowledge base* (collection of facts), *vocabulary* (shared terminology), *ontology* (shared logical conceptualization).

2.4 RDF Serializations

The initial official W3C RDF standard [7] comprised a serialization of the RDF data model in XML called *RDF/XML*. Its rationale was to integrate RDF with the existing XML standard, so it could be used smoothly in conjunction with the existing XML technology landscape. However, RDF/XML turned out to be difficult to understand for the majority of potential users because it requires to be familiar with two data models (i.e., the tree-oriented XML data model as well as the statement oriented RDF datamodel) and interactions between them, since RDF statements are represented in XML. As a consequence, with *N-Triples*, *Turtle* and *N3* a family of alternative text-based RDF serializations was developed, whose members have the same origin, but balance differently between readability for humans and machines. Later in 2009, *RDFa* (RDF Annotations, [1]) was standardized by the W3C in order to simplify the integration of HTML and RDF and to allow the joint representation of structured and unstructured content within a single source HTML document. Another RDF serialization, which is particularly beneficial in the context of JavaScript web applications and mashups is the serialization of RDF in JSON. Figure 4 presents an example serialized in the most popular serializations.

3   Integrating Heterogeneous Tools into the LOD2 Stack

The LOD2 Stack serves two main purposes. Firstly, the aim is to ease the distribution and installation of tools and software components that support the Linked

Data publication cycle. As a distribution platform, we have chosen the well established Debian packaging format. The second aim is to smoothen the information flow between the different components to enhance the end-user experience by a more harmonized look-and-feel.

3.1   Deployment Management Leveraging Debian Packaging

In the *Debian package management system* [9], software is distributed in architecture-specific binary packages and architecture-independent source code packages. A Debian software package comprises two types of content: **(1)** control information (incl. metadata) of that package, and **(2)** the software itself.

The control information of a Debian package will be indexed and merged together with all other control information from other packages available for the system. This information consists of descriptions and attributes for:

(a) The software itself (e.g. licenses, repository links, name, tagline, ...),
(b) Its relation to other packages (dependencies and recommendations),
(c) The authors of the software (name, email, home pages), and
(d) The deployment process (where to install, pre and post install instructions).

The most important part of this control information is its relations to other software. This allows the deployment of a complete stack of software with one action. The following dependency relations are commonly used in the control information:

Depends: This declares an absolute dependency. A package will not be configured unless all of the packages listed in its Depends field have been correctly configured. The Depends field should be used if the depended-on package is required for the depending package to provide a significant amount of functionality. The Depends field should also be used if the install instructions require the package to be present in order to run.

Recommends: This declares a strong, but not absolute, dependency. The Recommends field should list packages that would be found together with this one in all but unusual installations.

Suggests: This is used to declare that one package may be more useful with one or more others. Using this field tells the packaging system and the user that the listed packages are related to this one and can perhaps enhance its usefulness, but that installing this one without them is perfectly reasonable.

Enhances: This field is similar to Suggests but works in the opposite direction. It is used to declare that a package can enhance the functionality of another package.

Conflicts: When one binary package declares a conflict with another using a Conflicts field, dpkg will refuse to allow them to be installed on the system at the same time. If one package is to be installed, the other must be removed first.

N-Triples

```
1  <http://dbpedia.org/resource/Leipzig> <http://dbpedia.org/property/hasMayor>
2       <http://dbpedia.org/resource/Burkhard_Jung> .
3  <http://dbpedia.org/resource/Leipzig> <http://www.w3.org/2000/01/rdf-schema#label>
4       "Leipzig"@de .
5  <http://dbpedia.org/resource/Leipzig> <http://www.w3.org/2003/01/geo/wgs84_pos#lat>
6       "51.333332"^^<http://www.w3.org/2001/XMLSchema#float> .
```

Turtle

```
1  @prefix rdf: <http://www.w3.org/1999/02/22-rdf-syntax-ns#> .
2  @prefix rdfs="http://www.w3.org/2000/01/rdf-schema#> .
3  @prefix dbp="http://dbpedia.org/resource/> .
4  @prefix dbpp="http://dbpedia.org/property/> .
5  @prefix geo="http://www.w3.org/2003/01/geo/wgs84_pos#> .
6
7  dbp:Leipzig  dbpp:hasMayor  dbp:Burkhard_Jung ;
8               rdfs:label    "Leipzig"@de ;
9               geo:lat       "51.333332"^^xsd:float .
```

RDF/XML

```
1  <?xml version="1.0"?>
2  <rdf:RDF xmlns:rdf="http://www.w3.org/1999/02/22-rdf-syntax-ns#"
3                        xmlns:rdfs="http://www.w3.org/2000/01/rdf-schema#"
4          xmlns:dbpp="http://dbpedia.org/property/"
5                        xmlns:geo="http://www.w3.org/2003/01/geo/wgs84_pos#">
6   <rdf:Description rdf:about="http://dbpedia.org/resource/Leipzig">
7    <property:hasMayor rdf:resource="http://dbpedia.org/resource/Burkhard_Jung" />
8    <rdfs:label xml:lang="de">Leipzig</rdfs:label>
9    <geo:lat rdf:datatype="http://www.w3.org/2001/XMLSchema#float">51.3333</geo:lat>
10   </rdf:Description>
11  </rdf:RDF>
```

RDFa

```
1  <?xml version="1.0" encoding="UTF-8"?>
2  <!DOCTYPE html PUBLIC "-//W3C//DTD XHTML+RDFa 1.0//EN"
3       "http://www.w3.org/MarkUp/DTD/xhtml-rdfa-1.dtd">
4  <html version="XHTML+RDFa 1.0" xml:lang="en" xmlns="http://www.w3.org/1999/xhtml"
5          xmlns:rdf="http://www.w3.org/1999/02/22-rdf-syntax-ns#"
6                       xmlns:rdfs="http://www.w3.org/2000/01/rdf-schema#"
7          xmlns:dbpp="http://dbpedia.org/property/"
8                       xmlns:geo="http://www.w3.org/2003/01/geo/wgs84_pos#">
9   <head><title>Leipzig</title></head>
10   <body about="http://dbpedia.org/resource/Leipzig">
11    <h1 property="rdfs:label" xml:lang="de">Leipzig</h1>
12    <p>Leipzig is a city in Germany. Leipzig's mayor is
13        <a href="Burkhard_Jung" rel="dbpp:hasMayor">Burkhard Jung</a>. It is located
14           at latitude <span property="geo:lat" datatype="xsd:float">51.3333</span>.</p>
15   </body>
16  </html>
```

JSON-LD

```
1  {
2    "@context": {
3      "rdfs": "http://www.w3.org/2000/01/rdf-schema#",
4      "hasMayor": { "@id": "http://dbpedia.org/property/hasMayor", "@type": "@id" },
5      "Person": "http://xmlns.com/foaf/0.1/Person",
6         "lat": "http://www.w3.org/2003/01/geo/wgs84_pos#lat"
7    },
8    "@id": "http://dbpedia.org/resource/Leipzig",
9    "rdfs:label": "Leipzig",
10   "hasMayor": "http://dbpedia.org/resource/Burkhard_Jung",
11   "lat": { "@value": "51.3333", "@type": "http://www.w3.org/2001/XMLSchema#float"
12  }
```

Fig. 4. Different RDF serializations of three triples from Fig. 3

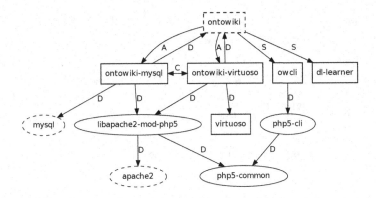

Fig. 5. Example DEB-package dependency tree (OntoWiki). Some explanation: Boxes are part of the LOD2 Stack, Ellipses are part of the Debian/Ubuntu base system, Dashed forms are meta-packages, Relations: Depends (D), Depends alternative list (A), Conflicts (C) and Suggests (S).

All of these relations may restrict their applicability to particular versions of each named package (the relations allowed are $<<$, $<=$, $=$, $>=$ and $>>$). This is useful in forcing the upgrade of a complete software stack. In addition to this, dependency relations can be set to a list of alternative packages. In such a case, if any one of the alternative packages is installed, that part of the dependency is considered to be satisfied. This is useful if the software depends on a specific functionality on the system instead of a concrete package (e.g. a mail server or a web server). Another use case of alternative lists are meta-packages. A meta-package is a package which does not contain any files or data to be installed. Instead, it has dependencies on other (lists of) packages.

Example of meta-packaging: OntoWiki.
To build an appropriate package structure, the first step is to inspect the manual deployment of the software, its variants and the dependencies of these variants. *OntoWiki* is a browser-based collaboration and exploration tool as well as an application for linked data publication. There are two clusters of dependencies: the runtime environment and the backend. Since OntoWiki is developed in the scripting language *PHP*, it's architecture-independent but needs a web server running PHP. More specifically, OntoWiki needs PHP5 running as an Apache 2 module. OntoWiki currently supports two different back-ends which can be used to store and query RDF data: *Virtuoso* and MySQL. Virtuoso is also part of the LOD2 Stack while *MySQL* is a standard package in all Debian-based systems. In addition to OntoWiki, the user can use the OntoWiki command line client *owcli* and the *DL-Learner* from the LOD2 Stack to enhance its functionality.

The dependency tree (depicted in Fig. 5) is far from being complete, since every component also depends on libraries and additional software which is omitted here. Given this background information, we can start to plan the packaging. We assume that users either use MySQL or Virtuoso as a backend on

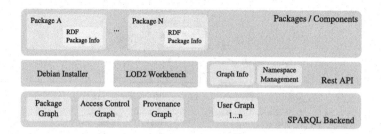

Fig. 6. Basic architecture of a local LOD2 Stack.

a server, so the first decision is to split this functionality into two packages: `ontowiki-mysql` and `ontowiki-virtuoso`. These two packages are abstracted by the meta-package `ontowiki`, which requires either `ontowiki-mysql` or `ontowiki-virtuoso`, and which can be used by other LOD2 Stack packages to require OntoWiki. Since both the MySQL backend and the Virtuoso backend version use the same system resources, we need to declare them as conflicting packages.

3.2 Data Integration Based on SPARQL, WebID and Vocabularies

The basic architecture of a local LOD2 Stack installation is depicted in Fig. 6. All components in the LOD2 Stack act upon RDF data and are able to communicate via SPARQL with the central system-wide RDF quad store (i.e. SPARQL backend). This quad store (Openlink Virtuoso) manages user graphs (knowledge bases) as well as a set of specific system graphs where the behaviour and status of the overall system is described. The following system graphs are currently used:

Package Graph:
In addition to the standard Debian package content, each LOD2 Stack package consists of a RDF package info which contains:

- The basic package description, e.g. labels, dates, maintainer info (this is basically DOAP data and redundant to the classic Debian control file)
- Pointers to the place where the application is available (e.g. the menu entry in the LOD2 Stack workbench)
- A list of capabilities of the packed software (e.g. resource linking, RDB extraction). These capabilities are part of a controlled vocabulary. The terms are used as pointers for provenance logging, access control definition and a future capability browser of the LOD2 workbench.

Upon installation, the package info is automatically added to the package graph to allow the workbench / demonstrator to query which applications are available and what is the user able to do with them.

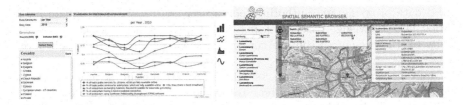

Fig. 7. The visualization widgets CubeViz (statistic) and SemMap (spatial data).

Access Control Graph:
This system graph is related to WebID[4] authentication and describes which users are able to use which capabilities and have access to which graphs. The default state of this graph contains no restrictions, but could be used to restrict certain WebIDs to specific capabilities. Currently, only OntoWiki takes this graph into account and the access control definition is based on the WebAccessControl schema[5].

Provenance Graph:
Each software package is able to log system wide provenance information to reflect the evolution of a certain knowledge base. Different ontologies are developed for that use-case. To keep the context of the LOD2 Stack, we use the controlled capability vocabulary as reference points.

In addition to the SPARQL protocol endpoint, application packages can use a set of APIs which allow queries and manipulation currently not available with SPARQL alone (e.g. fetching graph information and manipulating namespaces). Two authorized administration tools are allowed to manipulate the package and access control graphs:

- The Debian system installer application automatically adds and removes package descriptions during install / upgrade and remove operations.
- The LOD2 Workbench (Demonstrator) is able to manipulate the access control graph.

All other packages are able to use the APIs as well as to create, update and delete knowledge bases. Chapter 5 gives an comprehensive overview on the LOD2 Stack components.

3.3   REST Integration of User Interfaces

Many of the components come with their own user interface. For example, the Silk Workbench is a user interface for the Silk linking engine. This workbench supports the creation of linking specifications, executing them and improving them using the feedback from the user on the created links. With the OntoWiki

---

[4] http://www.w3.org/wiki/WebID
[5] http://www.w3.org/wiki/WebAccessControl

linked data browsing and authoring tool, a user can browse and update information in a knowledge base. By using both tools together, the user gains the ability to study the input sources' content structure and to create links between them.

Many stack components request similar information from the user. For example, selecting the graph of interest. To provide the end-user the feeling of a harmonized single application, we develop supportive REST-based WebAPIs. These APIs offer a common application view of the LOD2 Stack. The more tools support this API, the more harmonized and integrated the end-user experience gets. Currently, the LOD2 Stack WebAPI consists of:

- *Graph management*: The set of graphs is not easy to maintain. SPARQL does not support retrieval of all graphs. The only possible query which selects all graphs that have at least one triple is performance wise quite costly: `SELECT DISTINCT ?g WHERE GRAPH ?g ?s ?p ?o` The WebAPI also standardizes some meta information like *being a system graph*. When LOD2 Stack components use this common graph management WebAPI, the end-user obtains a uniform look-and-feel with respect to graph management.
- *Prefix management*: To make RDF resources more readable, prefixes are used to abbreviate URI namespaces. Typically, each application manages its own namespace mapping. Using this REST API, a central namespace mapping is maintained, thus producing consistency among stack components. The end-user is freed from updating the individual component mappings. Moreover, an update in one component is immediately available to another.

In addition to creating supportive REST-based APIs, the LOD2 Stack encourages component owners to open up their components using REST based WebAPIs. For example, the semantic-spatial browser, a UI tool that visualizes RDF data containing geospatial information on a map, is entirely configurable by parameters encoded within its invocation URL. Similarly other visualization and exploration widgets (such as the CubeViz statistical data visualization) can directly interact with the SPARQL endpoint (cf. Fig. 7). This makes it easy to integrate into (third party) applications into the stack.

4   Conclusion and Outlook

In this chapter we gave a brief introduction to Linked Data its management life-cycle on the Web and the LOD2 Stack, the result of a large-scale effort to provide technological support for the life-cycle of Linked Data. We deem this a first step in a larger research and development agenda, where derivatives of the LOD2 Stack are employed to create corporate enterprise knowledge hubs withing the Intranets of large companies. The overall stack architecture and guidelines can also serve as a blue-print for similar software stacks in other areas.

References

1. Adida, B., Birbeck, M., McCarron, S., Pemberton, S.: RDFa in XHTML: Syntax and processing - a collection of attributes and processing rules for extending XHTML to support RDF. W3C Recommendation, October 2008. http://www.w3.org/TR/rdfa-syntax/
2. Berners-Lee, T., Fielding, R.T., Masinter, L.: Uniform resource identifiers (URI): Generic syntax. Internet RFC 2396, August 1998
3. Fielding, R., Gettys, J., Mogul, J., Frystyk, H., Masinter, L., Leach, P., Berners-Lee, T.: Hypertext transfer protocol - http/1.1 (rfc 2616). Request for Comments. http://www.ietf.org/rfc/rfc2616.txt (1999). Accessed 7 July 2006
4. Heath, T., Bizer, C.: Linked data - evolving the web into a global data space. In: Hendler, J., van Harmelen, F. (eds.) Synthesis Lectures on the Semantic Web: Theory and Technology. Morgan & Claypool, San Rafael (2011)
5. HTML 5: A vocabulary and associated APIs for HTML and XHTML. W3C Working Draft, August 2009. http://www.w3.org/TR/2009/WD-html5-20090825/
6. Jacobs, I., Walsh, N.: Architecture of the world wide web, volume one. World Wide Web Consortium, Recommendation REC-webarch-20041215, December 2004
7. Klyne, G., Carroll, J.J.: Resource description framework (RDF): concepts and abstract syntax. Technical report W3C, 2 (2004)
8. Moats, R.: Urn syntax. Internet RFC 2141, May 1997
9. Murdock, I.: The Debian Manifesto (1994). http://www.debian.org/doc/manuals/project-history/ap-manifesto.en.html
10. Sauermann, L., Cyganiak, R.: Cool URIs for the semantic web. W3C Interest Group Note, December 2008
11. Tramp, S., Frischmuth, P., Ermilov, T., Auer, S.: Weaving a social data web with semantic pingback. In: Cimiano, P., Pinto, H.S. (eds.) EKAW 2010. LNCS (LNAI), vol. 6317, pp. 135–149. Springer, Heidelberg (2010)

Technology

Advances in Large-Scale
RDF Data Management

Peter Boncz[1], Orri Erling[2], and Minh-Duc Pham[1(✉)]

[1] CWI, Amsterdam, The Netherlands
{P.Boncz,duc}@cwi.nl
[2] OpenLink Software, Burlington, UK
erling@xs4all.nl

Abstract. One of the prime goals of the LOD2 project is improving
the performance and scalability of RDF storage solutions so that the
increasing amount of Linked Open Data (LOD) can be efficiently managed. Virtuoso has been chosen as the basic RDF store for the LOD2
project, and during the project it has been significantly improved by
incorporating advanced relational database techniques from MonetDB
and Vectorwise, turning it into a compressed column store with vectored
execution. This has reduced the performance gap ("RDF tax") between
Virtuoso's SQL and SPARQL query performance in a way that still
respects the "schema-last" nature of RDF. However, by lacking schema
information, RDF database systems such as Virtuoso still cannot use
advanced relational storage optimizations such as table partitioning or
clustered indexes and have to execute SPARQL queries with many self-
joins to a triple table, which leads to more join effort than needed in
SQL systems. In this chapter, we first discuss the new column store
techniques applied to Virtuoso, the enhancements in its cluster parallel
version, and show its performance using the popular BSBM benchmark
at the unsurpassed scale of 150 billion triples. We finally describe ongoing work in deriving an "emergent" relational schema from RDF data,
which can help to close the performance gap between relational-based
and RDF-based storage solutions.

1 General Objectives

One of the objectives of the LOD2 EU project is to boost the performance and
the scalability of RDF storage solutions so that it can, efficiently manage huge
datasets of Linked Open Data (LOD). However, it has been noted that given
similar data management tasks, relational database technology significantly out-
performed RDF data stores. One controlled scenario in which the two technologies can be compared is the BSBM benchmark [2], which exists equivalent
relational and RDF variants. As illustrated in Fig. 1, while the SQL systems
can process by up to 40–175K QMpH, the Triple stores can only reach 1–10K
QMpH, showing a factor of 15–40 of performances difference.

S. Auer et al. (Eds.): Linked Open Data, LNCS 8661, pp. 21–44, 2014.
DOI: 10.1007/978-3-319-09846-3_2

In the LOD2 project we investigated the causes of this large difference (the "RDF tax", i.e. the performance cost of choosing RDF instead of relational database technology). Here we identify three causes:

Table 12. Performance for multiple clients, 25M dataset (in QMpH).

Dataset size 25M	Number of clients				
	1	2	4	8	64
Sesame	1,343	1,485	1,204	1,300	1,271
Jena TDB	353	513	694	536	555
Jena SDB	968	1,346	1,021	883	927
Virtuoso TS	4,123	7,610	9,491	5,901	5,400
D2R Server	140	187	160	146	143
MySQL	18,578	31,093	39,647	40,599	40,470
Virtuoso SQL	69,585	85,146	135,097	173,665	148,813

Fig. 1. Triple stores vs. SQL: a heavy "RDF Tax" (2009)

- the particular case of BSBM is to the disadvantage of RDF as BSBM by its nature is very relational: its schema has just few classes, and all its properties occur exactly once for each subject, such that the data structure is very tabular. As such, the ease of use of SPARQL to formulate queries on irregularly structured data does not come into play, and the complications to which such irregular data leads in relational solutions (many more tables, and many more joins) are avoided.
- relational systems are quite mature in their implementations. For instance, the explore workload is an OLTP workload which relational systems target with key index structures and pre-compiled PL/SQL procedures. The BI workload of BSBM benefits from analytical execution techniques like columnar storage and vectorized execution and hash joins with bloom filters (to name just a few). While relational products over the years have implemented many such optimizations, RDF stores typically have not. Another area where analytical relational database engines have made important progress is the use of cluster technology. Whereas in 1990s only the very high end of RDBMS solutions was cluster-enabled (i.e. Teradata), many other systems have been added such as Greenplum, Paraccel, Vertica, SAP HANA and SQLserver Parallel data Warehouse (which without exceptional also leverage columnar storage and vectorized or JIT-compiled execution).
- RDF stores do not require a schema but also do not exploit it, even though the structure of the data in fact is highly regular. This hurts in particular in the very common SPARQL star-patterns, which need to be executed using multiple self-joins, where relational systems do not need joins at all. The structure that *is* heavily present in RDF triples further leads to the co-occurrence of properties to be heavily (anti-) correlated. The complexity of query optimization is not only exponential with respect to the amount of joins (and SPARQL needs many more than SQL) but also relies on cost models, yet cost models typically become very unreliable in the face of correlations. Unreliable cost models lead to bad query plans and this very strongly affects performance and scalability of RDF stores. In all, query optimization for SPARQL is both more costly and unreliable than for SQL.

Virtuoso6, a high-performance RDF Quad Store, was chosen as the main RDF store for LOD2 knowledge base at the start of the project. In order to reduce the "RDF tax", we first revised architectural ideas from the state-of-the-art of relational database systems, particularly, advanced column stores such as MonetDB [9] and Vectorwise [18]. Then, we brought some of the unique technologies and architectural principles from these column stores into Virtuoso7, making it work more efficiently on modern hardware. These techniques include tuning the access patterns of database queries to be CPU-cache conscious, and also making query processing amendable to deeply pipelined CPUs with SIMD instructions by introducing concepts like vector processing. We note that the insights gained in improving Virtuoso will also be useful for other RDF store providers to enhance their respective technologies as well.

Further, the cluster capabilities of Virtuoso were significantly improved. Note that by lack of table structures, RDF systems must distribute data by the triple (not tuple), which leads to more network communication during query execution. Network communication cost tends to be the limiting factor for parallel database systems, hence Virtuoso7 Cluster Edition introduced an innovative control flow framework that is able to hide network cost as much as possible behind CPU computation.

By the end of the LOD2 project, these improvements in Virtuoso7 on the BSBM BI workload strongly improved performance. A quantified comparison is hard as Virtuoso6 would not even complete the workload ("infinitely better" would be an exaggeration). Still, when comparing the SQL with the SPARQL implementation of BSBM-BI on Virtuoso7, we still see an "RDF tax" of a factor 2.5. This performance difference comes from the schema-last approach of RDF model: SPARQL plans need more joins than SQL and often the query plan is not optimal. To address this issue, CWI performed research in the line of the second bullet point above: the goal would be to give the RDF store more insight in the actual structure of RDF, such that SPARQL query plans need less self-joins and query optimization becomes more reliable. This goal should be achieved without losing the schema-last feature of RDF: there should be no need for an explicit user-articulated schema.

The idea of recovering automatically an "emergent" schema of actual RDF data is that RDF data in practice is quite regular and structured. This was observed in the proposal to make SPARQL query optimization more reliable by recognizing "characteristics sets" [10]. A characteristic set is a combination of properties that typically co-occur with the same subject. The work in [10] found that this number is limited to a few thousand on even the most complex LOD datasets (like DBpedia), and the CWI research on emergent schema detection that started in the LOD2 project [15] aims to further reduce the amount of characteristic sets to the point that characteristics sets become tables in a table of limited size (less than 100), i.e. further reducing the size. To that, the additional challenge of finding human-understandable labels (names) for tables, columns, and relationships was added. The goal of emergent schemata thus became two-fold: (1) to inform SPARQL systems of the schema of the data such that they need less self-joins and query optimization becomes more reliable, (2) to offer a fully relational view of an RDF dataset to end-users so that existing SQL applications can be leveraged on any RDF dataset. The latter goal could help to increase RDF adoption and further help make relational systems more semantic (because all tables, columns and relationships in an emergent schema are identified by URIs).

In all, this chapter shows tangible progress in reducing the "RDF tax" and a promising avenue to further reduce the performance gap between SPARQL and SQL systems and even some hope of making them converge.

2 Virtuoso Column Store

The objective of the Virtuoso7 column store release was to incorporate the state of the art in relational analytics oriented databases into Virtuoso, specifically for the use with RDF data. Ideally, the same column store engine would excel in both relational analytics and RDF.

Having RDF as a driving use case emphasizes different requirements from a purely relational analytics use case, as follows:

Indexed access. Some column stores geared purely towards relational analytics [18] obtain excellent benchmark scores without any use of index lookup, relying on merge and hash join alone. An RDF workload will inevitably have to support small lookups without setup cost, for which indexed access is essential.

Runtime data types. Runtime data typing is fundamental to RDF. There must be a natively supported any data type that can function as a key part in an index. Dictionary encoding all literal values is not an option, since short data types such all numbers and dates must be stored inline inside an index. This offers native collation order and avoids a lookup to a dictionary table, e.g. before doing arithmetic or range comparisons. This is a requirement for any attempt at near parity with schema-first systems. Thus dictionary encoding is retained only for strings.

Multi-part and partitionable indices. Many early column stores [9] were based on an implicit row number as a primary key. Quite often this would be dense and would not have to be materialized. Such a synthetic row number is however ill suited to a scale-out RDF store as a globally unique row number for a partitioned column is hard to be maintained. Thus, Virtuoso does not have any concept of row number but rather has multi-part sorted column-wise compressed indices for all persistent data structures. In this, Virtuoso most resembles [1,7]. This structure is scale-out friendly since partitioning can be determined by any high cardinality key part and no global synthetic row number needs to exist, even as an abstraction.

Adaptive compression. Column stores are renowned for providing excellent data compression. This comes from having all the values in a column physically next to each other. This means that values, even in a runtime typed system, tend to be of the same type and to have similar values. This is specially so for key parts where values are ascending or at least locally ascending for non-first key parts. However, since a single column (specially for the RDF object column) will store all the object values of all triples, there can be no predeclared hints for type or compression. Different parts of the column will have radically different data types, data ordering and number of distinct values. Thus local environment is the only indication available for deciding on compression type.

Transactionality. While a column-wise format is known to excel for read-intensive workloads and append-style insert, RDF, which trends to index quads at least from S to O and the reverse. Thus with one index there can be mostly ascending insert but there is no guarantee of order on the other index. Also row-level locking needs to be supported for transactional applications. This is by and large not an OLTP workload but short transactions must still be efficient. Thus Virtuoso departs from the typical read-intensive optimization of column stores that have a separate delta structure periodically merged into a read-only column-wise compressed format [7,18]. Virtuoso updates column-wise compressed data in place, keeping locks positionally and associating rollback information to the lock when appropriate. Thus there is no unpredictable latency having to do with flushing a write optimized delta structure to the main data. While doing so, Virtuoso has excellent random insert performance, in excess of the best offered by Virtuoso's earlier row store.

As a result of these requirements, Virtuoso uses a sparse row-wise index for each column-wise stored index. The row wise index is a B-Tree with one row for anywhere between 2000 to 16000 rows. This entry is called the row-wise leaf. To each row-wise leaf corresponds a segment of each column in the table. Each segment has an equal number of values in each column. Consecutive segments tend to be of similar size. When values are inserted into a segment, the segment will split after reaching a certain size, leading to the insertion of a new row-wise leaf row. This may cause the row-wise leaf page to split and so forth. Each column segment is comprised of one or more compression entries. A compression entry is a sequence of consecutive values of one column that share the same compression. The compression entry types are chosen based on the data among the following:

- **Run length.** Value and repeat count
- **Array.** Consecutive fixed length (32/64 nbit) or length prefixed strings
- **Run length delta.** One starting value followed by offsets and repeat counts for each offset
- **Bitmap.** For unique closely spaced integers, there is a start value and a one bit for each consecutive value, the bit position gives the offset from start value
- **Int delta.** From a start value, array of 16 bit offsets
- **Dictionary.** For low cardinality columns, there is a homogenous or heterogeneous array of values followed by an array of indices into the array. Depending on the distinct values, the index is 4 or 8 bits.

Using the Virtuoso [5] default index scheme with two covering indices (PSOG and POSG) plus 3 distinct projections (SP, OP, GS), we obtain excellent compression for many different RDF datasets. The values are in bytes per quad across all the five indices, excluding dictionary space for string literals.

| BSBM: 6 bytes | DBpedia: 9 bytes | Uniprot: 6 bytes | Sindice crawl: 14 bytes |

DBpedia has highly irregular data types within the same property and many very differently sized properties, thus compresses less. Uniprot and BSBM are highly regular and compress very well. The web crawl consists of hundreds of millions of graphs of 20 triples each, thus the graph column is highly irregular and less compressible, accounting for the larger space consumption. However one typically does not reference the graph column in queries, so it does not take up RAM at runtime.

2.1   Vectored Execution

A column store is nearly always associated with bulk operators in query execution, from the operator at a time approach of MonetDB [9] to vectored execution [4,7,18]. The idea is to eliminate query interpretation overhead by passing many tuples between operators in a query execution pipeline. Virtuoso is no exception, but it can also run vectored plans for row-wise structures. The main operators are index lookup and different variations of hash, from hash join to group by. An index lookup receives a vector of key values, sorts them, does a log(n) index lookup for the first and subsequently knows that all future matches will be to the right of the first match. If there is good locality, an index lookup is indistinguishable from a merge join. The added efficiency of vectoring is relative to the density of hits. Considering that over a million rows are typically under one row-wise leaf page (e.g. 16K rows per segment * 70 segments per page), there is a high likelihood that the next hit is within the next 16K or at least within the next 1M rows, hence there is no need to restart the index lookup from the tree top.

Hash based operations use a memory-only linear hash table. This is essentially the same hash table for hash join, group by and distinct. The hash table consists of a prime number of fixed size arrays that are aligned by CPU cache line. Different fields of a 64 bit hash number give the array and a place in the array. The entry is either found at this place or within the same cache line or is not in the hash table. If a cache line is full and the entry does not match, there is an extra exceptions list which is typically short. One can determine the absence of a value with most often one cache miss. Only if the line is full does one need to consult the exceptions, leading to a second cache miss. Since the hash operations are all vectored, prefetch is used to miss multiple consecutive locations in parallel. Further, if the hash table contains pointers to entries instead of single fixed length integers, the high bits of the pointer are used to contain a filed of the hash number. Thus one does not dereference a pointer to data unless the high bits of the pointer (not used for addressing) match the high bits of the hash number. In this way cache misses are minimized and each thread can issue large numbers of cache misses in parallel without blocking on any.

Further, Bloom filters are used for selective hash joins. We have found that a setting of 8 bits per value with 4 bits set gives the best selectivity. Typically the Bloom filter drops most of non-matching lookup keys before even getting to the hash table.

2.2   Vector Optimizations

Virtuoso can adjust the vector size at runtime in order to improve locality of reference in a sparse index lookup. Easily 30 % of performance can be gained if looking for 1M instead of 10K consecutive values. This comes from higher density of hits in index lookup. The vector size is adaptively set in function of available memory and actually observed hit density.

2.3   Query Optimization

All the advanced execution techniques described so far amount to nothing if the query plan is not right. During the last year of LOD2 we have made a TPC-H implementation to ensure that all state of the art query optimization techniques are present and correctly applied. TPC-H is not an RDF workload but offers an excellent checklist of almost all execution and optimization tricks [3].

The goal of LOD2 is RDF to SQL parity but such parity is illusory unless the SQL it is being compared to is on the level with the best. Therefore having a good TPC-H implementation is a guarantee of relevance plus opens the possibility of Virtuoso applications outside of the RDF space. Details are discussed in [13].

In the following we cover the central query optimization principles in Virtuoso.

Sampling. Virtuoso does not rely on up-front statistics gathering. Instead, the optimizer uses the literals in queries to sample the database. The results of sampling are remembered for subsequent use. In RDF, there is an indexed access path for everything. Thus if leading P, S or O are given, the optimizer can just look at how many hits there in the index. The hits, if numerous, do not have to be counted. Counting the number of hits per page and number of pages is accurate enough. Also, within each RDF predicate, there is a count of occurrences of the predicate, of distinct S's, distinct O's and G's. These allow estimating the fan-out of the predicate, e.g. a `foaf:name` has one O per S and `foaf:knows` has 100 O's per S. Also we recognize low cardinality properties, e.g. there is one city per person but 1M persons per city.

The statistics interact with runtime support of inference. Thus in one inference context, if tag is a super-property of about and mentions, but there are no triples with tag, the statistics automatically drill down to the sub-properties and sum these up for the super-property. This is however scoped to the inference context.

There can be conditions on dependent part columns, e.g. if P, S and G are given, G is likely a dependent part since in PSOG there is O between the leading parts and G. Thus sampling is used to determine the frequency of a specific G within a fixed P, S. The same is done for relational tables where there in fact are dependent columns that do not participate in ordering the table.

Cost Model. It has been recently argued [17] that SPARQL can be optimized just as well or even better without a cost model. We do not agree with this due to the following: It is true that a cost model has many complexities and possibilities for error. However, there are things that only a cost model can provide, in specific, informed decision on join type.

There is a definite break-even point between hash join and vectored index lookup. This is tied to the input counts on either side of the join. Both the number of rows on the build and the probe sides must be known in order to decide whether to use hash join. Also, when building the hash table, one has to put as many restrictions as possible on the build side, including restrictive joins. To get this right, a cost model of one kind or another is indispensable. The choice hinges on quantities, not on the structure of the query. If the goal is only to do look-ups efficiently, then one can probably do without a cost model. But here the goal is to match or surpass the best, hence a cost model, also for RDF is necessary even though it is very complex and has a high cost of maintenance. It is also nearly impossible to teach people how to maintain a cost model. Regardless of these factors, we believe that one is indispensable for our level of ambition.

2.4   State of the RDF Tax

We refer to the performance difference between a relational and RDF implementation of a workload as the RDF tax. This has been accurately measured with the Star Schema Benchmark (SSB) [12], a simplified derivative of TPC-H. While Virtuoso does TPC-H in SQL [13] on a par with the best, the RDF translation of all the query optimization logic is not yet complete, hence we will look at SSB.

SSB has one large fact table (*line order*) and several smaller dimension tables (*part*, *supplier*, *dw_date*, *nation* and *region*). The schema is denormalized into a simple star shape. Its RDF translation is trivial; each primary key of each table is a URI, each column is a property and each foreign key is a URI.

SSB was run at 30G scale on a single server with Virtuoso, MonetDB and MySQL. In SQL, Virtuoso beats MonetDB by a factor of 2 and MySQL by a factor of 300 (see Table 1). In SPARQL, Virtuoso came 10–20 % behind MonetDB but still 100x ahead of MySQL. These results place the RDF tax at about 2.5x in query execution time. Thanks to Virtuoso's excellent query performance, SPARQL in Virtuoso will outperform any but the best RDBMS's in analytics even when these are running SQL.

All plans consist of a scan of the fact table with selective hash joins against dimension tables followed by a simple aggregation or a group by with relatively few groups, e.g. YEAR, NATION. In the RDF variant, the fact table scan becomes a scan of a property from start to end, with the object, usually a foreign key, used for probing a hash table built from a dimension table. The next operation is typically a lookup on another property where the S is given by the first and the O must again satisfy a condition, like being in a hash table.

The RDF tax consists of the fact that the second column must be looked up by a self join instead of being on the same row with the previous column. This is

Table 1. Star Schema Benchmark with scales 30 GB and 300 GB (in seconds)

Query	30 GB					300 GB		
	Virtuoso SQL	Virtuoso SPARQL	RDF tax	MonetDB	MySQL	Virtuoso SQL	Virtuoso SPARQL	RDF tax
Q1	0.413	1.101	2.67	1.659	82.477	2.285	7.767	3.40
Q2	0.282	0.416	1.48	0.5	74.436	1.53	3.535	2.31
Q3	0.253	0.295	1.17	0.494	75.411	1.237	1.457	1.18
Q4	0.828	2.484	3.00	0.958	226.604	3.459	6.978	2.02
Q5	0.837	1.915	2.29	0.648	222.782	3.065	8.71	2.84
Q6	0.419	1.813	4.33	0.541	219.656	2.901	8.454	2.91
Q7	1.062	2.33	2.19	5.658	237.73	5.733	15.939	2.78
Q8	0.617	2.182	3.54	0.521	194.918	2.267	6.759	2.98
Q9	0.547	1.29	2.36	0.381	186.112	1.773	4.217	2.38
Q10	0.499	0.639	1.28	0.37	186.123	1.44	4.342	3.02
Q11	1.132	2.142	1.89	2.76	241.045	5.031	12.608	2.51
Q12	0.863	3.77	4.37	2.127	241.439	4.464	15.497	3.47
Q13	0.653	1.612	2.47	1.005	202.817	2.807	4.467	1.59
Total	8.405	21.989	2.62	17.622	2391.55	37.992	100.73	2.65

the best case for the RDF tax, as the execution is identical in all other respects. There are some string comparisons, e.g. brand contains a string but these are put on the build side of a hash join and are not run on much data.

In a broader context, the RDF tax has the following components:

Self-joins. If there are conditions on more than one column, every next one must be fetched via a join. This is usually local and ordered but still worse than getting another column. In a column store, predicates on a scan can be dynamically reordered based on their observed performance. In RDF, this is not readily feasible as it would alter the join order.

Cardinality estimation. In a multi-column table one can sample several predicates worth in one go, in RDF this requires doing joins in the cost model and is harder. Errors in cost estimation build up over many joins. Accurate choice of hash vs index based join requires reliable counts on either side. In SQL analytics, indices are often not even present, hence the join type decision is self-evident.

Optimization search space. A usage pattern of queries with tens of triple patterns actually hitting only a few thousand triples leads to compilation dominating execution times. A full exploration of all join orders is infeasible, as this is in the order of factorial of the count of tables and there can easily be 30 or 40 tables. Reuse of plans when the plans differ only in literals is a possibility and has been tried. This is beneficial in cases but still needs to revalidate if the cardinality estimates still hold with the new literal values. Exploring plans with many joins pushed to the build side of a hash join further expands the search space.

String operations. Since RDF is indexed many ways and arbitrary strings are allowed everywhere, implementations store unique strings in a dictionary and a specially tagged reference to the dictionary in the index. Going to the dictionary makes a scan with a *LIKE* condition extremely bad, specially if each string is distinct. Use of a full text index is therefore common.

URI's. For applications that do lookups, as most RDF applications do, translating identifiers to their external, usually very long, string form is an RDF-only penalty. This can be alleviated by doing this as late as possible but specially string conditions on URI's are disastrous for performance.

Indexing everything. Since there is usually an indexed access path for everything, space and time are consumed for this. TPC-H 100G loads in SQL in 15 min with no indices other than the primary keys. The 1:1 RDF translation takes 12 h. This is the worst case of the RDF tax but is limited to bulk load. Update intensive OLTP applications where this would be worse still are generally not done in RDF. Of course nobody forces one to index everything but this adds complexities to query optimization for cases where the predicate is not known at compile time.

Runtime data typing. This is a relatively light penalty since with vectored execution it is possible to detect a homogenous vector at runtime and use a typed data format. If a property is all integers, these can be summed by an integer-specific function. This usually works since RDF often comes from relational sources. DBpedia is maybe an exception with very dirty data, but then it is not large, hence the penalty stays small.

Lack of schema. There is usually no schema or the data does not comply with it. Therefore optimizations like late projection that are safe in SQL are not readily applicable. If you take the 10 youngest people and return their birth date, name and address you cannot defer getting the name and address after the top 10 since there might be people with many names or no names etc. These special cases complicate the matter but optimizations having to do with top k order are still possible. Similarly dependencies inside grouping columns in a group by cannot be exploited because one does not know that these are in fact functional even if the schema claims so.

Many of these penalties fall away when leaving the triple table format and actually making physical tables with columns for single valued properties. The exceptions may still be stored as triples/quads, so this does not represent a return to schema-first. Physical design, such as storing the same data in multiple orders becomes now possible since data that are alike occupy their own table. Also n:m relationships with attributes can be efficiently stored in a table with a multi-part key while still making this look like triples.

This is further analyzed in a later section of this chapter. Implementation in Virtuoso is foreseen in the near future.

3   Virtuoso Cluster Parallel

Virtuoso's scale out capability has been significantly upgraded during LOD2. The advances are as follows:

Elastic partitions. The data is sharded in a large number of self-contained partitions. These partitions are divided among a number of database server processes and can migrate between them. Usually each process should have one partition per hardware thread. Queries are parallelized to have at most one thread per partition. Partitions may split when growing a cluster. Statistics are kept per partition for detecting hot spots.

Free-form recursion between partitions. One can write stored procedures that execute inside a partition and recursively call themselves in another partition, ad infinitum. This is scheduled without deadlocking or running out of threads. If a procedure waits for its descendant and the descendant needs to execute something in the waiting procedure's partition, the thread of the waiting procedure is taken over. In this way a distributed call graph never runs out of threads but still can execute at full platform parallelism. Such procedures can be transparently called from queries as any SQL procedures, the engine does the partitioning and function shipping transparently.

Better vectoring and faster partitioning. Even the non-vectored Virtuoso cluster combined data for several tuples in messages, thus implementing a sort of vectoring at the level of interconnect while running scalar inside the nodes. Now that everything is vectored, the architecture is simpler and more efficient.

More parallel control flows. The basic query execution unit in cluster is a series of cross partition joins, called DFG (distributed fragment). Each set of co-located joins forms a stage of the DFG pipeline. Each stage runs one thread per partition if there is work to do in the partition. The results are partitioned again and sent onwards. The DFG ends by returning vectors of query variable bindings to the query coordinator or by feeding them in an aggregation. An aggregation itself will be partitioned on the highest cardinality grouping key if the cardinality is high enough. A subsequent DFG can pick the results of a previous partitioned aggregation and process these through more joins again with full platform utilization.

Different parallel hash joins. Tables are usually partitioned and in the case of RDF always partitioned. However, if a hash join build side is small, it is practical to replicate this into every server process. In this way, what would be a non-collocated join from foreign key to primary key becomes collocated because the hash table goes to its user. However, if the probe key is also the partitioning key of the probe, there is never a need to replicate because the hash table can be partitioned to be collocated with the probe without replicating. If the hash table would be large but the probe key is not the partitioning key of the probing operator, the hash table can still be partitioned. This will require a message exchange (a DFG stage). However, this is scalable since each server will only host a fraction of the whole hash table. Selective hash joins have Bloom filters. Since the Bloom filter is much smaller than the hash table itself, it can be replicated on all nodes even if the hash table is not. This allows most of the selectivity to take place before the inter-partition message exchange (DFG stage).

With SSB, the cluster shows linear throughput gains: 10x the data takes 5x longer on twice the hardware (see Table 1). This is the case for either RDF or SQL. The RDF tax is the same for cluster as for single server, as one would expect.

3.1 Performance Dynamics

Running complex queries such as the BSBM BI workload makes high use of cross partition joins (DFG) and of nested subqueries. This is a DFG inside a DFG, where the innermost DFG must run to completion before the invoking stage of the calling DFG can proceed. An existence test containing a non-collocated set of joins is an example of such pattern.

We find that message scheduling that must keep track of distributed dependencies between computations becomes a performance bottleneck. Messages can be relatively fragmented and numerous. Scheduling a message involves a critical section that can become a bottleneck. In subsequent work this critical section has been further split. The scheduling itself is complex since it needs to know which threads are waiting for which operations and whether a descendant operation ought to take over the parent's thread or get its own.

All the techniques and observed dynamics apply identically to RDF and SQL but are worse in RDF because of more joins. Use of hash joins and flattening of subqueries alleviates many of these problems. Hash joins can save messages by replicating the hash table, so there are messages only when building the hash table. In a good query plan this is done on far less data than probing the hash table.

3.2 Subsequent Development

Virtuoso is at present an excellent SQL column store. This is the prerequisite for giving RDF performance that is comparable with the best in relational data warehousing.

The next major step is storing RDF in tables when regular structure is present. This will be based on the CWI research, described in the next section. Query plans can be made as for triples but many self-joins can be consolidated at run time in into a table lookup when the situation allows. Cost model reliability will also be enhanced since this will know about tables and can treat them as such.

4   BSBM Benchmark Results

The BSBM (Berlin SPARQL Benchmark) was developed in 2008 as one of the first open source and publicly available benchmarks for comparing the performance of storage systems that expose SPARQL endpoints such as Native RDF stores, Named Graph stores, etc. The benchmark is built around an e-commerce use case, where a set of products is offered by different vendors and consumers have posted reviews about products. BSBM has been improved over this time and is current on release 3.1 which includes both Explore and Business Intelligence use case query mixes, the latter stress-testing the SPARQL1.1 group-by and aggregation functionality, demonstrating the use of SPARQL in complex analytical queries. To show the performance of Virtuoso cluster version, we present BSBM results [2] on the V3.1 specification, including both the Explore (transactional) and Business Intelligence (analytical) workloads (See the full BSBM V3.1 results for all other systems[1]).

We note that, comparing to the previously reported BSBM report[2] for 200M triples dataset, this BSBM experiment against 50 and 150 billion triple datasets on a clustered server architecture represents a major step (750 times more data) in the evolution of this benchmark.

4.1 Cluster Configuration

We selected the CWI scilens[3] cluster for these experiments. This cluster is designed for high I/O bandwidth, and consists of multiple layers of machines. In order to get large amounts of RAM, we used only its "bricks" layer, which contains its most powerful machines. Virtuoso V7 Column Store Cluster Edition was set up on 8 Linux machines. Each machine has two CPUs (8 cores and hyper threading, running at 2 GHz) of the Sandy Bridge architecture, coupled with 256 GB RAM and three magnetic hard drives (SATA) in RAID 0 (180 MB/s sequential throughput). The machines were connected through an InfiniBand Switch (Mellanox MIS5025Q). The cluster setups have 2 processes per machine, 1 for each CPU. A CPU has its own memory controller which makes it a NUMA node. CPU affinity is set so that each server process has one core dedicated to the cluster traffic reading thread (i.e. dedicated to network communication) and the other cores of the NUMA node are shared by the remaining threads. The reason for this set-up is that communication tasks should be handled with high-priority, because failure to handle messages delays all threads. These experiments have been conducted over many months, in parallel to the Virtuoso V7 Column Store Cluster Edition software getting ready for release. Large part of the effort spent was in resolving problems and tuning the software.

---

[1] http://wifo5-03.informatik.uni-mannheim.de/bizer/berlinsparqlbenchmark/results/V7/index.html

[2] http://wifo5-03.informatik.uni-mannheim.de/bizer/berlinsparqlbenchmark/results/V6/index.html

[3] This cluster is equipped with more-than-average I/O resources, achieving an Amdahl number >1. See www.scilens.org.

4.2 Bulk Loading RDF

The original BSBM data generator was a single-threaded program. Generating 150B triples with it would have taken weeks. We modified the data generator to be able to generate only a subset of the dataset. By executing the BSBM data generator in parallel on different machines, each generating a different part of the dataset, BSBM data generation has become scalable. In these experiments we generated 1000 data files, and then distributed them to each machine according to the modulo of 8 (i.e., the number of machine) so that files number 1, 9, ... go to machine 1, file number 2, 10, ... go to machine 2, and so on. This striping of the data across the nodes ensures a uniform load, such that all nodes get an equal amount of similar data (Table 2).

Table 2. BSBM data size and loading statistic

nr triples	Size (.ttl)	Size (.gz)	Database Size	Load Time
50 Billion	2.8 TB	240 GB	1.8 TB	6h 28m
150 Billion	8.5 TB	728 GB	5.6 TB	n/a

Each machine loaded its local set of files (125 files), using the standard parallel bulk-load mechanism of Virtuoso. This means that multiple files are read at the same time by the multiple cores of each CPU. The best performance was obtained with 7 loading threads per server process. Hence, with two server processes per machine and 8 machines, 112 files were being read at the same time. Also notice that in a cluster architecture there is constant need for communication during loading, since every new URIs and literals must be encoded identically across the cluster; hence shared dictionaries must be accessed. Thus, a single loader thread counts for about 250 % CPU across the cluster. The load was non-transactional and with no logging, to maximize performance. Aggregate load rates of up to 2.5M quads per second were observed for periods of up to 30 min. The total loading time for the dataset of 50 billion triples is about 6 h 28 min, which makes the average loading speed 2.14M triples per second.

The largest load (150B quads) was slowed down by one machine showing markedly lower disk write throughput than the others. On the slowest machine iostat showed a continuous disk activity of about 700 device transactions per second, writing anything from 1 to 3 MB of data per second. On the other machines, disks were mostly idle with occasional flushing of database buffers to disk producing up to 2000 device transactions per second and 100 MB/s write throughput. Since data is evenly divided and 2 of 16 processes were not runnable because the OS had too much buffered disk writes, this could stop the whole cluster for up to several minutes at a stretch. Our theory is that these problems were being caused by hardware malfunction.

To complete the 150B load, we interrupted the stalling server processes, moved the data directories to different drives, and resumed the loading again. The need for manual intervention, and the prior period of very slow progress makes it hard to calculate the total time it took for the 150B load.

4.3   Notes on the BI Workload

The test driver can run with single-user run or multi-user run, simulating the cases that one user or multiple users concurrently execute query mixes against the system under test.

All BSBM BI runs were with minimal disk IO. No specific warm-up was used and the single user run was run immediately following a cold start of the multi-user run. The working set of BSBM BI is approximately 3 bytes per quad in the database. The space consumption without literals and URI strings is 8 bytes with Virtuoso column store default settings. For a single user run, typical CPU utilization was around 190 of 256 core threads busy. For a multi-user run, all core threads were typically busy. Hence we see that the 4 user run takes roughly 3 times the real time of the single user run.

4.4   Benchmark Results

The following terms will be used in the tables representing the results.

- *Elapsed runtime* (seconds): the total runtime of all the queries excluding the time for warm-up runs.
- *Throughput*: the number of executed queries per hour. *Throughput = (Total # of executed queries) * (3600 / ElapsedTime) * scaleFactor*. Here, the scale factor for the 50 billion triples dataset and 150 billion triples dataset is 500 and 1500, respectively.
- *AQET*: Average Query Execution Time (seconds): The average execution time of each query computed by the total runtime of that query and the number of executions: *AQET(q) = (Total runtime of q) / (number of executions of q)*.

BI Use Case. Table 3 shows the results for the BI workload. Some results seem noisy, for instance Q2@50B, Q4@50B, Q4@150B are significantly cheaper in the multi-client-setup. Given the fact that the benchmark was run in drill-down mode, this is unexpected. It could be countered by performing more runs, but, this would lead to very large run-times as the BI workload has many long-running queries.

In the following, we discuss the above performance result over the query Q2. Further discussion on other queries can be found in [6].

```
SELECT ?otherProduct ?sameFeatures {
?otherProduct a bsbm:Product .
FILTER(?otherProduct != %Product%)
{SELECT ?otherProduct (COUNT(?otherFeature) AS ?sameFeatures) {
    %Product% bsbm:productFeature ?feature .
    ?otherProduct bsbm:productFeature ?otherFeature .
    FILTER(?feature=?otherFeature)
} GROUP BY ?otherProduct}}
ORDER BY DESC(?sameFeatures) ?otherProduct LIMIT 10
```

Table 3. BI Use Case: detailed results (Jan. 2013)

	50 Billion triples		150Billion triples	
	Single-Client	4-Clients	Single-Client	4-Clients
runtime	3733s	9066s	12649s	29991s
Tput	12.052K	19.851K	10.671K	18.003K
	AQET	AQET	AQET	AQET
Q1	622.80s	1085.82	914.39s	1591.37s
Q2	189.85s	30.18	196.01s	507.02s
Q3	337.64s	2574.65	942.97s	8447.73s
Q4	18.13s	6.3s	183.00s	125.71s
Q5	187.60s	319.75s	830.26s	1342.08s
Q6	47.64s	34.67s	24.45s	191.42s
Q7	36.96s	39.37s	58.63s	94.82s
Q8	256.93s	583.20s	1030.73s	1920.03s

Table 4. BI Use Case: updated results (Mar. 2013)

	50 Billion triples	
	Single-Client	4-Clients
runtime	1988s	4690s
Tput	22.629K	38.375K
	AQET	AQET
Q1	58.93	72.26
Q2	2.15	20.14
Q3	449.42	656.52
Q4	36.35	75.09
Q5	95.37	312.33
Q6	0.31	25.85
Q7	7.72	27.96
Q8	154.47	292.77

BSBM BI Q2 is a lookup for the products with the most features in common with a given product. The parameter choices (i.e., %Product%) produce a large variation in run times. Hence the percentage of the query's timeshare varies according to the repetitions of this query's execution. For the case of 4-clients, this query is executed for 4 times which can be the reason for the difference timeshare between single-client and 4-client of this query.

The benchmark results in the Table 3 are taken from our experiments running in January 2013. With more tuning in the Virtuoso software, we have re-run the benchmark with the dataset of 50B triples. The updated benchmark results in Table 4 show that the current version of Virtuoso software, namely Virtuoso7-March2013, can run the BSBM BI with a factor of 2 faster than the old version (i.e., the Virtuoso software in January). Similar improvement on the benchmark results is also expected when we re-run the benchmark with the dataset of 150B triples.

Explore Use Case. We now discuss the performance results in the Explore workload. We notice that these 4-client results seem more noisy than the single-client results and therefore it may be advisable in future benchmarking to also use multiple runs for multi-client tests. What is striking in the Explore results is that Q5 (see the query below) dominates execution time (Tables 5 and 6).

```
SELECT DISTINCT ?product ?productLabel WHERE {
    ?product rdfs:label ?productLabel .
    FILTER (%ProductXYZ% != ?product)
    %ProductXYZ% bsbm:productFeature ?prodFeature .
    ?product bsbm:productFeature ?prodFeature .
    %ProductXYZ% bsbm:productPropertyNumeric1 ?origProp1 .
    ?product bsbm:productPropertyNumeric1 ?simProp1 .
    FILTER (?simProp1<(?origProp1+120) && ?simProp1>(?origProp1-120))
    %ProductXYZ% bsbm:productPropertyNumeric2 ?origProp2 .
```

Table 5. Explore Use Case: detailed results

Table 6. Explore Use Case results: query mixes per hour

	50 Billion triples		150Billion triples	
	Single-Client	4-Clients	Single-Client	4-Clients
runtime	931s	15s	1894s	29s
	(100 runs)	(1 run)	(100 runs)	(1 run)
Tput	4.832M	11.820M	7.126M	18.386M
	AQET	AQET	AQET	AQET
Q1	0.066s	0.415s	0.113s	0.093s
Q2	0.045s	0.041s	0.066s	0.086s
Q3	0.112s	0.091s	0.111s	0.116s
Q4	0.156s	0.102s	0.308s	0.230s
Q5	3.748s	6.190s	8.052s	9.655s
Q7	0.155s	0.043s	0.258s	0.360s
Q8	0.100s	0.021s	0.188s	0.186s
Q9	0.011s	0.010s	0.011s	0.011s
Q10	0.147s	0.020s	0.201s	0.242s
Q11	0.005s	0.004s	0.006s	0.006s
Q12	0.014s	0.019s	0.013s	0.010s

	Single Client	4-Clients
50B	4253.157	2837.285
150B	2090.574	1471.032

```
?product bsbm:productPropertyNumeric2 ?simProp2 .
    FILTER (?simProp2<(?origProp2+170) && ?simProp2>(?origProp2-170))
} ORDER BY ?productLabel LIMIT 5
```

Q5 asks for the 5 most similar products to one given product, based on two numeric product properties (using range selections). It is notable that such range selections might not be computable with the help of indexes; and/or the boundaries of both 120 and 170 below and above may lead to many products being considered 'similar'. Given the type of query, it is not surprising to see that Q5 is significantly more expensive than all other queries in the Explore use case (the other queries are lookups that are index computable. – this also means that execution time on them is low regardless of the scale factor). In the Explore use case, most of the queries have the constant running time regardless of the scale factor, thus computing the throughput by multiplying the qph (queries per hour) with the scale factor may show a significant increase between the cases of 50 billion and 150 billion triples. In this case, instead of the throughput metric, it is better to use another metric, namely qmph (number of query mixes per hour).

5   Emergent Schemas

In this section, we describe solutions for deriving an *emergent relational schema* from RDF triples, that one could liken to an UML class diagram. These solutions have been implemented in the RDF parser of the open-source research column store, MonetDB, which we call MonetDB/RDF. A more extensive description of this work can be found in [8].

Our problem description is as follows. Given a (very) large set of RDF triples, we are looking an emergent schema that describes this RDF data consisting of *classes* with their *attributes* and their *literal types*, and the *relationships* between classes for URI objects, but:

(a) the schema should be *compact*, hence the amount of classes, attributes and relationships should be as small as possible, such that it is easily understood by humans, and data does not get scattered over too many small tables.

(b) the schema should have *high coverage*, so the great majority of the triples in the dataset should represent an attribute value or relationship of a class. Some triples may not be represented by the schema (we call these the "non-regular" triples), but try to keep this loss of coverage small, e.g. <10%.

(c) the schema should be *precise*, so the amount of *missing* properties for any subject that is member of such an recognized class is minimized.

Our solution is based on finding *Characteristic Sets* (CS) of properties that co-occur with the same subject. We obtain a more compact schema than [10], by using the TF/IDF (Term Frequency/Inverted Document Frequency) measure from information retrieval [16] to detect *discriminative* properties, and using semantic information to *merge* similar CS's. Further, a schema graph of CS's is created by analyzing the co-reference relationship statistics between CS's.

Given our intention to provide users an easy-to-understand emergent schema, our second challenge is to determine logical and short *labels* for the classes, attributes and relationships. For this we use ontology labels and class hierarchy information, if present, as well as CS co-reference statistics, to obtain class, attribute and relational labels.

5.1   Step1: Basic CS Discovery

Exploring CS's. We first identify the basic set of CS's by making one pass through all triples in the SPO (Subject, Predicate, Object) table created after bulk-loading of all RDF triples. These basic CS's are secondly further split out into combinations of (property, literal-type), when the object is a literal value. Thus, for each basic CS found, we may have multiple CS variants, one for each combination of occurring literal types. We need the information on literal types because our end objective is RDF storage in relational tables, which allow only a single type per column.

Exploring CS Relationships. A foreign key (FK) relationship between two CS's happens when a URI property of one CS typically refers in the object field to members of one other CS (object-subject references). Therefore, we make a second pass over all triples with a non-literal object, look up which basic CS the reference points, and count the frequencies of the various destination CS's.

5.2   Step2: Dimension Tables Detection

There tends to be a long tail of infrequently occurring CS's, and as we want a compact schema, the non-frequent CS's should be pruned. However, a low-frequency

CS which is referred to many times by high-frequency CS's in fact represents important information of the dataset and should be part of the schema. This is similar to a *dimension table* in a relational data warehouse, which may be small itself, but may be referred to by many millions of tuples in large fact tables, over a foreign key. However, detecting dimension tables should not be handled just based on the number of *direct* relationship references. The relational analogy here are *snowflake* schemas, where a finer-grained dimension table like NATION refers to an even smaller coarse-grained dimension table CONTINENT. To find the transitive relationships and their relative importance, we use the recursive PageRank [14] algorithm on the graph formed by all CS's (vertexes) and relationships (edges). As a final result, we mark low-frequency CS's with a high rank as "dimension" tables, which will protect them later from being pruned.

5.3   Step3: Human-Friendly Labels

When presenting humans with a UML or relational schema, short labels should be used as aliases for machine-readable and unique URIs for naming classes, attributes and relationships. For assigning labels to CS's, we exploit both structural and semantic information (ontologies).

Type Properties. Certain specific properties (e.g., rdf:type) explicitly specify the *class* or *concept* a subject belongs to. By analyzing the *frequency distribution* of different RDF type property values in the triples that belong to a CS, we can find a class label for the CS. As ontologies usually contain *hierarchies*, we create a histogram of type property values per CS that is aware of hierarchies. The type property value that describes most of the subjects in the CS, but is also as specific as possible is chosen as the URI of the class. If a ontology class URI is found, we can use its label as the CS's label. In Fig. 3, the value "Ship" is chosen.

Ontologies. Even if no type property is present in the CS, we can still try to match a CS to an ontology class. We compare the property set of the CS with the property sets of ontology classes using the TF/IDF similarity score [16]. This method relies on identifying "discriminative" properties, that appear in few ontology classes only, and whose occurrence in triple data thus gives a strong hint for the membership of a specific class. An example is shown in Fig. 2.

The ontology class correspondence of a CS, if found, is also used to find labels for properties of the CS (both for relationships and literal properties).

Relationships between CS's. If the previous approaches do not apply, we can look at which other CS's refer to a CS, and then use the URI of the referring property to derive a label. For example, a CS that is referred as <*author*> indicates that this CS represents instances of a <*Author*> class. We use the most frequent relationship to provide a CS label. Figure 4 shows an example of such "foreign key" names.

URI shortening. If the above solutions cannot provide us a link to ontology information, for providing attribute and relationship labels we resort to a

CS₂
rdf:type
gor:validFrom
gor:validThrough
gor:hasCurrency
gor:hasCurrencyValue
gor:hasUnitOfMeasurement
gor:valueAddedTaxIncluded
gor:eligibleTransactionVolume
(prefix gor:
http://purl.org/goodrelations/v1#)

PriceSpecification
gor:description
gor:name
gor:eligibleTransactionVolume
gor:validFrom
gor:validThrough
gor:hasCurrency
gor:hasCurrencyValue
gor:hasUnitOfMeasurement
gor:valueAddedTaxIncluded
gor:hasMaxCurrencyValue
gor:hasMinCurrencyValue

Fig. 2. Example CS vs. ontology class

Level	Type	%
0	Thing	100
1	MeanOfTransportation	100
2	Ship	97
2	Automobile	2
2	SpaceShuttle	1

Fig. 3. CS type property values

FK name	#CS	#tuples
instrument	3	93532
author	1	5

Fig. 4. References to a CS

practical fall-back, based on the observation that often property URI values do convey a hint of the semantics. That is, for finding labels of CS properties we shorten URIs (e.g., http://purl.org/goodrelations/v1#offers becomes offers), by removing the ontology prefix (e.g., http://purl.org/goodrelations/v1#) or simply using the part after the last slash, as suggested by [11].

5.4   Step4: CS Merging

To have a compact schema, we further reduce the number of tables in the emergent relational schema by merging CS's, using either *semantic* or *structural* information.

Semantic Merging. We can merge two CS's on semantic grounds when both CS class labels that we found were based on ontology information. Obviously, two CS's whose label was created using the same ontology class URI represent the same concept, and thus can be merged. If the labels stem from *different* ontology classes we can observe the subclass hierarchy and identify the common concept/class shared by both CS's (e.g., <Athlete> is a common class for <BasketballPlayer> and <BaseballPlayer>), if any, and then justify whether these CS's are similar based on the "generality" of the concept. Here the "generality" score of a concept is computed by the percentage of instances covered by it and its subclasses among all the instances covered by that ontology. Two CS's whose labels share a non-general ancestor in an ontology class hierarchy can be merged.

Structural Merging. The structural similarity between two CS's can be assessed by using the set of properties in each CS and the found relationships to them with other CS's. As original class can be identified based on "discriminating" properties (based on TF/IDF scoring), we merge two CS if their property sets have a high TF/IDF similarity score. Additionally, as a subject typically refers to only one specific entity via a property, we also merge two CS's which are both referred from the same CS via the same property.

5.5   Step5: Schema and Instance Filtering

We now perform final post-processing to clean up and optimize both the schema and the data instances in it. At part of this phase, all RDF triples are visited again, and either become stored in relational tables (typically >90 % of the triples, which we consider regular), and the remainder gets stored separately in a PSO table. Hence, our final result is a set of relational tables with foreign keys between them, and a single triple table in PSO format.

Filtering small tables. After the merging process, most of these merged classes (i.e., surviving merged CS's) cover a large amount of triples. However, it may happen that some classes still cover a limited number of RDF subjects, (i.e. less than 0.1 of all data). As removing these classes will only marginally reduce coverage, we remove them from the schema (except classes that were recognized as dimension tables with the described PageRank method). All triples of subjects belonging to these classes will be moved to the separate PSO table.

Maximizing type homogeneity. Literal object values corresponding to each attribute in a class can have several different types e.g., number, string, date-Time, etc. The relational model can only store a single type in each column, so in case of type diversity multiple columns will be used for a single property. As the number of columns can be large just due to a few triples having the wrong type (dirty data), we minimize this number by filtering out all the infrequent literal types (types that appear in less than 5 % of all object values) for each property. The triples with infrequent literal types are moved to the separate PSO table.

Minimizing the number of infrequent columns. Infrequent columns are those that have lots of NULL values. If the property coverage is less than a certain threshold value (i.e., 5 %), that property is infrequent and all the RDF triples of that property are treated as irregular data and moved to the separate PSO table.

Filtering the relationships. We further filter out *infrequent* or "dirty" relationships between classes. A relationship between cs_i and cs_j is infrequent if the number of references from cs_i to cs_j is much smaller than the frequency of cs_i (e.g., less than 1 % of the CS's frequency). A relationship is considered dirty if most but not all the object values of the referring class (e.g., cs_i) refer to the instances of the referred class (cs_j). In the former case, we simply remove the relationship information between two classes. In the latter case, the triples in cs_i that do not refer to cs_j will be filtered out (placed in the separate PSO table).

Multi-valued attributes. The same subject may have 0, 1 or even multiple triples with the same property, which in our schema leads to an attribute with cardinality >1. While this is allowed in UML, direct storage of such values is not possible in relational databases. Practitioners handle this by creating a separate table that contains the primary key (subject oid) and the value (which given literal type diversity may be multiple columns). The MonetDB/RDF system does this, but only creates such separate storage if really necessary. That is, we analyze the mean number of object values (*meanp*) per property. If the *meanp* of a property p is not much greater than 1 (e.g., less than 1.1), we consider p as a single-valued property and only keep the first value of that property while moving all the triples with other object values of this property to the non-structural part of the RDF dataset. Otherwise, we will add a table for storing all the object values of each multi-valued property.

5.6   Final Schema Evaluation

For evaluating the quality of the final schema, we have conducted extensive experiments over a wide range of real-world and synthetic datasets (i.e., DBpedia[4], PubMed[5], DBLP[6], MusicBrainz[7], EuroStat[8], BSBM[9], SP2B[10], LUBM[11] and WebDataCommons[12]). The experimental results in Table 7 show that we can derive a compact schema from each dataset with a relative small number of tables. We see that the synthetic RDF benchmark data (BSBM, SP2B, LUBM) is fully relational, and also all dataset with non-RDF roots (PubMed, MusicBrainz, EuroStat) get >99 % coverage. Most surprisingly, the RDFa data that dominates WebDataCommons and even DBpedia are more than 90 % regular.

Table 7. Number of tables and coverage percentage after merging & filtering steps

Datasets	Number of tables				Coverage – Metric C (%)		
	before merging		after	remove	remove	prune	final
	basic CS's	frequent CS's	merging	small tables	small tables	infrequent prop.	schema
Pubmed	3340	1754	14	10	99.99	99.74	**99.72**
DBpedia	472244	213851	517	298	94.12	91.73	**90.82**
BSBM	51	51	8	8	100	100	**100.00**
DBLP	251	181	9	6	99.99	99.68	**99.60**
SP2B	554	410	13	9	99.99	99.65	**99.65**
MusicBrainz	27	27	12	12	100	99.9	**99.19**
LUBM	17	16	12	11	100	100	**100.00**
WebDataCommons	13913	8319	780	113	98.79	94.55	**92.90**
EuroStat	44	27	5	5	99.51	99.32	**99.32**

Labeling Evaluation. We evaluate the quality of the labels in the final schema by showing the schema of DBpedia and WebDataCommons (complex and, may be, "dirty" datasets) to 19 humans. The survey asking for rating label quality

---

[4] http://dbpedia.org - we used v3.9.
[5] http://www.ncbi.nlm.nih.gov/pubmed
[6] http://gaia.infor.uva.es/hdt/dblp-2012-11-28.hdt.gz
[7] http://linkedbrainz.c4dmpresents.org/data/musicbrainz_ngs_dump.rdf.ttl.gz
[8] http://eurostat.linked-statistics.org
[9] http://wifo5-03.informatik.uni-mannheim.de/bizer/berlinsparqlbenchmark/
[10] http://dbis.informatik.uni-freiburg.de/forschung/projekte/SP2B/
[11] http://swat.cse.lehigh.edu/projects/lubm/
[12] A 100M triple file of http://webdatacommons.org.

with the 5-point Likert scale from 1 (bad) to 5 (excellent) shows that 78 (Web-DataCommons) and 90 % (DBpedia) of the labels are rated with 4 points (i.e., "good") or better.

Computational cost & Compression. Our experiments also show that the time for detecting the emerging schema is negligible comparing to bulk-loading time for building a single SPO table, and thus the schema detection process can be integrated into the bulk-loading process without any recognizable delay. Additionally, the database size stored using relational tables can be 2x smaller than the database size of a single SPO triple table since in the relational representation the S and P columns effectively get compressed away and only the O columns remain.

Final words. We think the emergent schema detection approach we developed and evaluated is promising. The fact that all tested RDF datasets turned out highly regular, and that good labels for them could be found already provides immediate value, since MonetDB/RDF can now simply be used to load RDF data in a SQL system; hence existing SQL applications can now be leveraged on RDF without change. We expect that all systems that can store both RDF and relational data (this includes besides Virtuoso also the RDF solutions by Oracle and IBM) could incorporate the possibility to load RDF data and query it both from SQL and SPARQL.

Future research is to verify the approach on more RDF dataset and further tune the recognition algorithms. Also, the second and natural step is now to make the SPARQL engine aware of the emergent schema, such that its query optimization can become more reliable and query execution can reduce the join effort in evaluating so-called SPARQL star-patterns. In benchmarks like LUBM and BSBM our results show that SPARQL systems could become just as fast as SQL systems, but even on "real" RDF datasets like DBpedia 90 % of join effort can likely be accelerated. Work is underway to verify this both in MonetDB and Virtuoso.

6 Conclusion

In this chapter we have described the advanced column store techniques and architectural ideas implemented in Virtuoso RDF store and its cluster edition, which help reduce the "RDF tax" by an order of magnitude (i.e., from 150 to 2.5). Extensive experiments using the BSBM benchmark on both short-running index lookup queries (the Explore use case) and the complex analytical queries (the BI use case) demonstrate that the new cluster architecture allows to perform RDF data management on a unprecedented scale (i.e., 150 billion triples).

In addition to the promising approach of exploiting the column store techniques, which significantly reduces the "RDF tax", to make the performances of SPARQL and SQL systems converge, RDF store needs to be aware of the actual structure of RDF data, allowing it to decrease the inherent large number of self-joins and making query optimization more reliable. For that, we have presented practical techniques for discovering an emergent relational schema in RDF dataset, that recovers a compact and precise relational schema with high coverage and useful labels as alias for all machine-readable URIs (which it preserves). The emergent schemas not only open up many opportunities to improve physical data indexing for RDF, but also respect the schema-last nature of the semantic web as being automatically detected. Implementation of these techniques will soon be realized in Virtuoso, and hopefully will close the performance gap between the SPARQL and SQL systems.

References

1. Abadi, J.: Query execution in column-oriented database systems, MIT Ph.D. thesis (2008)
2. Bizer, C., Schultz, A.: The Berlin SPARQL benchmark. Int. J. Semant. Web Inf. Syst. (IJSWIS) **5**(2), 1–24 (2009)
3. Boncz, P., Neumann, T., Erling, O.: TPC-H analyzed: hidden messages and lessons learned from an influential benchmark. In: Nambiar, R., Poess, M. (eds.) TPCTC 2013. LNCS, vol. 8391, pp. 61–76. Springer, Heidelberg (2014)
4. IBM DB2. www.ibm.com/software/data/db2/
5. Erling, O.: Virtuoso, a hybrid RDBMS/graph column store. IEEE Data Eng. Bull. **35**(1), 3–8 (2012)
6. Harth, A., Hose, K., Schenkel, R.: Linked Data Management. CRC Press, Boca Raton (2014)
7. Lamb, A., et al.: The vertica analytic database: C-store 7 years later. Proc. VLDB Endowment **5**, 1790–1801 (2012)
8. Minh-Duc, P., et al.: Deriving an emergent relational schema from RDF data. In: ISWC (submitted) (2014)
9. MonetDB column store. https://www.monetdb.org/
10. Neumann, T., et al.: Characteristic sets: accurate cardinality estimation for RDF queries with multiple joins. In: ICDE (2011)
11. Neumayer, R., Balog, K., Nørvåg, K.: When simple is (more than) good enough: effective semantic search with (almost) no semantics. In: Baeza-Yates, R., de Vries, A.P., Zaragoza, H., Cambazoglu, B.B., Murdock, V., Lempel, R., Silvestri, F. (eds.) ECIR 2012. LNCS, vol. 7224, pp. 540–543. Springer, Heidelberg (2012)
12. O'Neil, P., et al.: The star schema benchmark (SSB). PAT (2007)
13. Openlink Software Blog. http://www.openlinksw.com/weblog/oerling/
14. Page, L., et al.: The pagerank citation ranking: bringing order to the web. Technical report, Stanford InfoLab (1999)
15. Pham, M.-D.: Self-organizing structured RDF in MonetDB. In: ICDE Workshops (2013)
16. Salton, G., McGill, M.J.: Introduction to Modern Information Retrieval. McGraw-Hill, New York (1983)
17. Tsialiamanis, P., et al.: Heuristics-based query optimisation for SPARQL. In: EDBT (2012)
18. Zukowski, M., Boncz, P.A.: Vectorwise: beyond column stores. IEEE Data Eng. Bull **35**(1), 21–27 (2012)

Knowledge Base Creation, Enrichment and Repair

Sebastian Hellmann[1]($\boxtimes$), Volha Bryl[2], Lorenz Bühmann[1], Milan Dojchinovski[4], Dimitris Kontokostas[1], Jens Lehmann[1], Uroš Milošević[3], Petar Petrovski[2], Vojtěch Svátek[4], Mladen Stanojević[3], and Ondřej Zamazal[4]

[1] University of Leipzig, Leipzig, Germany
{hellmann,buehmann,kontokostas,lehmann}@informatik.uni-leipzig.de
[2] University of Mannheim, Mannheim, Germany
{volha,petar}@informatik.uni-mannheim.de
[3] Institute Mihajlo Pupin, Belgrade, Serbia
{uros.milosevic,mladen.stanojevic}@pupin.rs
[4] University of Economics Prague, Prague, Czech Republic
{milan.dojchinovski,svatek,ondrej.zamazal}@vse.cz

Abstract. This chapter focuses on data transformation to RDF and Linked Data and furthermore on the improvement of existing or extracted data especially with respect to schema enrichment and ontology repair. Tasks concerning the triplification of data are mainly grounded on existing and well-proven techniques and were refined during the lifetime of the LOD2 project and integrated into the LOD2 Stack. Triplification of legacy data, i.e. data not yet in RDF, represents the entry point for legacy systems to participate in the LOD cloud. While existing systems are often very useful and successful, there are notable differences between the ways knowledge bases and Wikis or databases are created and used. One of the key differences in content is in the importance and use of schematic information in knowledge bases. This information is usually absent in the source system and therefore also in many LOD knowledge bases. However, schema information is needed for consistency checking and finding modelling problems. We will present a combination of enrichment and repair steps to tackle this problem based on previous research in machine learning and knowledge representation. Overall, the Chapter describes how to enable tool-supported creation and publishing of RDF as Linked Data (Sect. 1) and how to increase the quality and value of such large knowledge bases when published on the Web (Sect. 2).

1 Linked Data Creation and Extraction

1.1 DBpedia, a Large-Scale, Multilingual Knowledge Base Extracted from Wikipedia

Wikipedia is the 6th most popular website[1], the most widely used encyclopedia, and one of the finest examples of truly collaboratively created content. There are

---

[1] http://www.alexa.com/topsites. Retrieved in May 2014.

© The Author(s)
S. Auer et al. (Eds.): Linked Open Data, LNCS 8661, pp. 45–69, 2014.
DOI: 10.1007/978-3-319-09846-3_3

official Wikipedia editions in 287 different languages which range in size from a couple of hundred articles up to 3.8 million articles (English edition)[2]. Besides of free text, Wikipedia articles consist of different types of structured data such as infoboxes, tables, lists, and categorization data. Wikipedia currently offers only free-text search capabilities to its users. Using Wikipedia search, it is thus very difficult to find all rivers that flow into the Rhine and are longer than 100 km, or all Italian composers that were born in the 18th century.

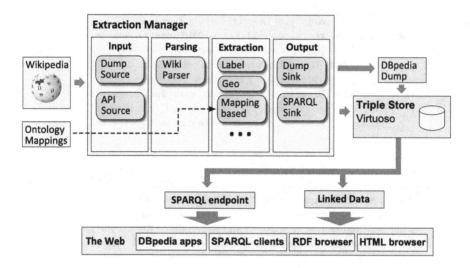

Fig. 1. Overview of DBpedia extraction framework

The DBpedia project [9,13,14] builds a large-scale, multilingual knowledge base by extracting structured data from Wikipedia editions in 111 languages. Wikipedia editions are extracted by the open source "DBpedia extraction framework" (cf. Fig. 1). The largest DBpedia knowledge base which is extracted from the English edition of Wikipedia consists of over 400 million facts that describe 3.7 million things. The DBpedia knowledge bases that are extracted from the other 110 Wikipedia editions together consist of 1.46 billion facts and describe 10 million additional things. The extracted knowledge is encapsulated in modular dumps as depicted in Fig. 2. This knowledge base can be used to answer expressive queries such as the ones outlined above. Being multilingual and covering an wide range of topics, the DBpedia knowledge base is also useful within further application domains such as data integration, named entity recognition, topic detection, and document ranking.

The DBpedia knowledge base is widely used as a test-bed in the research community and numerous applications, algorithms and tools have been built around or applied to DBpedia. Due to the continuous growth of Wikipedia and

---

[2] http://meta.wikimedia.org/wiki/List_of_Wikipedias

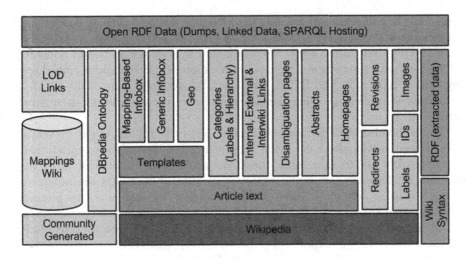

Fig. 2. Overview of the DBpedia data stack.

improvements in DBpedia, the extracted data provides an increasing added value for data acquisition, re-use and integration tasks within organisations. While the quality of extracted data is unlikely to reach the quality of completely manually curated data sources, it can be applied to some enterprise information integration use cases and has shown to be relevant in several applications beyond research projects. DBpedia is served as Linked Data on the Web. Since it covers a wide variety of topics and sets RDF links pointing into various external data sources, many Linked Data publishers have decided to set RDF links pointing to DBpedia from their data sets. Thus, DBpedia became a central interlinking hub in the Web of Linked Data and has been a key factor for the success of the Linked Open Data initiative.

The structure of the DBpedia knowledge base is maintained by the DBpedia user community. Most importantly, the community creates mappings from Wikipedia information representation structures to the DBpedia ontology. This ontology unifies different template structures, both within single Wikipedia language editions and across currently 27 different languages. The maintenance of different language editions of DBpedia is spread across a number of organisations. Each organisation is responsible for the support of a certain language. The local DBpedia chapters are coordinated by the DBpedia Internationalisation Committee. The *DBpedia Association* provides an umbrella on top of all the DBpedia chapters and tries to support DBpedia and the DBpedia Contributors Community.

1.2   RDFa, Microdata and Microformats Extraction Framework

In order to support web applications to understand the content of HTML pages, an increasing number of websites have started to semantically markup their pages, that is, embed structured data describing products, people, organizations, places, events, etc. into HTML pages using such markup standards as Microformats[3], RDFa[4] and Microdata[5]. Microformats use style definitions to annotate HTML text with terms from a fixed set of vocabularies, RDFa allows embedding any kind of RDF data into HTML pages, and Microdata is part of the HTML5 standardization effort allowing the use of arbitrary vocabularies for structured data.

The embedded data is crawled together with the HTML pages by search engines, such as Google, Yahoo! and Bing, which use these data to enrich their search results. Up to now, only these companies were capable of providing insights [15] into the amount as well as the types of data that are published on the web using different markup standards as they were the only ones possessing large-scale web crawls. However, the situation changed with the advent of the Common Crawl[6], a non-profit foundation that crawls the web and regularly publishes the resulting corpora for public usage on Amazon S3.

For the purpose of extracting structured data from these large-scale web corpora we have developed the *RDFa, Microdata and Microformats extraction framework* that is available online[7].

The extraction consists of the following steps. Firstly, a file with the crawled data, in the form of ARC or WARC archive, is *downloaded* from the storage. The archives usually contain up to several thousands of archived web pages. The framework relies on the Anything To Triples (Any23)[8] parser library for *extracting* RDFa, Microdata, and Microformats from HTML content. Any23 outputs RDF quads, consisting of subject, predicate, object, and a URL which identifies the HTML page from which the triple was extracted. Any23 parses web pages for structured data by building a DOM tree and then evaluates XPath expressions to extract the structured data. As we have found that the tree generation accounts for much of the parsing cost, we have introduced the *filtering* step: We run regular expressions against each archived HTML page prior to extraction to detect the presence of structured data, and only run the Any23 extractor when potential matches are found. The *output* of the extraction process is in NQ (RDF quads) format.

We have made available two implementations of the extraction framework, one based on the Amazon Web Services, and the second one being a Map/Reduce implementation that can be run over any Hadoop cluster. Additionally, we provide a plugin to the Apache Nutch crawler allowing the user to configure the crawl and then extract structured data from the resulting page corpus.

To verify the framework, three large scale RDFa, Microformats and Microdata extractions have been performed, corresponding to the Common Crawl

---

[3] http://microformats.org/
[4] http://www.w3.org/TR/xhtml-rdfa-primer/
[5] http://www.w3.org/TR/microdata/
[6] http://commoncrawl.org/
[7] https://subversion.assembla.com/svn/commondata/
[8] https://any23.apache.org/

data from 2009/2010, August 2012 and November 2013. The results of the 2012 and 2009/2010 are published in [2] and [16], respectively. Table 1 presents the comparative summary of the three extracted datasets. The table reports the number and the percentage of URLs in each crawl containing structured data, and gives the percentage of these data represented using Microformats, RDFa and Microdata, respectively.

Table 1. Large-scale RDF datasets extracted from Common Crawl (CC): summary

	CC 2009/2010	CC August 2012	CC November 2013
Size(TB), compressed	28.9	40.1	44
Size, URLs	2,565,741,671	3,005,629,093	2,224,829,946
Size, Domains	19,113,929	40,600,000	12,831,509
Parsing cost, USD	576	398	263
Structured data, URLs with triples	147,871,837	369,254,196	585,792,337
Structured data, in %	5.76	12.28	26.32
Microformats, in %	96.99	70.98	47.48
RDFa, in %	2.81	22.71	26.48
Microdata, in %	0.2	6.31	26.04
Average num. of triples per URL	3.35	4.05	4.04

The numbers illustrate the trends very clearly: in the recent years, the amount of structured data embedded into HTML pages keeps increasing. The use of Microformats is decreasing rapidly, while the use of RDFa and especially Microdata standards has increased a lot, which is not surprising as the adoption of the latter is strongly encouraged by the biggest search engines. On the other hand, the average number of triples per web page (only pages containing structured data are considered) stays the same through the different version of the crawl, which means that the data completeness has not changed much.

Concerning the topical domains of the published data, the dominant ones are: persons and organizations (for all three formats), blog- and CMS-related metadata (RDFa and Microdata), navigational metadata (RDFa and Microdata), product data (all three formats), and event data (Microformats). Additional topical domains with smaller adoption include job postings (Microdata) and recipes (Microformats). The data types, formats and vocabularies seem to be largely determined by the major consumers the data is targeted at. For instance, the RDFa portion of the corpora is dominated by the vocabulary promoted by Facebook, while the Microdata subset is dominated by the vocabularies promoted by Google, Yahoo! and Bing via schema.org.

More detailed statistics on the three corpora are available at the Web Data Commons page[9].

By publishing the data extracted from RDFa, Microdata and Microformats annotations, we hope on the one hand to initialize further domain-specific studies by third parties. On the other hand, we hope to lay the foundation for enlarging the number of applications that consume structured data from the web.

1.3 Rozeta

The ever-growing world of data is largely unstructured. It is estimated that information sources such as books, journals, documents, social media content and everyday news articles constitute as much as 90 % of it. Making sense of all this data and exposing the knowledge hidden beneath, while minimizing human effort, is a challenging task which often holds the key to new insights that can prove crucial to one's research or business. Still, understanding the context, and finding related information are hurdles that language technologies are yet to overcome.

Rozeta is a multilingual NLP and Linked Data tool wrapped around STRU-TEX, a structured text knowledge representation technique, used to extract words and phrases from natural language documents and represent them in a structured form. Originally designed for the needs of Wolters Kluwer Deutschland, for the purposes of organizing and searching through their database of court cases (based on numerous criteria, including case similarity), Rozeta provides automatic extraction of STRUTEX dictionaries in Linked Data form, semantic enrichment through link discovery services, a manual revision and authoring component, a document similarity search tool and an automatic document classifier (Fig. 3).

1.3.1 Dictionary Management

The Rozeta dictionary editor (Fig. 4) allows for a quick overview of all dictionary entries, as well as semi-automatic (supervised) vocabulary enrichment/link discovery and manual cleanup. It provides a quick-filter/AJAX search box that helps users swiftly browse through the dictionary by retrieving the entries that start with a given string, on-the-fly. The detailed view for a single entry shows its URI, text, class, any existing links to relevant LOD resources, as well as links to the files the entry originated from. Both the class and file origin information can be used as filters, which can help focus one's editing efforts on a single class or file, respectively.

To aid the user in enriching individual entries with links to other relevant linked data sources, Wiktionary2RDF recommendations are retrieved automatically. The user can opt for one of the available properties (`skos:exactMatch` and `skos:relatedMatch`) or generate a link using a custom one. Furthermore, the *Custom link* and *More links* buttons give the user the ability to link the

---

[9] http://webdatacommons.org

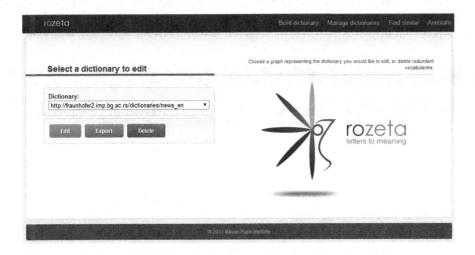

Fig. 3. Rozeta: dictionary selection

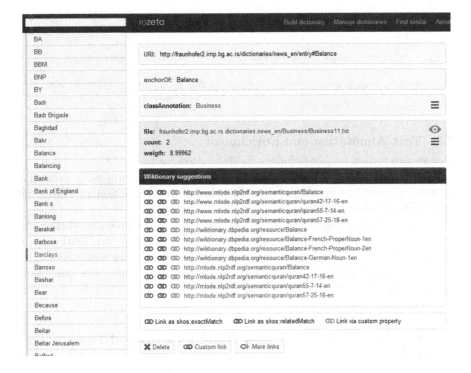

Fig. 4. Rozeta: dictionary management

selected dictionary phrase to any LOD resource, either manually, or by letting the system provide them with automatic recommendations through one of the available link discovery services, such as Sindice or a custom SPARQL endpoint.

Fig. 5. Rozeta: text annotation and enrichment

1.3.2   Text Annotation and Enrichment

The text annotation and enrichment module, used for highlighting the learned vocabulary entries in any natural language document and proposing potential links through custom services, can be launched from the dictionary editor, or used as a stand-alone application.

The highlighted words and phrases hold links to the corresponding dictionary entry pages, as well as linking recommendations from DBpedia Spotlight, or custom SPARQL endpoints (retrieved on-the-fly; sources are easily managed through an accompanying widget). The pop-up widget also generates quick-link buttons (skos:exactMatch and skos:relatedMatch) for linking the related entries to recommended Linked Open Data resources (Fig. 5).

2   Analysis, Enrichment and Repair of Linked Data with ORE Tool

The ORE tool supports knowledge engineers in enriching the schema of OWL based knowledge bases, either accessible as file or via SPARQL. Additionally, it allows for the detection and repair of logical errors as well as the validation of instance data by defining constraints in forms of OWL axioms. ORE also integrates the PaOMat framework (see Sect. 3), thus, it allows for the detection and repair of naming issues. The ORE tool is published as an open source project[10,11].

2.1 Logical Debugging

2.1.1 Motivation

Along with the uptake of Semantic Web technologies, we observe a steady increase of the amount of available OWL ontologies as well as an increase of the complexity of such ontologies. While the expressiveness of OWL is indeed a strong feature, it can also lead to a *misunderstanding* and *misusage* of particular types of constructs in the language. In turn, this can lead to modeling errors in the ontology, i.e. *inconsistency* or *unsatisfiable classes*. Inconsistency, in simple terms, is a logical contradiction in the knowledge base, which makes it impossible to derive any meaningful information by applying standard OWL reasoning techniques. Unsatisfiable classes usually are a fundamental modeling error, in that they cannot be used to characterize any individual, that means they cannot have any individual.

Both kinds of modeling errors are quite easy to detect by standard OWL reasoners, however, determining why the errors hold can be a considerable challenge even for experts in the formalism and in the domain, even for modestly sized ontologies. The problem worsens significantly as the number and complexity of axioms of the ontology grows. Clearly, only with the understanding of why such an undesired entailment holds, it is possible to get rid of the errors, i.e. to *repair* the ontology.

In the area of *ontology debugging*, a specific type of explanation called *justifications* [1,7,8,18] was introduced by the research community, which is basically a minimal subset of the ontology that is sufficient for the entailment to hold. The set of axioms corresponding to the justification is minimal in the sense that if an axiom is removed from the set, the remaining axioms no longer support the entailment. One such justification could be the following example, which gives an explanation why the class `metal` is unsatisfiable.

```
metal EquivalentTo chemical and (atomic-number some integer)
                           and (atomic-number exactly 1 Thing)
nonmetal EquivalentTo chemical and (atomic-number some integer)
                           and (atomic-number exactly 1 Thing)
metal DisjointWith nonmetal
```

2.1.2 Support in ORE

The debugging view for OWL ontologies (see Fig. 6), here described for unsatisfiable classes, consists mainly of four parts: The first part on the left side (①) gives

---

[10] http://ore-tool.net/Projects/ORE
[11] https://github.com/AKSW/ORE

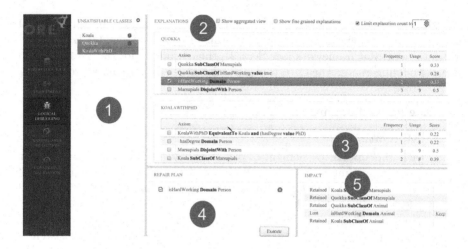

Fig. 6. Screenshot of the debugging view for OWL ontologies.

a list of the unsatisfiable classes which were detected in the selected knowledge base. In this list itself, root unsatisfiable classes, i.e. classes which unsatisfiability does not depend on the unsatisfiability of other classes, are tagged with "Root". Usually, in a repair process it is recommended to handle such root unsatisfiable classes first, as other conflicts will be solved then too. The second main part contains the presentation of the explanations, which are computed once an unsatisfiable class is selected, and shown as tables (③). In addition to the axioms of the justification, each of the tables contains two metrics which give some insights into how an axiom is involved in other justifications (frequency) and how strong an axiom is connected in the ontology (usage), both metrics finally aggregated in total score (score). The menu (②) allows for the choice between the computation of regular or laconic justifications as well as for the limitation of the maximum number of computed justifications. Furthermore, it gives the option to show an aggregated view of all the axioms contained in the computed justifications, compared to the presentation of each justification in its own table. In the third part (④) - the repair plan - a list of all changes a user has chosen in order to repair the knowledge base is displayed. The changes can either be the removal or addition of axioms and will be executed once a user has decided to do so by clicking the "Execute" button. The last part of the debugging view, located at the bottom right (⑤), contains an outline of the effects the changes of the repair plan would have to the knowledge base, i.e. it contains lost and retained entailments. If an entailment is found to be lost when executing the repair plan, it is possible to add an axiom to the knowledge base which retains that entailment. This part is only available during the debugging of unsatisfiable classes, as it is (currently) impossible to compute such entailments in inconsistent knowledge bases.

2.2 Schema Enrichment

2.2.1 Motivation

The Semantic Web has recently seen a rise in the availability and usage of knowledge bases, as can be observed within the Linking Open Data Initiative, the TONES and Protégé ontology repositories, or the Watson search engine. Despite this growth, there is still a lack of knowledge bases that consist of sophisticated schema information and instance data adhering to this schema. Several knowledge bases, e.g. in the life sciences, only consist of schema information, while others are, to a large extent, a collection of facts without a clear structure, e.g. information extracted from data bases or texts. The combination of sophisticated schema and instance data would allow powerful reasoning, consistency checking, and improved querying possibilities. Schema enrichment allows to create a sophisticated schema base based on existing data (sometimes referred to as "grass roots" approach or "after the fact" schema creation).

Example 1. As an example, consider a knowledge base containing a class Capital and instances of this class, e.g. London, Paris, Washington, Canberra, etc. A machine learning algorithm could, then, suggest that the class Capital may be equivalent to one of the following OWL class expressions in Manchester OWL syntax[12]:

```
City and isCapitalOf min 1 GeopoliticalRegion
City and isCapitalOf min 1 Country
```

Both suggestions could be plausible: The first one is more general and includes cities that are capitals of states, whereas the latter one is stricter and limits the instances to capitals of countries. A knowledge engineer can decide which one is more appropriate, i.e. a semi-automatic approach is used, and the machine learning algorithm should guide the user by pointing out which one fits the existing instances better.

Assuming the knowledge engineer decides for the latter, an algorithm can show the user whether there are instances of the class Capital which are neither instances of City nor related via the property isCapitalOf to an instance of Country.[13] The knowledge engineer can then continue to look at those instances and assign them to a different class as well as provide more complete information; thus improving the quality of the knowledge base. After adding the definition of Capital, an OWL reasoner can compute further instances of the class which have not been explicitly assigned before.

---

[12] For details on Manchester OWL syntax (e.g. used in Protégé, OntoWiki) see http://www.w3.org/TR/owl2-manchester-syntax/.

[13] This is not an inconsistency under the standard OWL open world assumption, but rather a hint towards a potential modelling error.

Fig. 7. Screenshot of the enrichment view for SPARQL knowledge bases.

2.2.2   Support in ORE

The enrichment view for SPARQL knowledge bases(see Fig. 7), can be subdivided into two main parts: The first part on the left side (①) allows for configuring the enrichment process like to denote for which entity and which types ORE will search for schema axioms. The second part on the right side(②) shows the generated axiom suggestions as well as their confidence score for each chosen axiom type in forms of tables. Additionally, it is possible to get some more details about the confidence score by clicking on the question mark symbol(?). This shows up a new dialog as shown in Fig. 8. The dialog gives some natural language based explanation about the F-score depending on the axiom type. Moreover, positive and negative examples (if exists) according to the axiom are shown, thus, giving some more detailed insights in how the axiom fits the data of the knowledge base.

2.3   Constraint Based Validation

2.3.1   Motivation

Integrity constraints provide a mechanism for ensuring that data conforms to guidelines specified by the defined schema. The demand for validating instance data as in relational databases or XML tools also holds for knowledge modeled in languages of the Semantic Web.

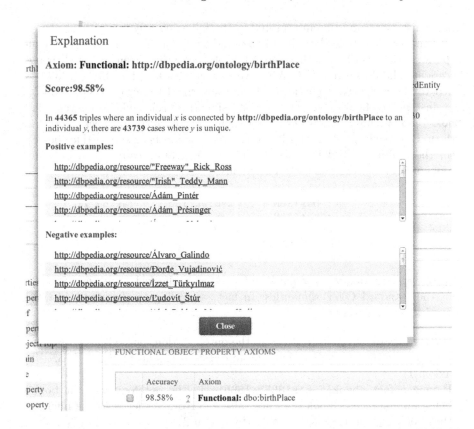

Fig. 8. Screenshot of confidence score explanation in enrichment view for SPARQL knowledge bases.

In some use cases and for some requirements, OWL users assume and intend OWL axioms to be interpreted as Integrity Constraints. However, the direct semantics of OWL[14] does not interpret OWL axioms in this way; thus, the consequences that one can draw from such ontologies differ from the ones that some users intuitively expect and require. In other words, some users want to use OWL as a validation or constraint language for RDF instance data, but that is not possible using OWL based tools that correctly implement the standard semantics of OWL.

To see the nature of the problem, consider an OWL ontology that describes terms and concepts regarding a book store. The ontology includes the classes Book and Writer, the object property hasAuthor, and the data property hasISBN. Suppose we want to impose the following ICs on the data:

1. Each book must have an ISBN
2. Only books can have ISBNs
3. Books must not have more than one author

---

[14] http://www.w3.org/TR/owl2-direct-semantics/

These constraints could be interpreted in the following way:

Whenever an instance bookX of Book is added to the ontology, a check should be performed to verify whether the ISBN of bookX has been specified; if not, the update should be rejected. Whenever a fact <bookX, hasISBN, ISBNX> is added to the ontology, a check should be performed to verify whether bookX is an instance of Book; if not, the update should be rejected. Whenever a fact <bookX, hasAuthor, writerX> is added to the ontology, a check should be performed to verify whether another writer writerY has been specified for bookX; if so, the update should be rejected. These constraints can be concisely and unambiguously represented as OWL axioms:

```
Class: Book
   SubClassOf: hasISBN some xsd:string        (axiom 1)
DataProperty: hasISBN
   Domain: Book                               (axiom 2)
ObjectProperty: hasAuthor
   Characteristics: Functional                (axiom 3)
```

However, these axioms will not be interpreted as checks by tools which implement the standard OWL semantics. In fact, according to the standard OWL semantics, we have that:

1. Having a book without an ISBN in the ontology does not raise an error, but leads to the inference that the book in question has an unknown ISBN. (by axiom 1)
2. Having a fact <bookA, hasISBN, ISBN1> in the ontology without bookA being an instance of Book does not raise an error, but leads to the inference that bookA is an instance of Book. (by axiom 2)
3. Having a fact <bookA, hasAuthor, writerA> having specified a previous writer writerB for bookA does not raise an error, but leads to the inference that writerA and writerB denote the same individual. (by axiom 3)

In some cases, users want these inferences; but in others, users want integrity constraint violations to be detected, reported, repaired, etc.

One approach for using OWL as an expressive schema language, but giving it an alternative semantics such that OWL axioms can be used as ICs, was proposed in [20]. The idea behind it is to interpret OWL axioms with Closed World Assumption (CWA) and a weak form of Unique Name Assumption (UNA). Assuming a CWA interpretation basically means that an assertion is false if it is not explicitly known it is true or false. Weak UNA means that if two individuals are not inferred to be the same, then they will be assumed to be distinct. Based on these assumptions, translating an OWL axiom into one or more SPARQL queries is suggested to validate the given constraint. This approach is integrated in ORE, thus, it is possible to define and validate ICs by reusing OWL as a language.

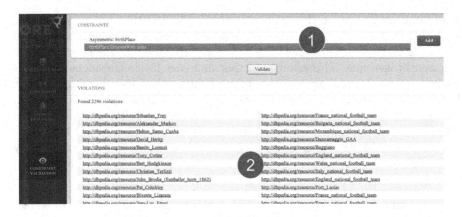

Fig. 9. Screenshot of constraint validation view.

2.3.2   Support in ORE

Basically, the constraint validation view (see Fig. 9) consists of two parts. In the upper table (①) the user can define a list of constraints by adding OWL axioms, here for instance that the object properties `birthPlace` and `team` are disjoint, i.e. there are no pairs of instances that are related by both properties. The bottom part (②) is used to visualize violations of the given constraints. In the example on Fig. 9, it was found that `Pat Critchley` was born in `Port Laoise`, but also was a team member of it, which is obviously a contradiction to the disjointness statement.

3   Ontology Repair with PatOMat

The *PatOMat* is a pattern-based ontology transformation framework specifically designed for OWL ontologies [23]. By applying transformation it enables
a designer to modify the structure of an ontology or its fragments to make it
more suitable for a target application. While it can adapt any ontology aspect
(logical, structural, naming or annotation aspect), within the context of LOD2
project the PatOMat focuses on ontology naming aspect.

During the decades of knowledge engineering research, there has been recur-
rent dispute on how the natural language structure influences the structure of
formal knowledge bases and vice versa. A large part of the community seems
to recognise that the content expressed in formal representation languages, such
as the semantic web ones, should be accessible not only to logical reasoning
machines but also to humans and NLP procedures, and thus resemble the natural language as much as possible [17].

Often, an ontology naming practice can be captured as a *naming pattern*.
For instance, it is quite common in ontologies that a subclass has the same

head noun as its parent class (Non-Matching Child Pattern).[15] By an earlier study [22] it was estimated that in ontologies for technical domains this simple pattern is verified in 50–80 % of class-subclass pairs such that the subclass name is a multi-token one. This number further increases if one considers thesaurus correspondence (synonymy and hypernymy) rather than literal string equality. In fact, the set-theoretic nature of taxonomic path entails that the correspondence of head nouns along this path should be close to 100 % in principle; the only completely innocent deviations from it should be those caused by incomplete thesauri. In other words, any violation of head noun correspondence may potentially indicate a (smaller or greater) problem in the ontology. Prototypical situations are:

- Inadequate use of class-subclass relationship, typically in the place of whole-part or class-instance relationship, i.e., a conceptualisation error frequently occurring in novice ontologies.
- Name shorthanding, typically manifested by use of adjective, such as "State-Owned" (subclass of "Company").

While the former requires complex refactoring of the ontology fragment, the latter can be healed by propagation of the parent name down to the child name.

While in the biomedical field there have already been efforts in naming analysis, e.g., in [6,19], naming in the broad field of linked data vocabularies (where domain- specific heuristics cannot be applied) has rarely been addressed.

A pattern in the PatOMat framework, called transformation, consists of three parts: two *ontology patterns* (source OP and target OP) and the description of the transformation between them, called *pattern transformation* (PT). Naming pattern, such as non-matching child pattern, can be captured by specifying violation of a naming pattern to be detected (i.e. source OP) and its refactored variant (e.g. non-matching child pattern as target OP). Transformation patterns can be designed directly as XML files or by using graphical editor. For general usage the framework can be applied directly from the code by importing the PatOMat Java library[16] or by using *Graphical User Interface for Pattern-based Ontology Transformation* [21].

Naming issue detection and repair is supported by integrating the PatOMat framework into the ORE. The whole process is basically done in three subsequent steps, all of them visualized in a single view shown in Fig. 10. Here the user can select a naming pattern in the leftmost list (①). PatOMat then detects instances of the selected pattern in the currently loaded ontology, e.g. [$?OP1P = Contribution; ?OP1A = Poster$](②). For the selected pattern instances the user will be provided a list of renaming instructions (see ③), for example to rename the class *Poster* to *PosterContribution*, which can then be used to transform the ontology and solve the detected naming issues.

---

[15] The head noun is typically the last token, but not always, in particular due to possible prepositional constructions, as, e.g., in "HeadOfDepartment".

[16] http://owl.vse.cz:8080/

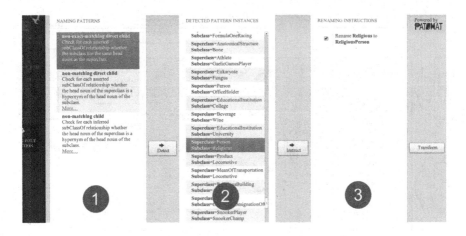

Fig. 10. Screenshot of naming pattern detection and repair view in the ORE.

4   Linked Data Quality Assessment with RDFUnit

RDFUnit [10–12][17] is a framework for test-driven Linked Data quality assessment, which is inspired by test-driven software development. A key principle of test-driven software development is to start the development with the implementation of automated test-methods before the actual functionality is implemented. Compared to software source code testing, where test cases have to be implemented largely manually or with limited programmatic support, the situation for Linked Data quality testing is slightly more advantageous. On the Data Web we have a unified data model – RDF – which is the basis for both, data *and* ontologies. RDFUnit exploits the RDF data model by devising a pattern-based approach for the data quality tests of knowledge bases. Ontologies, vocabularies and knowledge bases can be accompanied by a number of test cases, which help to ensure a basic level of quality. This is achieved by employing SPARQL query templates, which are instantiated into concrete quality test SPARQL queries. We provide a comprehensive library of quality test patterns, which can be instantiated for rapid development of more test cases. Once test cases are defined for a certain vocabulary, they can be applied to all datasets reusing elements of this vocabulary. Test cases can be re-executed whenever the data is altered. Due to the modularity of the approach, where test cases are bound to certain vocabulary elements, test cases for newly emerging datasets, which reuse existing vocabularies can be easily derived.

RDFUnit is capable of performing quality assessments with only a minimal amount of manual user intervention and is easily applicable to large datasets. Other tools like the TopBraid Composer[18] use the *SPARQL Inferencing Notation*

---

[17] http://rdfunit.aksw.org
[18] www.topbraidcomposer.com

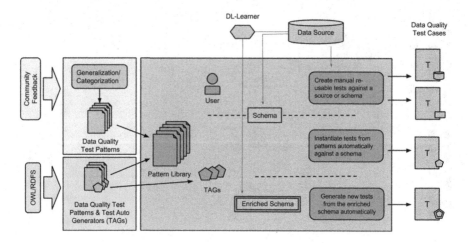

Fig. 11. Flowchart showing the test-driven data quality methodology. The left part displays the input sources of our pattern library. In the middle part the different ways of pattern instantiation are shown which lead to the data quality test cases on the right.

(SPIN)[19] to define SPARQL queries for quality assessment. However, RDFUnit utilizes an own SPARQL template notation, which better suits our methodology. An overview of the methodology is depicted in Fig. 11.

5   Analysis of Link Validity

5.1   Web Linkage Validator

With the integration of data into the LOD cloud, it is essential that links between datasets are discoverable as well as efficiently and correctly assessed. The Web Linkage Validator is a web-based tool that allows for knowledge base owners to improve their data with respect to linkage and to assess their linked data for integration with the LOD cloud.

The goal is to provide a tool to the LOD2 stack to aid in assessing links between LOD datasets. It analyses the links between entities that a dataset has as well as links to entities from other datasets. It will help knowledge base users in improving the quality of links of their datasets.

The Web Linkage Validator's assessment is based on the concept of a *data graph summary* [3,4]. A data graph summary is a concise representation of the RDF data graph and is composed of the structural elements, i.e., class and property. The information it contains, such as RDF class and predicate, usage frequency, provenance and linkage, are the basis for suggesting to knowledge base owners ways in which they may create or improve the links within their datasets and with other external datasets.

---

[19] http://spinrdf.org/

5.2   Data Graph Summary Model

In general, an RDF graph consists of datasets which in turn contain a number of entities. These entities are organised into classes. Links can exist at any of these levels; either between datasets, between class of entities or between the entities themselves. The data graph summary is a meta-graph that highlights the structure of a data graph (e.g. RDF).

For the graph summary process, we need to represent the data graph using three conceptual layers: the *dataset* layer, the *node collection* layer and the *entity* layer. The entity layer represents the original data graph. The node collection layer captures the schema and structure of the data graph in a concise way by grouping similar entities into a parent node that we call a *node collection*. This grouping is required as it allows for the graph summary to correctly determine collection specific information about those entities. The dataset layer captures the link structure across datasets as well as the provenance of the information on the entity and node collection layers. The Fig. 12 gives an example of the three layer representation of a data graph. Note that the ⋆ symbol represents terminating or leaf entities, e.g., RDF literal values. The node collection layer represents a summary computed by grouping together entities having the same classes. The node collection layer is composed of node collections and linksets, i.e., a set of links having the same labels between two node collections. For example, in the figure the links "author" between articles and people on the entity layer are mapped to two linksets "author" on the node collection layer.

5.3   Link Analysis

A data graph summary provides a unique view on the linkage information of a dataset. Using this meta-graph, it is possible to analyse the links of a dataset from the "point of view" of said dataset: links from/to other datasets, internal links between classes, etc. The Web Linkage Validator shown in Fig. 13a presents various "point of views" for the purpose of aiding the owners of datasets in the assessment of their linked data.

Besides giving a structural breakdown of the dataset, the graph summary is a utility for validating the internal and external links of a particular graph of data. In terms of external links, it shows what a dataset is "saying" about other datasets and vice-versa. This is important as it gives knowledge base owners the ability to validate what the links represent.

5.4   Provenance

The provenance represents the *origin* of entities and links. The provenance includes a classification of the relationships as *intra-dataset* or *inter-dataset* respectively based on entity linkage inside singular datasets or across multiple datasets. For example, a link between two entities can be classified as internal to a dataset because it was published within it, but can also be further classified as inter-dataset because the relationship contains an entity **outside** of the

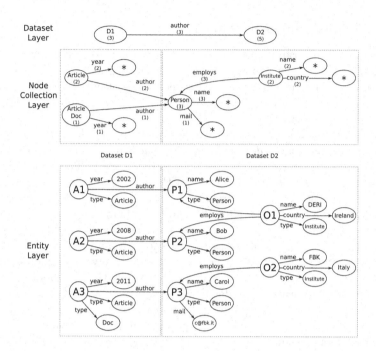

Fig. 12. A three layer representation of our Web Data model. On the node collection layer, nodes labelled with a star ⋆ represent blank collections.

publishing context. The Fig. 13b presents a view of the Web Linkage Validator showing the links internal to a dataset.

Direction. Inter-dataset triples are classified as *incoming* or *outgoing* depending on the direction of the link, relative to its origin (the subject entity) and to its destination (the object entity), based on its perspective (the context or publishing domain of the triple). For example, a triple published on the knowledge base (or domain) "xyz.com" that has a subject entity from "123.com" and object entity from "xyz.com" would be classified as incoming.

Authority. Similar to provenance and direction, the authority is based on the datasets and entities linked in a relationship. A link is classified as *authoritative* if at least one entity of the link originates from the publishing domain. For example, if a triple was published on "xyz.com" and the subject was from "xyz.com" and the object was from "123.com", then this link would be considered authoritative because "xyz.com" is asserting it. However, if the domain in which this triple was published was changed to "123.com", then it would become a non-authoritative link.

Third-Party Links. In regards to validating datasets, the authority classification helps knowledge base owners to distinguish another important aspect: third-party links. These represent non-authoritative links where both the subject and object of the link are defined in a dataset other than the publishing

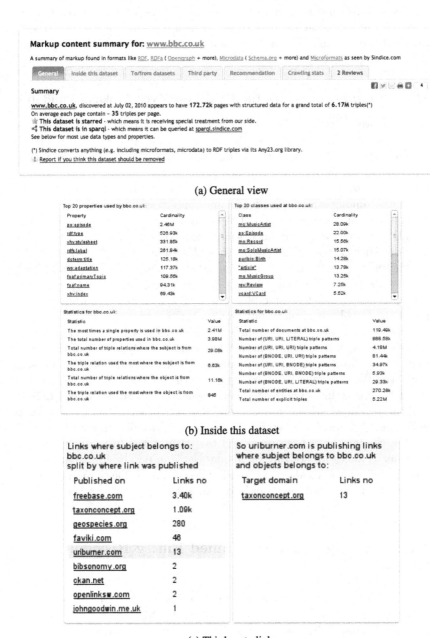

(a) General view

(b) Inside this dataset

(c) Third-party links

Fig. 13. Views on a dataset provided by the Web Linkage Validator application.

one. Also, they are useful to discover if they consist of links that are incorrect or specify relationships that the owner does not explicitly agree with. In some cases, these links can be connotative to the idea of e-mail spam. Figure 13c presents the view of the Web Linkage Validator that provides information on the links classified as non-authoritative.

5.5   How to Improve Your Dataset with the Web Linkage Validator

In this section we show how the results of the Web Linkage Validator can be used as suggestions for improving one's dataset. Being able to see the classes and the properties of his dataset, the dataset owner is able to have a deep understanding of his dataset. He can determine if the dataset graph looks as he planned. For example, let's assume the dataset contains the "foaf:Person" class which has, among others, the "foaf:name" and "foaf:homepage" properties. From the number of the occurrences of these properties, the dataset owner can decide if his dataset is as he intended too: if he knows that most of the people in the dataset should have a homepage, then this should be reflected in similar numbers for the occurences of the "foaf:name" and "foaf:homepage" properties.

Also, the dataset owner can identify possible mistakes like typos in the classes/properties names. For example, it is well known that "foaf:name" is a property of the FOAF vocabulary but "foaf:naem" is not.

Moreover, having access to the number of links to and from other datasets, the dataset owner can determine whether his dataset really is part of the LOD. If the number of links to/from other datasets is quite small or even missing completely, the Web Linkage Validator supports the dataset owner in improving the dataset by suggesting similar datasets to which the dataset owner can link. Based on the top most similar dataset, the dataset owner identify concepts in the recommended dataset similar to the ones he uses and link them.

Once the changes have been done and the dataset has been improved, the dataset owner changes his website or his dataset dump. The infrastructure on which the Web Linkage Validator is based will recompute the data graph summary for the resubmitted dataset and next time the user will see his improvements.

6   Benchmarking Semantic Named Entity Recognition Systems

Named entity recognition (NER) became one of the most exploited means for information extraction and content enrichment. The NER systems detect text fragments identifying entities and provide classification of the entities into a set of pre-defined categories. This is usually a fixed set of raw classes such as the CoNLL set (PERSON, ORGANIZATION, LOCATION, MISCELLANEOUS), or classes from an ontology, such as the DBpedia Ontology. However, it is a recent trend that the NER systems such as DBpedia Spotlight to go beyond this type classification and also perform unique identification of the entities using

URIs from a knowledge bases such as DBpedia or Wikipedia. During LOD2, we have created a collection of tools adhering to this new class of *Wikification, Semantic NER* or *Entity Linking* systems and contributed it the Wikipedia page about Knowledge Extraction[20].

While these Semantic NER systems are gaining popularity, there is yet no oversight on their performance in general, and their performance in specific domains. To fill this gap, we have developed a framework for benchmarking NER systems [5][21]. It is developed as a stand-alone project on top of the GATE text engineering framework[22]. It is primarily developed for off-line evaluation of NER systems. Since different NER systems might perform better in one and worse in another domain, we have also developed two annotated datasets with entities, the News and the Tweets dataset. The Tweets datasets, consists of very large number of short texts (tweets), while the News dataset consists of standard-length news articles.

A prerequisite for benchmarking different NER tools is achieving interoperability at the *technical, syntactical* and *conceptual* level. Regarding the technical interoperability, most of the NER tools provide a REST API over the HTTP protocol. At the syntactical and conceptual level we opted for the NIF format, which directly addresses the syntactical and the conceptual aspects. The syntactical interoperability is addressed using the RDF and OWL as standards for common data model, while the conceptual interoperability is achieved by identifying the entities and the classes using global unique identifiers. For identification of the entities we opted for re-using URIs from DBpedia. Since different NER tools classify the entities with classes from different classification systems (classification ontologies), we perform alignment of those ontologies to the DBpedia Ontology[23].

In the future, we hope to exploit the availability of interoperable NIF corpora as described in [10].

7   Conclusion

In this chapter we have presented tools for conversion and extraction of data into RDF that were developed in the context of the LOD2 project. Specifically, the DBpedia Extraction Framework supports the extraction of knowledge from Wikis such as Wikipedia, the RDFa, Microdata and Microformats Extraction Framework crawls and collects data from the Web and Rozeta enables users to create and refine terminological data such as dictionaries and thesauri from natural language text. Once this data has been extracted and lifted to RDF, tools such as ORE and RDFUnit can analyse data quality and repair errors via a GUI. The presented tools are open source and make part of the Linked Data

---

[20] A frequently updated list can be found here http://en.wikipedia.org/wiki/Knowledge_extraction#Tools.

[21] http://ner.vse.cz/datasets/evaluation/

[22] http://gate.ac.uk/

[23] http://wiki.dbpedia.org/Ontology

stack (see Chap. 6). The tools have been extensively evaluated, for the details the reader is referred to the respective sections, cited articles and tools' webpages. These tools have been applied within LOD2 project, e.g. in a media publishing, enterprise and public procurement use cases, for the details see Chaps. 7, 8 and 10 of the present book, respectively.

References

1. Baader, F., Hollunder, B.: Embedding defaults into terminological knowledge representation formalisms. In: Nebel, B., Rich, C., Swartout, W.R., (eds.) KR, pp. 306–317. Morgan Kaufmann (1992)
2. Bizer, C., Eckert, K., Meusel, R., Mühleisen, H., Schuhmacher, M., Völker, J.: Deployment of RDFA, microdata, and microformats on the web - a quantitative analysis. In: Proceedings of the In-Use Track of the 12th International Semantic Web Conference (2013)
3. Campinas, S., Perry, T.E., Ceccarelli, D., Delbru, R., Tummarello, G.: Introducing RDF graph summary with application to assisted SPARQL formulation. In: 23rd International Workshop on Database and Expert Systems Applications, DEXA 2012, pp. 261–266, Sept 2012
4. Campinas, S., Delbru, R., Tummarello, G.: Efficiency and precision trade-offs in graph summary algorithms. In: Proceedings of the 17th International Database Engineering and Applications Symposium, IDEAS '13, pp. 38–47. ACM, New York (2013)
5. Dojchinovski, M., Kliegr, T.: Datasets and GATE evaluation framework for benchmarking wikipedia-based NER systems. In: Proceedings of 1st International Workshop on NLP and DBpedia, 21–25 October 2013, Sydney, Australia, volume 1064 of NLP & DBpedia 2013, Sydney, Australia, October 2013, CEUR Workshop Proceedings (2013)
6. Fernandez-Breis, J.T., Iannone, L., Palmisano, I., Rector, A.L., Stevens, R.: Enriching the gene ontology via the dissection of labels using the ontology pre-processor language. In: Cimiano, P., Pinto, H.S. (eds.) EKAW 2010. LNCS, vol. 6317, pp. 59–73. Springer, Heidelberg (2010)
7. Kalyanpur, A.: Debugging and repair of OWL ontologies. Ph.D. thesis, University of Maryland, College Park, College Park, MD, USA (2006) (Adviser-James Hendler)
8. Kalyanpur, A., Parsia, B., Horridge, M., Sirin, E.: Finding all justifications of OWL DL entailments. In: Aberer, K., Choi, K.-S., Noy, N., Allemang, D., Lee, K.-I., Nixon, L.J.B., Golbeck, J., Mika, P., Maynard, D., Mizoguchi, R., Schreiber, G., Cudré-Mauroux, P. (eds.) ASWC 2007 and ISWC 2007. LNCS, vol. 4825, pp. 267–280. Springer, Heidelberg (2007)
9. Kontokostas, D., Bratsas, Ch., Auer, S., Hellmann, S., Antoniou, I., Metakides, G.: Internationalization of linked data: the case of the greek DBpedia edition. Web Semant. Sci. Serv. Agents World Wide Web **15**, 51–61 (2012)

10. Kontokostas, D., Brümmer, M., Hellmann, S., Lehmann, J., Ioannidis, L.: NLP data cleansing based on linguistic ontology constraints. In: Proceedings of the Extended Semantic Web Conference 2014 (2014)

11. Kontokostas, D., Westphal, P., Auer, S., Hellmann, S., Lehmann, J., Cornelissen, R.: Databugger: a test-driven framework for debugging the web of data. In: Proceedings of the Companion Publication of the 23rd International Conference on World Wide Web Companion, WWW Companion '14, pp. 115–118, Republic and Canton of Geneva, Switzerland, 2014, International World Wide Web Conferences Steering Committee

12. Kontokostas, D., Westphal, P., Auer, S., Hellmann, S., Lehmann, J., Cornelissen, R., Zaveri, A.: Test-driven evaluation of linked data quality. In: Proceedings of the 23rd International Conference on World Wide Web, WWW '14, pp. 747–758, Republic and Canton of Geneva, Switzerland, 2014, International World Wide Web Conferences Steering Committee

13. Lehmann, J., Bizer, Ch., Kobilarov, G., Auer, S., Becker, Ch., Cyganiak, R., Hellmann, S.: DBpedia - a crystallization point for the web of data. J. Web Semant. 7(3), 154–165 (2009)

14. Lehmann, J., Isele, R., Jakob, M., Jentzsch, A., Kontokostas, D., Mendes, P.N., Hellmann, S., Morsey, M., van Kleef, P., Auer, S., Bizer, C.: DBpedia - a large-scale, multilingual knowledge base extracted from wikipedia. Semant. Web J. (2014)

15. Mika, P., Potter, T.: Metadata statistics for a large web corpus. In: LDOW: Linked Data on the Web. CEUR Workshop Proceedings, vol. 937 (2012)

16. Mühleisen, H., Bizer, C., Web data commons - extracting structured data from two large web corpora. In: LDOW: Linked Data on the Web. CEUR Workshop Proceedings, vol. 937 (2012)

17. Nirenburg, S., Wilks, Y.: What's in a symbol: ontology, representation and language. J. Exp. Theor. Artif. Intell. 13(1), 9–23 (2001)

18. Schlobach, S., Cornet, R.: Non-standard reasoning services for the debugging of description logic terminologies. In: Proceedings of the 18th International Joint Conference on Artificial Intelligence, pp. 355–360. Morgan Kaufmann Publishers, San Francisco (2003)

19. Schober, D., Smith, B., Lewis, S.E., Kusnierczyk, W., Lomax, J., Mungall, C., Taylor, C.F., Rocca-Serra, P., Sansone, S.-A.: Survey-based naming conventions for use in OBO foundry ontology development. BMC Bioinform. 10(1), 125 (2009)

20. Sirin, E., Tao, J.: Towards integrity constraints in OWL. In: Hoekstra, R., Patel-Schneider, P.F., (eds.) OWLED, volume 529 of CEUR Workshop Proceedings (2008). http://CEUR-WS.org

21. Šváb-Zamazal, O., Dudáš, M., Svátek, V.: User-friendly pattern-based transformation of OWL ontologies. In: ten Teije, A., Völker, J., Handschuh, S., Stuckenschmidt, H., d'Acquin, M., Nikolov, A., Aussenac-Gilles, N., Hernandez, N. (eds.) EKAW 2012. LNCS, vol. 7603, pp. 426–429. Springer, Heidelberg (2012)

22. Šváb-Zamazal, O., Svátek, V.: Analysing ontological structures through name pattern tracking. In: Gangemi, A., Euzenat, J. (eds.) EKAW 2008. LNCS (LNAI), vol. 5268, pp. 213–228. Springer, Heidelberg (2008)

23. Zamazal, O., Svátek, V.: Patomat - versatile framework for pattern-based ontology transformation. Comput. Inf. (2014) (Accepted)

Interlinking and Knowledge Fusion

Volha Bryl[1]([⊠]), Christian Bizer[1], Robert Isele[2], Mateja Verlic[3],
Soon Gill Hong[4], Sammy Jang[4], Mun Yong Yi[4], and Key-Sun Choi[4]

[1] University of Mannheim, Mannheim, Germany
{volha,chris}@informatik.uni-mannheim.de
[2] Brox IT-Solutions GmbH, Hannover, Germany
mail@robertisele.com
[3] Zemanta d.o.o, Ljubljana, Slovenia
mateja.verlic@zemanta.com
[4] KAIST, Daejeon, Korea
{soonhong,sammy1221,munyi,kschoi}@kaist.ac.kr

Abstract. The central assumption of Linked Data is that data providers ease the integration of Web data by setting RDF links between data sources. In addition to linking entities, Web data integration also requires the alignment of the different vocabularies that are used to describe entities as well as the resolution of data conflicts between data sources. In this chapter, we present the methods and open source tools that have been developed in the LOD2 project for supporting data publishers to set RDF links between data sources. We also introduce the tools that have been developed for translating data between different vocabularies, for assessing the quality of Web data as well as for resolving data conflicts by fusing data from multiple data sources.

1 Introduction

The amount of Linked Open Data (LOD) already available on the Web of Data, or extracted using e.g. the methods presented in Chap. 3, is huge, as well as its potential for applications. However, the *quality* of the LOD sources varies greatly across domains and single datasets [1], making the efficient use of data problematic. An important quality-related problem is the lack of *data consistency*: same real world entities are described in different datasets using different vocabularies and data formats, and the descriptions often contain conflicting values.

According to the architecture of a Linked Data application illustrated in Fig. 1, four steps are necessary before the input coming from the Web of Data can be consumed by an application: *vocabulary mapping, identity resolution, data quality assessment* and *data fusion.*

This chapter presents methods and open source tools developed within the LOD2 project, which cover the above four steps of the process of integrating and cleansing the Linked Data from the Web.

Vocabulary mapping, or schema alignment step is inevitable as different LOD providers may use different vocabularies to represent the same type of information. E.g. *population* property of a country or city can come under different names

S. Auer et al. (Eds.): Linked Open Data, LNCS 8661, pp. 70–89, 2014.
DOI: 10.1007/978-3-319-09846-3_4

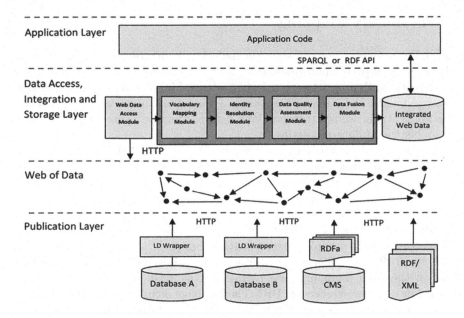

Fig. 1. Schematic architecture of a Linked Data application [7]

such as *population, populationTotal, numberOfInhabitants, hasPopulation,* etc. Therefore, tools that translate terms from different vocabularies into a single target schema are needed. Section 2 presents the R2R Framework, which enables Linked Data applications to discover and apply vocabulary mappings to translate the Web data to the application's target vocabulary.

Identity resolution aims at interlinking URIs that are used by different Linked Data sources to identify the same entity, for instance, a person or a place. Data sources may provide *owl:sameAs* links connecting data about the same real-world entity, but in many cases methods and tools for discovering these links are needed. In Sect. 3 we present the Silk Link Discovery Framework that supports identity resolution and data interlinking in the LOD context. Section 4 presents the LOD-enabled version of OpenRefine for data cleansing and reconciliation, which is also enhanced with crowdsourcing capabilities.

Data quality assessment and data fusion steps ensure the quality and consistency of data coming from the web. Depending on the application, different data quality aspects may become relevant: trustworthiness, precision, recency, etc. Section 5 presents Sieve – Linked Data Quality Assessment and Fusion tool, which allows filtering and then fusing the Web data according to user-defined data quality assessment and conflict resolution policies. One of the crowdsourcing use cases in Sect. 4 is related to improving the data quality via data enrichment.

In addition, Sect. 6 addresses the specific challenges of identity resolution and data fusion for some of the most wide-spread Asian languages: Korean, Chinese and Japanese.

2 Vocabulary Mapping

Linked Data sources use different vocabularies to describe the same type of objects. It is also common practice to mix terms from different widely used vocabularies[1] with proprietary terms. In contrast, Linked Data applications usually expect data to be represented using a consistent target vocabulary. Thus these applications need to translate Web data to their local schema before doing any sophisticated data processing.

To overcome these problems, we have developed the **R2R Framework**[2][3]. This open source framework consists of a *mapping language* for expressing term correspondences, *best practices* on how to publish mappings on the Web, and a *Java API* for transforming data to a given target vocabulary according to the mappings. We also provide the R2R Graphical User Interface, a web application that allows loading, editing and executing R2R mappings on data sources that are either located in a triple store or in RDF dumps.

As the *R2R mapping language* is designed for publishing mappings as Linked Data on the Web, mappings are represented as RDF and each mapping is assigned its own dereferenceable URI. The language defines the link type *r2r:has Mapping* to interlink mappings with RDFS or OWL term definitions and voiD dataset descriptions. The syntax of the R2R mapping language[3] is very similar to the SPARQL query language, which eases the learning curve.

The mapping language covers value transformation for use cases where RDF datasets use different units of measurement, and can handle one-to-many and many-to-one correspondences between vocabulary elements. R2R also offers modifiers to be used for assigning data types and language tags or converting a literal into a URI reference using a pattern. The language provides a set of common string functions, such as *concat* or *split*, arithmetic and list functions. See Listing 1 for a mapping example (prefix definition omitted), in which the *firstName* and *lastName* properties are concatenated into the *name* property.

```
1  p:manyToOnePropertyMapping
2    a r2r:Mapping ;
3    r2r:sourcePattern "?SUBJ foaf:firstName ?f . ?SUBJ foaf:lastName ?l" ;
4    r2r:targetPattern "?SUBJ dbpedia:name ?n" ;
5    r2r:transformation "?n = concat(?l,',', ?f)" ;
```

Listing 1. R2R mapping example

The R2R Mapping Engine applies a *mapping composition* method for selecting and chaining partial mappings from different sources based on a mapping quality assessment heuristic. The assumptions are that mappings provided by vocabulary maintainers and data publishers themselves are likely to be of a higher quality, and that the quality of data translations decreases with the length of the mapping chains.

---

[1] E.g FOAF for representing data about people – http://www.foaf-project.org/

[2] http://wifo5-03.informatik.uni-mannheim.de/bizer/r2r/

[3] Full specification at http://wifo5-03.informatik.uni-mannheim.de/bizer/r2r/spec/

We evaluated the R2R Mapping Language by formulating mappings between DBpedia and 11 data sources that are interlinked with DBpedia, see [3] for further details. The language proved to be expressive enough in this experiment to represent all mappings that were required. The experiment also showed that far more expressivity is required to properly translate data to a target schema than currently provided by standard terms such as *owl:equivalentClass, owl:equivalentProperty* or *rdfs:subClassOf, rdfs:subPropertyOf.*

3   The Silk Link Discovery Framework

A central problem of the Web of Linked Data as well as of data integration in general is to identify entities in different data sources that describe the same real-world object. While the amount of Linked Open Data has grown significantly over the last years, most data sources are still not sufficiently interlinked. Out of the over 31 billion RDF statements published as Linked Data less than 500 million represent RDF links between data sources; analysis confirms that the LOD cloud represents a weakly connected graph with most publishers only linking to one other data source [2].

This section presents the **Silk Link Discovery Framework**, which generates RDF links between data items based on user-provided or automatically learned *linkage rules*. Silk can be used by data providers to generate RDF links pointing at existing Web datasets, and then publish them together with the primary datasets. Furthermore, applications that consume Linked Data can use Silk as an identity resolution component to augment the data with additional RDF links that have not been discovered and/or published.

In Silk linkage rules are expressed using a declarative language, and define the conditions that data items must conform to in order to be interlinked. For instance, a linkage rule defines which properties should be compared (e.g. *movieTitle* in one dataset and *label* in another), which similarity measures should be used for comparison and how they are to be combined.

Writing good linkage rules by hand is a non-trivial problem, which requires considerable effort and expertise. To address this, Silk implements the *ActiveGenLink* algorithm which combines *genetic programming* and *active learning* techniques to generate high-quality expressive linkage rules interactively, minimizing the involvement of a human expert. In this section, we will briefly introduce the tool and the underlying algorithms. For further details readers are referred to [8,9].

3.1   Silk: Functionality and Main Concepts

The Silk Link Discovery Framework can be downloaded from its official homepage[4], which is also the source for the documentation, examples and updates.

---

[4] http://wifo5-03.informatik.uni-mannheim.de/bizer/silk/

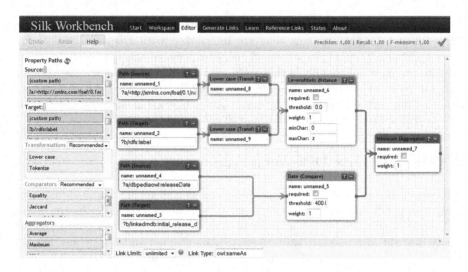

Fig. 2. Silk Workbench: linkage rule editor

It is an open source tool with the source code and the detailed developer documentation available online[5]. Silk can be used through the *Silk Workbench* graphical user interface or from the command line.

The Silk Workbench, developed in the course of the LOD2 project, aims at guiding the user through the process of interlinking different data sources. It is a web application offering the following functionality:

- Possibility to manage different data sources and linking tasks (with RDF dump files as well as local and remote SPARQL endpoints as input).
- Graphical editor to create and edit linkage rules (see Fig. 2).
- Possibility to evaluate links generated by the current linkage rule.
- User interface for learning linkage rules from existing reference links.
- Active learning interface, which learns a linkage rule by interactively asking the user to confirm or decline a number of candidate links.
- Possibility to create and edit a set of reference links used to evaluate the current link specification.

Additionally, Silk provides 3 command line applications: *Silk Single Machine* generates RDF links on a single machine, with input datasets either residing on the same machine or accessed via the SPARQL protocol; *Silk MapReduce* generate RDFs links between datasets using a cluster of multiple machines, is based on Hadoop and thus enables Silk to scale out to very big datasets. Finally, *Silk Server* [10] can be used as an identity resolution component within applications that consume Linked Data from the Web.

The basic concept in Silk is that of a *linkage rule*, which specifies the conditions under which two entities are considered to be referring to the same

---

[5] https://www.assembla.com/spaces/silk/wiki

real-world entity. A linkage rule assigns a similarity value to a pair of entities. We represent a linkage rule as a tree built from 4 types of operators.

Property Operator: Retrieves all values of a specific property of each entity, such as of values of the *label* property.

Transformation Operator: Transforms the values according to a specific data transformation function, e.g. case normalization, tokenization, concatenation. Multiple transformation operators can be nested in order to apply a sequence of transformations.

Comparison Operator: Evaluates the similarity between the values of two input operators according to a specific distance measure, such as Levenshtein, Jaccard, or geographic distance. A user-specified threshold specifies the maximum distance, and is used to normalize the measure.

Aggregation Operator: As often the similarity of two entities cannot be determined by evaluating a single comparison, an aggregation operator combines the scores from multiple comparison or aggregation operators according to an aggregation function, e.g. weighted average or minimum.

The resulting linkage rule forms a tree where the terminal nodes are represented by property operators and the internal nodes are represented by transformation, comparison and aggregation operators, see Fig. 2 for an example.

3.2   The GenLink Algorithm

Creating a good linkage rule by hand, that is choosing and combining appropriate operators and thresholds, is non-trivial and time-consuming. One way to reduce this effort is to use *supervised learning* to generate links from existing reference links, which contain pairs of entities labeled as matches or non-matches. Creating such reference links is much easier than writing linkage rules as it requires no previous knowledge about similarity measures or the specific linkage rule format used by the system. Usually, reference links are created by domain experts who confirm or reject the equivalence of a number of entity pairs from the input datasets.

In [8] we have presented the **GenLink algorithm** for automatically learning linkage rules from a set of reference links. The algorithm is based on *genetic programming* and generates linkage rules that can be understood and further improved by humans.

Genetic programming starts with a randomly created population of individuals, where each individual is represented by a tree which is a potential solution to the given problem. In Silk, in order to reduce the search space, before generating the initial population we build, given a set of positive reference links, a list of property pairs which hold similar values, and then use this set to build a random linkage rule.

Starting with the initial population, the genetic algorithm breeds a new population by evolving selected linkage rules using the reproduction, crossover and mutation genetic operators. A *fitness function* is used to assign a value to each linkage rule which indicates how close the rule is to the desired solution. We use the fitness measure based on *Matthews correlation coefficient,* and penalize linkage rules based on their number of operators. Based on the fitness of each linkage rule, the *selection method,* tournament selection in our case, selects the rules to be evolved. The algorithm iteratively evolves the population until either a linkage rule has been found which covers all reference links or a configured maximum number of 50 iterations is reached.

The experimental evaluation [8] shows that the GenLink produces better results than the state-of-art genetic programming approaches for identity resolution.

3.3   The ActiveGenLink Algorithm

For most real-world datasets it is not feasible, however, to manually create reference links covering a big enough subset of pairs of entities. Moreover, in order for the supervised learning algorithms to perform well on unknown data, reference links need to include all relevant *corner cases.* For example, while for most pairs of movie descriptions comparing titles is enough to establish that the two refer to the same movie, there might exist variations in titles of the same movie, or different movies having the same title but different release dates. The user has to label a very large number of *randomly selected* pairs in order to include these rare corner cases reliably.

To reduce the number of candidates to be labeled, we employ *active learning,* which in our case means iteratively selecting the most informative entity pair to be labeled by the user as matching or non-matching. In [9] we introduced the **ActiveGenLink algorithm,** which evolves a population of candidate solutions iteratively while building a set of reference links. The algorithm starts with a random population of linkage rules and an initially empty set of reference links. In each iteration, it selects a link candidate for which the current population of linkage rules is uncertain, from a pool of unlabeled links using a so called *query strategy.* After the link has been labeled by a human expert, the algorithm evolves the population of linkage rules using the GenLink algorithm and the extended set of reference links.

The query strategy Silk implements is based on a *query-by-committee* strategy: the selected link candidate is determined from the voting of all members of a committee, which consists of the current linkage rules in the population. We take as a baseline the widely used *query-by-vote-entropy,* which selects the candidate for which the members in the committee disagree the most, and introduce an improved strategy as follows. Firstly, as the unlabeled links are not distributed uniformly across the similarity space, we aim at distributing the links onto different clusters by selecting links that, based on the Jensen-Shannon divergence, are different from already labeled links. Secondly, the voting committee, i.e. the evolved population of linkage rules, may contain suboptimal linkage rules that do not cover all reference links. We implement the *restricted committee voting,* in which only linkage rules which fulfill a specific reference link are allowed to vote. Our experiments show that the improved query strategy outperforms the query-by-vote-entropy baseline.

The performance of the ActiveGenLink algorithm was evaluated on the same datasets as we used to evaluate the supervised GenLink algorithm [8]. The results show that by labeling a small number of links, ActiveGenLink achieves a comparable performance to GenLink on the complete reference link set. One of the datasets on which the evaluation was performed is *SiderDrugBank* from the *Ontology Alignment Evaluation Initiative* (OAEI) 2010 data interlinking track[6]. Our evaluation showed that with ActiveGenLink only about 30 links had to be labeled until a linkage rule could be learned which achieves an F-measure similar to the one GenLink gets using all 1718 reference links.

Two other experiments were done on the datasets that have been used frequently to evaluate the performance of different record linkage approaches: *Cora* and *Restaurant* datasets[7]. The results show that labeling a small number of links is enough to reach high performance. In addition, we successfully evaluated how the learned linkage rules compare to rules manually created by a human expert for the same dataset, and studied the scalability of the proposed approach. For the details of all the evaluation experiments the reader is referred to [9].

In order to further improve the linking precision we have developed the Silk Free Text Preprocessor [12], an extension of Silk for producing a structured representation for linking the data that contains or is derived from free text.

4   Data Cleansing and Reconciliation with LODRefine

Data cleansing and linking are very important processes in the life cycle of linked data, especially when creating new linked data. Nowadays data comes from different sources and it is published in many formats, e.g. XML, CSV, HTML, as dumps from relational databases or different services.

Unfortunately, cleansing and linking are rarely trivial, and can be very tedious, especially with the lack of good tools. A good cleansing tool should be able to assist users in detecting non-consistent data, removing duplicates, quickly performing transformations on a relatively large amount of data at once, and exporting cleansed data into different formats. It should be relatively simple to use and available on different operating systems. Fortunately, there is a open source (BSD licensed) solution available meeting all the above criteria. *OpenRefine*, previously Google Refine, was specifically created for dealing with messy data, is extendable, works on all three major operating systems and provides functionalities to reconcile data against Freebase. For needs of the LOD2 project we developed a LOD-enabled version of *OpenRefine* – **LODRefine**[8].

---

[6] http://oaei.ontologymatching.org/2010/im/index.html

[7] XML version: http://www.hpi.uni-potsdam.de/naumann/projekte/dude_duplicate_detection.html

[8] Available for download at http://sourceforge.net/projects/lodrefine/ or as a source code at https://github.com/sparkica/LODRefine

Even with tools available, data cleansing and linking in the LOD cycle still require a lot of manual work, and the current algorithms and fully automatated tools cannot completely replace human intuition and knowledge: it can be too complicated or costly to encode all our knowledge and experience into rules and procedures computers can understand. Although we already have good cleansing and linking tools at our disposal requiring only minimal human intervention, with huge amounts of data even simple tasks add up and time resources become an issue.

However, such tasks are often simple and include evaluation of automatically obtained results, finding missing information or, in rare cases, demand special domain knowledge. *Crowdsourcing* seems to be a promising solution for such situations and offers hiring affordable working power for certain repetitive but relatively simple tasks, especially when automated processing does not give good enough results, e.g. when classifying spam, categorizing images, and disambiguating data. To bring crowdsourcing closer to the needs of the LOD2 project we added support for using *CrowdFlower*[9], a popular and versatile crowdsourcing platform, directly from the LODRefine environment. In the rest of this section we introduce LODRefine and shortly describe three use cases of using crowdsourcing for different tasks, namely, data cleansing and disambiguation of reconciliation results.

4.1 LODRefine

LODRefine, a powerful tool for cleansing and automatically reconciling data with external databases, includes all core features of *OpenRefine* and extends them with LOD-specific ones. *Core features* include:

- Importing data from various formats.
- Cleansing data: finding duplicates, removing them, finding similar values.
- Filtering data using faceted browsing.
- Filtering data with regular expressions.
- Google Refine Expression language (GREL): a powerful language for transforming data.
- Reconciling with Freebase: the ability of linking your data to Freebase.
- Extending data from Freebase: the ability of adding data from Freebase to your reconciled data.

Figure 3 features faceted browsing, using regular expressions and GREL. *LOD-enabling features* added support for:

- Reconciliation and extending data with DBpedia.
- Named-entity recognition: recognizing and extracting named entities from text using different services.
- Using crowdsourcing: creating crowdsourcing jobs and uploading data to crowdsourcing platforms.

---

[9] http://www.crowdflower.com/

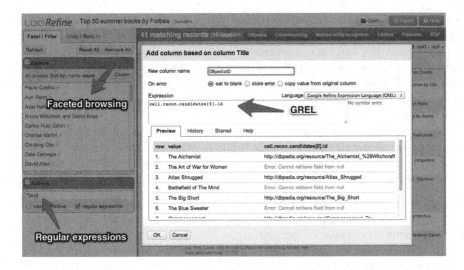

Fig. 3. LODRefine: faceted browsing, support for regular expressions and using GREL

4.2   Use Cases

The quality of reconciliation may vary with data and manual evaluation of those results is needed. In case we do not have available human resources crowdsourcing might be considered as a viable solution.

In the following we describe three use cases of using crowdsourcing from and within LODRefine. For further details readers are referred to the corresponding project deliverable [13].

Evaluating reconciliation results. Quality of linking (reconciliation) in the context of Linked Data can be evaluated by using rather sophisticated algorithms or manually with human evaluators. In the last case crowdsourcing can significantly speed up the process, especially when LODRefine is used to create a job from reconciliation evaluation template.

In this use case crowdsourcing was used to evaluate the quality of reconciled dataset of National Football League players[10]. Data contains names of players and links to their official profiles on NFL webpage. Freebase was used for reconciliation, and manual evaluation was done first by a group of in-house trained evaluators and then by workers at CrowdFlower. Because we already had verified evaluation results, we were able to asses the quality of results obtained by crowdsourcing.

Validation using crowdsourcing was split in two batches. For the first batch we collected three judgments per unit and for the second batch we lowered the overall costs by collecting only two judgments per unit. Although the quality of judgments dropped slightly for the second batch, the ratio costs versus quality of results was satisfiable.

---

[10] Official NFL webpage: http://www.nfl.com/

Validating named entities extracted from blogs. Integrating new entities into recommendation system is crucial for suggesting relevant contents to bloggers. New entities can be discovered by extracting links from blog posts. New links are considered as potential new named entities and links' anchors as entity aliases. In this use case we use crowdsourcing to verify extracted links from blog posts and mark them as entities if appropriate. If link was considered an entity, contributors also provided the type of entity.

We published this job on all available channels, which was reflected in the high number of overall units per hour, while in other two use cases we only used 2–4 labor channels (Amazon MTurk was always selected) and thus obtained much lower overall units per hour.

Data enrichment – finding missing information about festivals. Finding missing bits of information and enriching data is a frequently appearing type of assignment on crowdsourcing platforms.

In this use case we used crowdsourcing to enrich a dataset about festivals, which was extracted from blog posts mentioning festival and conference-like events either with their short names or using the full titles. In some cases blog posts mentioned words "festival" or "fest", but in a different context, and were wrongly extracted as a festival. We wanted to identify such cases and enrich data about actual festivals.

Data enrichment took much longer than other two use cases. Searching for data about festivals was more time consuming and questions were slightly more difficult. The price set was also relatively low, which was the other factor impacting time needed to collect responses.

4.3   Quality Evaluation of Crowdsourcing Results

All results obtained by crowdsourcing have been evaluated by comparing them to results provided by in-house trained evaluators. A lot depends on how instructions and questions are formulated, how much quality control is involved and which labor channels tasks are published on. In our case we got the best results in the first use case, in which contributors had to choose one of the provided suggestions or find a link in Freebase and thus there was not much room for subjectivity. Second best use case was data enrichment, where contributors had to check, whether the link contains information about a certain type of event – a festival – and provide a full name, a short name and a homepage for it. Again, the instructions and questions did not allow for too much subjectivity. The least good results were obtained in the second use case involving the evaluation of named entities. There are many possible causes for this: it might be not easy to grasp the notion of a named entity for an average contributor, contributors might not read instructions carefully enough, or instructions might have been too complicated.

Crowdsourcing is a relatively new business model and still requires some time before it will be fully mature and properly supported by legislation, but it can be regarded as a useful and feasible approach at least for some types of

LOD-related problems and tasks that were described and demonstrated above. There are several considerations that need to be taken into account while using crowdsourcing: quality assurance measures and constraints have to be applied and ethical issues related to fair price and reward for all contributors have to be considered. Although we would not use it for sensitive data or for gigabytes of data at once, crowdsourcing can serve as a starting point for developing automated solutions. It can provide means to collect enough data to train algorithms and to evaluate results obtained by those algorithms.

5 Data Quality Assessment and Fusion

The vocabulary alignment and interlinking steps presented in Sects. 2 and 3, result in interlinked entity descriptions originating from a number of heterogeneous data sources. The *quality* of data from these sources is very diverse [1], as values may be out of date, incomplete or incorrect, either because of data extraction errors or due to the errors by human data editors. Situations in which *conflicting values* for a property of a real-world object are provided often occur. In order for Linked Data applications to efficiently consume data, the latter should be assessed and integrated based on their quality.

Quality is a subjective matter, often defined as a "fitness for use", meaning that the interpretation of the quality of a data item depends on who will use it and for what task. Data quality has many dimensions such as accuracy, timeliness, completeness, relevancy, objectivity, believability, understandability, consistency, conciseness, availability, verifiability, etc. These dimensions are not independent of each other and typically only a subset of them is relevant in a specific situation. With the objective of supporting user applications in dealing with data quality and conflict resolution issues, we created **Sieve – Linked Data Quality Assessment and Fusion framework**[11] [11], which we summarize in this section.

Sieve consists of two components: Data Quality Assessment and Data Fusion, and takes as input data to be fused and an XML file containing both quality assessment and data fusion configurations. The input XML-based specification language allows a user to manually define conflict resolution strategies and quality assessment metrics to use for each data property.

Sieve takes as input two or more RDF data sources, along with the data provenance information. It is assumed that schema and object identifiers have been normalized, namely, if two descriptions refer to the same real-world object then they have the same identifier (URI), and if two properties refer to the same real-world attribute then there should be two values for the same property URI for a given subject URI. Each property value in the input is expressed by a quad *(subject,property,object,graph)* where the *graph* is a named graph, which is used to attach provenance information to a fact or a set of facts. For an example see Listing 2, where the input data for the population of Amsterdam coming from three different DBpedia editions is given, along with the last edit

---

[11] http://sieve.wbsg.de

date information. Note that the 4th quad component, the provenance graph for
lastedit property, is the same for all three triples and is omitted due to space
reasons.

```
1  dbp:Amsterdam  dbpedia-owl:population"820654"  en:Amsterdam:population
2  dbp:Amsterdam  dbpedia-owl:population  "758198"  ca:Amsterdam:population
3  dbp:Amsterdam  dbpedia-owl:population  "820654"  it:Amsterdam:population
4  en:Amsterdam:population  dpb-meta:lastedit  "2013-01-13T14:52:13Z"
5  ca:Amsterdam:population  dpb-meta:lastedit  "2009-06-14T10:36:30Z"
6  it:Amsterdam:population  dpb-meta:lastedit  "2013-03-24T17:04:16Z"
```

Listing 2. Data Fusion with Sieve: input data

5.1 Quality Assessment Metrics

Three main concepts Sieve uses in the quality assessment configuration are *quality indicators*, *scoring functions* and *assessment metrics*. A *data quality indicator*
is an aspect of a data item or dataset that may indicate the suitability of the
data for some intended use. The types of information used as quality indicators
may stem from the metadata about the circumstances in which information was
created, to information about the information provider, to data source ratings.
A *scoring function* produces a numerical representation of the suitability of the
data, based on some quality indicator. Each indicator may be associated with
several scoring functions, e.g. max or average functions can be used with the
data source rating indicator. *Assessment metrics* are procedures for measuring
information quality based on a set of quality indicators and scoring functions.
Additionally, assessment metrics can be *aggregated* through the average, sum,
max, min or threshold functions.

For an example see Listing 3, where *recency* assessment metric uses the *last
update* timestamp of a dataset or a single fact, a quality indicator which is transformed by *TimeCloseness* scoring function into a numeric score using a range
parameter (in days) to normalize the scores. Other scoring functions available
in Sieve include normalizing the value of a quality indicator, or calculating the
score based on whether the indicator value belongs to some interval or exceeds
a given threshold. The complete list of supported scoring functions is available
at the Sieve webpage; users can define their own scoring functions using Scala
and the guidelines provided at the webpage.

The output of the quality assessment module is a set of quads, where the
calculated scores are associated with each graph. A graph can contain the whole
dataset (e.g. Dutch DBpedia) or a subset of it (all properties of Berlin in Freebase) or a single fact. The scores represent the user-configured interpretation of
quality and are then used by the Data Fusion module.

```
1  <QualityAssessment>
2    <AssessmentMetric id="sieve:recency">
3      <ScoringFunction class="TimeCloseness">
4        <Param name="timeSpan" value="500"/>
5        <Input path="?GRAPH/dpb-meta:lastedit"/>
6      </ScoringFunction>
7    </AssessmentMetric>
8  </QualityAssessment>
```

```
 9   <Fusion>
10     <Class name="dbpedia-owl:PopulatedPlace">
11       <Property name="dbpedia-owl:population">
12         <FusionFunction class="KeepFirst" metric="sieve:recency"/>
13       </Property>
14     </Class>
15   </Fusion>
```

Listing 3. Data Fusion with Sieve: specification

5.2 Fusion Functions

In the context of data integration, Data Fusion is defined as the "process of fusing multiple records representing the same real-world object into a single, consistent, and clean representation" [5]. Data Fusion is commonly seen as a third step following schema mapping and identity resolution, as a way to deal with conflicts that either already existed in the original sources or were generated by integrating them.

The Sieve Data Fusion module is inspired by [4], a framework for data fusion in the context of relational databases that includes three major categories of conflict handling strategies:

- Conflict-ignoring strategies, which defer conflict resolution to the user. For instance, *PassItOn* strategy simply relays conflicts to the user or applications consuming integrated data.
- Conflict-avoiding strategies, which apply a unique decision to all data. For instance, strategy *TrustYourFriends* strategy prefers data from specific data sources.
- Conflict-resolution strategies, which decide between existing data (e.g. *Keep-UpToDate*, which takes the most recent value), or mediate the creation of a new value from the existing ones (e.g. *Average*).

In Sieve, fusion functions are of two types. *Filter functions* remove some or all values from the input, according to some quality metric, for example *keep the value with the highest score* for a given metric (e.g. recency or trust) or *vote* to select the most frequent value. *Transform functions* operate over each value in the input, generating a new list of values built from the initially provided ones, e.g. computing the *average* of the numeric values. The complete list of supported fusion functions is available at the Sieve webpage, and users have the possibility to implement their own functions.

The example of the specification in Listing 3 illustrates how a fusion function for the *population* property of a populated place is configured to use *KeepFirst* fusion function (i.e. keep the highest score) applied to *recency* quality assessment metric.

The output of the data fusion module is a set of quads, each representing a fused value of a subject-property pair, with the 4th component of the quad identifying the named graph from which a value has been taken. An extension of Sieve for automatically learning an optimal conflict resolution policy is presented in [6].

6   Data Interlinking and Fusion for Asian Languages

As the proportion of non-Western data that went to open is relatively small, recently many projects have been initiated to extend the boundary of Linked Open Data to non-European language resources, especially in such writing systems as Korean, Chinese and Japanese. Interlinking and integrating multilingual resources across languages and writing systems will allow exploiting the full potential of Linked Data.

This section presents the tools we developed to support interlinking and integrating Asian resources: **Asian Resource Linking Assistant** and **Asian Data Fusion Assistant**. The Asian Resource Linking Assistant extends Silk with Korean Phonemic Distance metric, Korean Transliteration Distance metric, and Han Edit Distance metric. The Asian Data Fusion Assistant extends Sieve by providing functions for translating phrases among Korean, Chinese, Japanese and English.

6.1   Interlinking Korean Resources in the Korean Alphabet: Korean Phoneme Distance

Using string distance metrics such as Levenshtein, or edit distance, is a popular way to measure distance between two strings in Western languages. When we apply Levenshtein distance to Korean strings, the output is based not on the number of letters but on the number of combinations of letters. This is because the unit of comparison is different between a single-byte code set and a multi-byte code set. The unit of comparison for single-byte code is a single letter. In Korean, however, a combination of two or three (occasionally four but rarely more) letters, which constitutes a syllable, is assigned to one code point. So when the edit distance between Korean strings is 1, it could mean 1 (as in case of English strings), but also 2, 3 or occasionally more letters. Therefore, we have developed a new Korean distance metric that reflects the nature of a multi-byte code set.

Our approach is based on the idea that the more the phonemes are distributed across the syllables, the less is the possibility the two string have the same meaning. For example, if two target strings have two different phonemes, then one target string with one syllable containing two different phonemes is closer to a source string than the other target string with two syllables each containing one different phoneme. For example, the distance between "바람" ("wind" in English) and "보름" ("15 days" in English) with a syllable-based metric is 2β whereas the distance between them is $1\beta+1\alpha$ (α: weight for syllable, β: weight for phoneme) with our metric.

The Korean Phoneme Distance metric is defined in Eq. (1), where sD is the syllable distance, and pDn is a list of phoneme distances of each syllable.

$$\text{if } (sD_0 > 0) \min_{0 \leq i \leq I} [(sD_i - 1) * \beta + \min_{0 \leq n \leq N} (spD_{in}) * \alpha], \text{ else } 0 \qquad (1)$$

This new metric can control the range of the target string more precisely, especially for those string pairs that have only one or two phonemes different from only one syllable. For example, if a threshold of two is applied, then a search for "호랑이" ("tiger" in English) would find its dialect "호래이" as a candidate (only the first syllable is different). But a syllable-based metric would find many of its variations such as "오라이" ("OK" in English) as well (the first and second syllables are different). This algorithm is especially useful for finding matching words in dialects and words with long histories, which have many variations across the country, and the variations have some similar patterns. This metric can fine-tune the distribution of different phonemes, and precision can be improved by reducing irrelevant information to be retrieved. Therefore, this metric is especially effective in enhancing precision by reducing the number of irrelevant records compared with Levenshtein.

6.2   Interlinking Korean Resources in Korean and English: Korean Transliteration Distance

During translation some terms may be transliterated from one language to another in case translators cannot find proper corresponding terminology in that local language. Transliteration is a way of converting letters from one writing system into another without concern for representing the original phonemics. For example, a Korean popular food called "칼국수" (translated as knife-cut Korean noodles) can be transliterated as *kalguksu* in English.

The best approach to measure distance between transliterated strings would be to apply Korean Phoneme Distance to the strings transliterated back. This approach, however, is complicated because a transliterated Korean string could be back transliterated into several possible original Korean strings in case the transliterated string has no explicit notation for identifying syllables. Unfortunately, existing transliteration systems do not consider back-transliteration, so no explicit borders of syllables, which is important to restore the original Korean words, exist. Although many efforts have focused on the back transliteration to help people identify the original string better, many existing Korean-English transliteration systems lack this mechanism.

Due to this difficulty, we decided to take a simpler but more practical approach for measuring distance between transliterated Korean strings, namely, Korean Transliteration Distance, which chooses one random letter for each consonant group from the International Phonetic Alphabet (IPA) chart. For example, as 'b' and 'p' belong to the bilabial plosive group, Korean Transliteration Distance replaces every 'b' with 'p'. Similarly, it replaces 'g' with 'k', 'd' with 't', and 'l' with 'r' (although 'l' and 'r' do not belong to the same group, they are used interchangeably in Korea). The main difference between Soundex and Korean Transliteration Distance is that Korean Transliteration Distance does not eliminate vowels or other consonants, does not remove duplicates, and does not limit the number of letters for comparison. There are three reasons for this. First, the Korean alphabet has 10 vowels and 14 consonants compared with 5 vowels and 21 consonants in English, so Korean vowels play a more important role in matching words than English vowels do. Second, the Korean alphabet has letters with fortis, which is expressed with two identical consonants in succession, so the meaning of the string will be lost if duplicate consonants are removed. Third, keeping all the letters is a more conservative and safer way to measure distance. This metric is especially useful for enhancing recall while keeping precision almost intact compared with Levenshtein and for enhancing precision compared with Soundex, thereby contributing to obtaining a higher number of correct links when used in Silk.

6.3   Interlinking Asian Resources in Chinese Alphabet: Han Edit Distance

China, Japan and Korea (CJK) are geographically close and have influenced each other language systems for thousand years. CJK share Han Chinese even though Japan and Korea have their own writing systems, and many currently used words in the three countries were derived from ancient Han Chinese. That means language resources existing in the three countries can be better matched and interlinked when the lineage is properly utilized. Therefore, a new linguistic similarity metric was developed to measure distances between commonly used Chinese letters among the three languages.

Han Edit Distance (HED) is a new similarity metric for Chinese, Japanese and Korean based on the Unihan database. The Unihan database covers more than 45,000 codes and contains mapping data to allow conversion to and from other coded character sets and additional information to help implement support for the various languages that use the Han ideographic script. As the Unihan database provides a variety of information associated with Han Chinese, HED measures similarities between two words by using this information.

As Han Chinese has been used in many Asian countries for a long period of time, Han characters are pronounced differently, and some of the shapes have changed over time in different regions. *Reading* category in the Unihan database shows the pronunciation of the same unified ideographs in Mandarin, Cantonese, Tang-dynasty Chinese, Japanese, Sino-Japanese, Korean and Vietnamese. The *Variants* category includes a variety of relationships with Han Chinese that can be used for interlinking. In Han Edit Distance, each piece of information about Han Chinese characters was classified into Reading and Semantic categories. That is, kMandarin, kJapaneseOn, kJapaneseKun, kKorean and kHangul are classified into the Reading category, and kSemanticVariant, kCompatibilityVariant, kSimplifiedVariant, kRSUnicode and kTotalStroke are classified into the Semantic category.

Figure 4 shows how HED is measured: it calculates Reading and Semantic distances using each category, sums the total distance, and normalizes the distance. The number of matching properties from the Reading category is the distance between two characters. Therefore, the maximum reading distance is 5 because Reading category has 5 properties. Semantic distance is calculated by comparing 3 semantic properties (semantic, compatibility, simplified variant). If any of the three matches, the two characters are believed to have a semantic relationship. If no match exists, then a semantic distance is calculated by counting radical strokes. That is, the number of total strokes of two characters when the

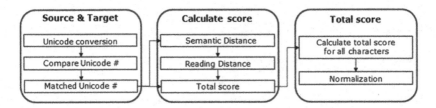

Fig. 4. Detailed process of Han Edit Distance algorithm

family root is the same becomes the distance. We defined 30 to be the maximum number of total strokes, even though the total number of strokes is larger than 30, but the number of Chinese characters that have more than 30 strokes is rare (about 0.23 %) in the Unihan database.

As Han Chinese words can be composed of one or more characters, we performed two types of experiments to compare with Levenshtein distance by using commonly used Han Chinese characters (1,936 pairs) and by using Han Chinese words (618 pairs). The F-measure scores of both experiments show better performance, specially as high as 23 % for Han Chinese words. From the experiment, the HED method shows performance improvements in comparison with Levenshtein distance for Han characters commonly used in Chinese, Japanese and Korean.

6.4   Asian Data Fusion Assistant

Integrating multilingual resources to derive new or unified values has not shown the full potential in the context of Linked Data partly because of language barriers. Asian Fusion Assistant, an extension of Sieve, aims at facilitating the fusion process by adding translation functionality from one Asian language to another. While machine translation systems pursue full automatic translation without human intervention by using a large bilingual corpora, building a machine translation system for each pairs of languages is hard to achieve. Therefore, we adopted a *translation memory* approach for two reasons. First, existing human translations can be fully utilized. Second, not every part of RDF triples ought to be translated, but only plain literals that have language tags.

A translation memory system provides similar translation pairs upon translator's requests and stores new translation pairs produced by human translators. Wikipedia (and hence, DBpedia) texts with inter-language links for many languages is a valuable source of translation memories. Therefore, parallel text pairs were collected from Korean, English, Chinese and Japanese DBpedia and stored separately. Although RDF triple translation follows the architecture of translation memory systems, one major difference is that human translators are substituted with (free) internet translation services. The advantages of using the Internet translation API services (e.g. Microsoft Bing) are that they usually support many language pairs and because the concerns about translation quality are reduced as texts to be translated are not sentences but nouns or noun phrases.

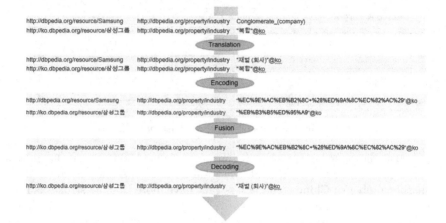

Fig. 5. Asian fusion process

Asian resource fusion process consists of 4 steps: translation, encoding, quality assessment/conflict resolution and decoding as shown at Fig. 5. Translation is only invoked when input triples contain plain literals with language tags. Encoder encodes multi-byte letters (e.g. Korean) into a stream of single-byte letters, and then Sieve performs quality assessment and conflict resolution to produce an integrated result. Finally, Decoder decodes all encoded strings into the original language again. We expect that translation memory systems can be globally interconnected and can boost the multilingual data fusion.

7 Conclusion

In this chapter we have presented the tools for vocabulary mapping, data interlinking, quality assessment and fusion, developed in the context of the LOD2 project. Specifically, R2R supports vocabulary mappings, Silk and LODRefine facilitate the process of creating and evaluating the quality of links among datasest, Sieve assists its users in assessing the data quality and resolving value conflicts. Additionally, Silk and Sieve has been extended to address interlinking and fusion issues specific to CJK (Chinese, Japanese and Korean) languages.

The presented tools are open source and make part of the Linked Data stack (see Chap. 6). The tools have been extensively evaluated, for the details the reader is referred to the respective sections, cited articles and tools' webpages. These tools have been applied within LOD2 project, e.g. in a media publishing, enterprise and public procurement use cases, for the details see Chaps. 7, 8 and 10 of the present book, respectively.

References

1. Acosta, M., Zaveri, A., Simperl, E., Kontokostas, D., Auer, S., Lehmann, J.: Crowd-sourcing linked data quality assessment. In: Alani, H., Kagal, L., Fokoue, A., Groth, P., Biemann, C., Parreira, J.X., Aroyo, L., Noy, N., Welty, Ch., Janowicz, K. (eds.) ISWC 2013, Part II. LNCS, vol. 8219, pp. 260–276. Springer, Heidelberg (2013)
2. Bizer, C., Jentzsch, A., Cyganiak, R.: State of the LOD cloud. Technical report, Freie Universität Berlin (2011). http://lod-cloud.net/state/
3. Bizer, C., Schultz, A.: The R2R framework: publishing and discovering mappings on the web. In: Proceedings of the 1st International Workshop on Consuming Linked Data (COLD) (2010)
4. Bleiholder, J., Naumann, F.: Declarative data fusion – syntax, semantics, and implementation. In: Eder, J., Haav, H.-M., Kalja, A., Penjam, J. (eds.) ADBIS 2005. LNCS, vol. 3631, pp. 58–73. Springer, Heidelberg (2005)
5. Bleiholder, J., Naumann, F.: Data fusion. ACM Comput. Surv. **41**(1), 1:1–1:41 (2009)
6. Bryl, V., Bizer, C.: Learning conflict resolution strategies for cross-language Wikipedia data fusion. In: 4th Workshop on Web Quality Workshop (WebQuality) at WWW 2014 (2014)
7. Heath, T., Bizer, C.: Linked data: evolving the web into a global data space. Synthesis Lectures on the Semantic Web: Theory and Technology. Morgan & Claypool Publishers, San Rafael (2011)
8. Isele, R., Bizer, C.: Learning expressive linkage rules using genetic programming. Proc. VLDB Endowment **5**(11), 1638–1649 (2012)
9. Isele, R., Bizer, C.: Active learning of expressive linkage rules using genetic programming. J. Web Semant. **23**, 2–15 (2013)
10. Isele, R., Jentzsch, A., Bizer, C.: Silk server - adding missing links while consuming linked data. In: Proceedings of the 1st International Workshop on Consuming Linked Data (COLD 2010), pp. 85–97 (2010)
11. Mendes, P.N., Mühleisen, H., Bizer, C.: Sieve: linked data quality assessment and fusion. In: EDBT/ICDT Workshops, pp. 116–123 (2012)
12. Petrovski, P., Bryl, V., Bizer, C.: Integrating product data from websites offering Microdata markup. In: 4th Workshop on Data Extraction and Object Search (DEOS2014) at WWW 2014 (2014)
13. Verlic, M.: Release of documentation and software infrastructure for using Google Refine along with Amazon Mechanical Turk, 2013. LOD2 project deliverable D4.6.2. http://static.lod2.eu/Deliverables/D4.6.2.pdf

Facilitating the Exploration and Visualization of Linked Data

Christian Mader[1], Michael Martin[2(✉)], and Claus Stadler[2]

[1] Semantic Web Company, Vienna, Austria
christian.mader@semantic-web.at
[2] University of Leipzig, Leipzig, Germany
{martin,cstadler}@informatik.uni-leipzig.de

Abstract. The creation and the improvement of tools that cover exploratory and visualization tasks for Linked Data were one of the major goals focused in the LOD2 project. Tools that support those tasks are regarded as essential for the Web of Data, since they can act as a user-oriented starting point for data customers. During the project, several development efforts were made, whose results either facilitate the exploration and visualization directly (such as OntoWiki, the Pivot Browser) or can be used to support such tasks. In this chapter we present the three selected solutions *rsine*, *CubeViz* and *Facete*.

1 Introduction

The increasing number of datasets that are available as Linked Data on the Web makes it difficult for dataset curators to review additions, removals or updates of assertions involving resources they authored. Existing approaches like central registries do not scale with the fast-changing nature of the Web, thus being outdated or incomplete. In this chapter we propose a set of approaches that deal with the exploration and visualization of Linked Data. First we present the Resource SubscrIption and Notification sErvice (rsine) in Sect. 2 which enables subscribers to register for notifications whenever changes to RDF datasets occur. Thereby, we outline our approach based on a controlled vocabulary development scenario and integrate it into two exemplary LOD2 stack components to show its applicability. Based on requirements that come from practical experience in thesaurus development at Wolters Kluwer Germany, we describe how rsine can be used to check and avoid introduction of potential thesaurus quality problems.

Secondly, we showcase in Sect. 3 CubeViz, a flexible exploration and visualization platform for statistical data represented adhering to the RDF Data Cube vocabulary. If statistical data is represented according to that vocabulary, CubeViz exhibits a faceted browsing widget allowing to interactively filter observations to be visualized in charts. Based on the selected structural part, CubeViz offers suitable chart types and options for configuring the visualization by users. We present the CubeViz visualization architecture and components, sketch its underlying API and the libraries used to generate the desired output.

© The Author(s)
S. Auer et al. (Eds.): Linked Open Data, LNCS 8661, pp. 90–107, 2014.
DOI: 10.1007/978-3-319-09846-3_5

By employing advanced introspection, analysis and visualization bootstrapping techniques CubeViz hides the schema complexity of the encoded data in order to support a user-friendly exploration experience.

Lastly, we present Facete in Sect. 4, which is an application tailored for the exploration of SPARQL-accessible spatial data. Facete is built from a set of newly developed, highly modular and re-usable components, which power the following features:

- advanced faceted search with support of inverse properties and nested properties;
- automatic detection of property paths that connect the resources that matches the facet selection with those resources that can be shown on the map; and
- a map component that operates directly on a SPARQL endpoint and automatically adopts its data retrieval strategy based on the amount of available spatial information.

2 Rsine - Getting Notified on Linked Data Changes

With the growing amount of content available on the Web of Data it becomes increasingly difficult for human users to track changes of resources they are interested in. This even holds true for "local" use cases where, e.g., contributors are working on a dataset in a collaborative way, linking and annotating each other's resources.

For example, contributors who develop controlled vocabularies, typically want to know whenever the meaning of a concept is fundamentally changed. This is because the concept might have been used for indexing documents and the changed meaning impairs search precision. However, with increasing frequency of change and size of the curated information resources, pull-based approaches do not scale anymore.

In this section we introduce the Resource SubscrIption and Notification sErvice (rsine), a framework that notifies subscribers whenever assertions to resources they are interested in are created, updated or removed. It is based on the W3C standards RDF and SPARQL and designed to be used alongside with existing triple storage solutions supporting these technologies. Multiple instances of the framework can communicate dataset changes also among each other. This allows to subscribe for changes of resources that are created or modified in other datasets on the Web that are managed by rsine.

An application of rsine is for instance the support of integrated quality management in controlled vocabulary development. We have shown in our previous work [8,9] that potential quality problems in controlled Web vocabularies can be detected from patterns ("quality issues") in the underlying RDF graph. We believe that immediate notification of the responsible contributors after such quality issues have been introduced will lead to faster development and higher quality of the created vocabularies.

2.1 Related Work

SparqlPuSH [13] is a subscription/notification framework that allows for "proactive notification of data updates in RDF stores". Users express the resources they are interested in as SPARQL queries which are used by the service to create RSS or Atom feeds. These feeds are published on "hubs" using the PubSubHubbub protocol which handles the dissemination of notifications. Our approach is closely related to SparqlPuSH but is designed to operate on a more general level. In particular, creation and subscription to feeds, as proposed in SparqlPuSH, is only one of the possible options for notifying subscribers in rsine. Furthermore, SparqlPuSH only relies on the extensiveness of the data contained in the underlying RDF store. Thus, it is not possible to, e.g., find out about all resources deleted in a certain period of time. Rsine supports these scenarios by using a standard ontology for storing changeset metadata.

SDShare[1] is a protocol for the distribution of changes to resources that are represented in RDF. A server that exposes data provides four different Atom feeds that provide information about the state of the data and update information. The protocol is designed to support replications of linked data sources and relies on clients actively monitoring the provided feeds. Furthermore, clients only get information about the updated resource URIs and are expected to fetch the actual changes of resources themselves.

In the course of the REWERSE [10] project, a "general framework for evolution and reactivity in the Semantic Web" has been proposed that is based on Event-Condition-Action (ECA) rules. The framework is designed to be independent from the languages used to specify define events, conditions and actions. We stick to this approach but utilize a custom RDF ontology to express the ECA rules. Additionally we decided to use SPARQL for definitions of both events and conditions because of its wide acceptance and our focus on RDF data. This results in a light-weight approach, eliminating the need for custom event matchers and detection engines in favour of SPARQL endpoints and incremental RDF changesets. Actions are represented in our rsine ECA rules by specifying one or multiple notifiers.

2.2 Approach

Figure 1 describes the proposed architecture of the rsine service (Notification Service frame). The service on the left side of the figure is intended to give an overview on the components interacting internally, whereas the notification service on the right side is a second instance of the framework installed on a remote location on the Web.

Our approach uses a *Change Handler* that mediates between the *Managed RDF store* and the rsine service. In our implementation we provide a Change Handler (rsineVad[2]) that can be used for Virtuoso Servers. However, in environments that rely on different RDF storage backends such as openRDF Sesame,

---

[1] Final Draft:http://www.sdshare.org/spec/sdshare-20120710.html
[2] https://github.com/rsine/rsineVad

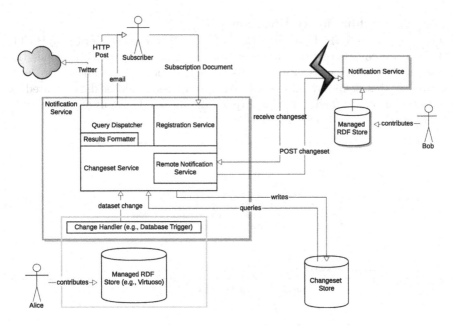

Fig. 1. Conceptual overview

a custom Change Handler that fits to the internals of the used storage solution must be implemented.

The rsine service continuously observes changes to the data held by a *Managed RDF Store* on the triple level, i.e., every time a triple is added, updated or removed the framework is triggered. The triple change events are then passed to the *Changeset Service* which converts the received triple changes to changesets expressed in the Changeset[3] ontology and persists them to an internal *Changeset Store*.

A subscriber who is interested in receiving notifications can subscribe by sending a subscription document to the service that contains SPARQL queries and information about the preferred notification channel (e.g., email, Twitter). The queries from the subscription document select resources the subscriber is interested in and access both the data contained in the *Managed RDF Store* as well as in the *Changeset Store*. The results of these queries, can then be disseminated through the desired channels. Before dissemination, the *Results Formatter* formats the query results into human-readable form by using the template provided in the subscription document.

Rsine can also send ("forward") local dataset changes to remote rsine instances on the Web (small Notification Service box). This feature is useful to get notifications whenever resources in datasets on different servers reference each other. Due to space limitations we refer to deliverable D5.3.1 for a detailed coverage of the workflows for both local and forwarded dataset changes.

---

[3] http://vocab.org/changeset/schema.html

2.2.1   Subscribing for Notifications

Subscriptions are RDF documents that are sent to the rsine service by HTTP POST. They consist of two mandatory parts: (i) a *query* which specifies the resources the subscriber is interested to get notifications about and (ii) at least one *notifier* that defines the way notification messages should be disseminated. A basic example is provided in Listing 1 (prefixes omitted, for an in-depth coverage we refer to the online documentation[4]).

```
1    [] a rsine:Subscription;
2        rsine:query [
3            spin:text"SELECT * WHERE {
4                ?cs a cs:ChangeSet .
5                ?cs cs:addition ?addition .
6                ?addition rdf:subject ?concept .
7                ?addition rdf:predicate skos:prefLabel .
8                ?addition rdf:object ?newLabel}";];
9
10       rsine:notifier [
11           a rsine:emailNotifier;
12           foaf:mbox <mailto:me@myoffice.com>].
```

Listing 1. Rsine Subscription.

2.3   Stack Integration

In order to showcase the capabilities of rsine, we integrated it with two exemplary components of the LOD2 stack: The *PoolParty Thesaurus Server* (PPT) and *Pebbles*. PPT is a tool for taxonomy experts to develop thesauri and publish them as Linked Data using SKOS. Pebbles is a Web application that provides a GUI to manage RDF metadata for XML documents. For testing the integration we used the stack installation operated by Wolters Kluwer Germany (WKD).

PPT builds on OpenRDF Sesame infrastructure for persisting RDF data. In order to provide interoperability between PPT and rsine, we implemented a subclass of `RepositoryConnectionListenerAdapter`. It intercepts the triple changes and, before handing them down to the triple store for persistence, announces them to rsine's HTTP interface.

Pebbles uses Virtuoso as storage backend. The only task for integrating rsine with Pebbles was thus to deploy the rsineVad package from the rsine repository to the Virtuoso instance. RsineVad is an extension to Virtuoso that configures database triggers and stored procedures so that all triple changes Pebbles performs to are communicated to rsine.

2.4   Notification Scenarios

WKD specified in total 13 scenarios for notifications that are described in detail in deliverable D7.3. They are divided into scenarios that are important in a thesaurus development process (e.g., to "follow all changes such as deletion,

---

[4] https://github.com/rsine/rsine#subscriptions

linking or editing of concepts") and scenarios from metadata editing with Pebbles (e.g., "Follow all changes of the document metadata"). We were able to support all but one requirements from the thesaurus development scenario and implemented one metadata editing scenario as a proof-of-concept. Furthermore, we adapted 9 checks for potential controlled vocabulary quality problems from our earlier work[5] and converted them for use with rsine. Among them are, e.g., checks for cyclic hierarchical relations or concepts with conflicting (i.e., identical) preferred labels.

3   CubeViz – Exploration and Visualization of Statistical Linked Data

A vast part of the existing Linked Data Web consists of statistics (cf. LOD-Stats[6] [3]) being represented according to the RDF Data Cube Vocabulary [2]. To hide the inherently complex, multidimensional statistical data structures and to offer a user-friendly exploration the RDF Data Cube Explorer CubeViz[7] has been developed. In this chapter we showcase how large data cubes comprising statistical data from different domains can be analysed, explored and visualized. CubeViz is based on the OntoWiki Framework [7] and consists of the following OntoWiki extensions:

- The *Integrity Analysis Component* (cf. Sect. 3.2) evaluates the existence and the quality of selected RDF graphs according to given integrity constraints.
- The *Facetted Data Selection Component* (cf. Sect. 3.3) is retrieving the structure of the selected Data Cube using SPARQL [5] in order to generate filter forms. Those forms allow to slice the data cube according to user interests.
- The *Chart Visualization Component* (cf. Sect. 3.4) receives all observation as input, that correspond to the given filter conditions, in order to generate a chart visualization.

All components support the comprehensive CubeViz GUI shown in Fig. 2. Before we introduce the three components in more detail, we give a brief introduction of the RDF Data Cube Vocabulary in the next section. We conclude the paper with links to publicly available deployments and a list of some upcoming features planned for the next release. Further information about CubeViz can be obtained in the repository wiki[8] or via a recorded webinar[9] comprising a comprehensive screencast.

3.1   The RDF Data Cube Vocabulary

The *RDF Data Cube vocabulary* is a W3C recommendation for representing statistical data in RDF. The vocabulary is compatible with the Statistical Data and

---

[5] qSKOS controlled vocabulary quality checker, https://github.com/cmader/qSKOS
[6] http://stats.lod2.eu/rdf_classes?search=Observation
[7] http://aksw.org/Projects/CubeViz
[8] https://github.com/AKSW/cubeviz.ontowiki/wiki
[9] http://www.youtube.com/watch?v=ZQc5lk1ug3M#t=1510

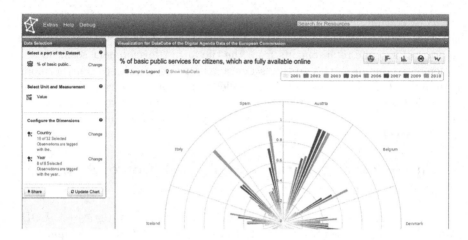

Fig. 2. The CubeViz GUI visualizing a slice of a 2-dimensional RDF DataCube in a combined polar-column chart.

Medadata eXchange XML format (SDMX) [4], which is defined by an initiative chartered in 2001 to support the exchange of statistical data. Sponsoring institutions[10] of SDMX are among others *the Bank for International Settlements*, the *European Central Bank*, *Eurostat*, the *International Monetary Fund*, the *Organisation for Economic Co-operation and Development* (OECD), the *United Nations Statistics Division* and the *World Bank*. Experiences while publishing statistical data on the Web using SDMX were summarized by the *United Nations* in [11] and by the OECD in [12].

The core concept of the Data Cube vocabulary is the class `qb:Observation`[11], that is used to type all statistical observations being part of a Data Cube. Every observation has to follow a specific structure that is defined using the class `qb:DataStructureDefinition` (DSD) and referenced by a dataset resource (DS) of type `qb:DataSet`. Since every observation should refer to one specific DS (which again refers to the corresponding DSD) the structure of the observation is fully specified. DSD components are defined as set of dimensions (`qb:DimensionProperty`), attributes (`qb:AttributeProperty`) and measures (`qb:MeasureProperty`) to encode the semantics of observations. Those component properties are used to link the corresponding elements of dimensions, measure values and units with the respective observation resource. Furthermore, it is possible to materialize groups and slices of observations as well as hierarchical orders of dimension elements using respective concepts.

---

[10] http://sdmx.org/?page_id=6
[11] Prefix qb:http://purl.org/linked-data/cube#

3.2   Integrity Analysis

As described in the W3C RDF Data Cube Recommendation document data cubes are structurally well-formed if they comply to specific integrity constraints[12]. Those constraints can be used to validate and if necessary to improve the quality of a data cube. For CubeViz, we translated those constraints into SPARQL queries using an ASK-clause returning boolean values. The queries were integrated into the Integrity Analysis Component of CubeViz, whose GUI is depicted in Fig. 3. If a query returns false, the corresponding constraint is marked in the GUI in red and can be selected in order to reuse and modify them with a configured query editor. This functionality supports the discovery of potential modelling or conversion flaws.

Additionally, this component is used to introspect the selected RDF model for all included data cubes. If the introspection query (given in Listing 2) returns a positive result, the Faceted Data Selection and Chart Visualization components are activated.

```
1  PREFIX qb:<http://purl.org/linked-data/cube#>
2  ASK FROM <http://example.org/> {
3    ?observation     a                qb:Observation .
4    ?observation     qb:dataSet       ?dataset .
5    ?observation     ?dimension       ?dimelement .
6    ?observation     ?measure         ?value .
7    ?dataset         a                qb:DataSet .
8    ?dataset         qb:structure     ?dsd .
9    ?dsd             a                qb:DataStructureDefinition .
10   ?dsd             qb:component     ?dimspec .
11   ?dsd             qb:component     ?measurespec .
12   ?dimspec         a                qb:ComponentSpecification .
13   ?dimspec         qb:dimension     ?dimension .
14   ?measurespec     a                qb:ComponentSpecification .
15   ?measurespec     qb:measure       ?measure}
```

Listing 2. Data cube introspection query.

3.3   Faceted Exploration

Given that the introspection was successful, specific structural parts of the identified data cube are queried in order to create a faceted search interface. All components of a DSD have to be integrated into any observation of the respective DS. In order to discover those observations the user has to select values that are referenced by those components. First the user needs to select a DS of a data cube in order to analyse the DSD that is the basis for all further facets. Second the user has to select the measure and attribute property used to identify the representation of values. The last mandatory facet is used to offer the selection of dimensions and its respective elements of interest. CubeViz is processing and visualizing values exactly as they are represented in the data cube and does not support aggregate functions such as SUM, AVG, MIN and MAX. As a consequence, users have to select at least one element of each dimension. Furthermore, if materialized slices are aggregated within the selected DS an optional facet will be generated to offer a selection from the retrieved slices.

---

[12] http://www.w3.org/TR/vocab-data-cube/#wf-rules

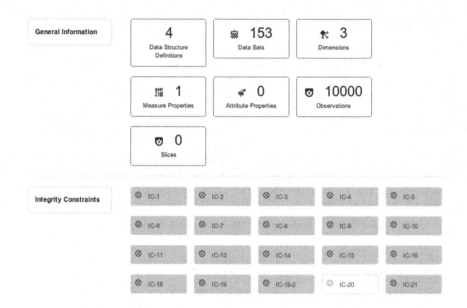

Fig. 3. GUI presenting results of the statistical and integrity analysis.

3.3.1 · Generation of Dialogues

The detected facets and their generated GUI representations are integrated into a filter form. To select/deselect elements of facets for extracting subsets of the DS, respective interface elements are dynamically created. According to the type of facet (mandatory/optional) a configurable amount of elements (min/max) is selectable. Additionally, the label and textual description of components are retrieved using SPARQL queries and added to the interface. As illustrated in Fig. 4 the selected amount of facet elements is displayed after confirmation. Already discovered RDF resources are cached on the client-side and will be re-used in the Chart Visualization component.

One of the major advantages of faceted exploration is the avoidance of possibly empty result sets. To avoid empty sets of observations after facet selection, the set of selectable elements of all further facets in combination with its respective count of observations is being calculated using respective SPARQL queries. Every selected combination of a component and its respective element is represented by a triple pattern that is conditionally used to retrieve the set of observations and all facet elements.

3.3.2 Initial Pre-selection

To lower the barrier of exploring a data cube from scratch, an initial pre-selection algorithm is started after a positive introspection. As described in Sect. 3.4 it is possible to integrate and configure charts visualizing one or multiple dimensions. The determined maximum amount of dimensions respectively chart axis is used

Fig. 4. Facets and dialogues.

as input for the pre-selection algorithm. After extracting all obligatory facets exactly one element per facet is pre-selected. According to the number of discovered dimensions and the maximum amount of processable chart axis, dimensions are randomly selected for which more than one element can be selected. To avoid confusing visualizations the amount of pre-selected elements is limited to 10 respectively 30 % of the set of elements. During manual selection these limits are not relevant.

3.4   Chart Visualisation

In order to extract observations according to user interests, filter criteria from the facet selection component are translated into a corresponding SPARQL query. The resulting set of observation resources is serialized in JSON and sent back to the client. On the client-side the result set will be analysed according the amount of disjunctive dimensions and the respective amount of elements in order to select suitable charts. After identifying suitable chart implementations the first one is launched and renders the visualization using the received set of observations. All further suitable charts can be selected using a respective GUI element without querying the observations again.

APIs

CubeViz comprises an abstraction layer to mediate between the retrieval of observations and the APIs used to generate and visualize charts. Currently, charts such as pie, bar, column, line and polar chart are implemented using the

APIs *Data Driven Documents*[13] (D3js) and *HighCharts*[14]. Every chart is implemented using a defined interface and comprises a mechanism to convert the set of observations in combination with the meta data about dimension properties into the chart-specific input format.

Chart Options

Most of the implemented chart visualizations can be adjusted using preconfigured chart options. Hence, it is possible to enable the display of measure values in addition to its graphical representation, to switch axis / dimensions, to switch the value scale between linear and logarithmic or to enable a normal or percentage stacking. Additionally it is possible to combine charts such as a polar chart with a column chart (see Fig. 2).

Element Recognition

On the Linked Data Web, URIs are used to identify resources. In a domain-agnostic tool such as CubeViz, it is not feasible to integrate static mappings between data items and their graphical representations. Most of the chart APIs have a limited amount of pre-defined colors used for colouring dimension elements or select colors completely arbitrarily. In order to display dimension elements in a deterministic manner and to support users to quickly recover selected elements in different charts we integrated a colouring algorithm that uniquely assigns URIs of each dimension element corresponding RGB color codes[15].

Interactive Legend

Below the generated charts an additional tabular representations of the selected data items is given (cf. Fig. 5). On the one hand they can be used as legend containing additional meta data. On the other hand this view offers support for resolving data inaccuracies with functionality for editing values, that automatically updates the chart representation.

Sharing Views

After exploring, configuring and possible adaption of values users are able to share the created output. Sharing functionality is implemented via a button, which triggers the gathering of all information necessary to reproduce the created output, storing them server-side and returning a shareable link containing an identifying hash code for the particular view configuration. Furthermore, it is possible to export selected data as CSV and RDF in Turtle notation.

---

[13] http://d3js.org/

[14] http://www.highcharts.com/

[15] http://cold.aksw.org/

↓ Country ↓≟ ↓F	↓ Year ↓≟ ↓F	↓ Value ↓≟ ↓F	
10 different dimension elements are in use	3 different dimension elements are in use	min: 0.08333333	max: 0.65
1 ↓ Belgium	↓ 2002	0.0833333333	Link
2 ↓ Germany	↓ 2002	0.1666666667 Save	Link
3 ↓ Belgium	↓ 2004	0.1666666667	Link
4 ↓ Belgium	↓ 2003	0.1666666667	Link

Fig. 5. Interactive CubeViz legend.

4   Facete - A Generic Spatial Facetted Browser for RDF

Facete is a web application for the exploration of SPARQL-accessible spatial data, which offers several distinguishing features. First, there is the advanced faceted search component which enables users to filter the data by inverse properties and nested properties. Counts are provided for both facets and facet values. Second, the system will always attempt to detect (possible indirectly) related geometric information for the set of resources matched by the faceted search. For example, if a user filters by the class *Person*, then the system could detect that *birthPlace* and *deathPlace* provide geo-coordinates and appropriate suggestions about what to display on the map would be shown to the user. Third, Facete provides a map display capable of dealing with large amounts of geometric information. Finally, users are able to customize a tabular view for the data related to their facet selection. Information about Facete is available on its project site[16]. All of Facete's user interface components are based on the popular AngularJS[17] framework, and are published as a separate library called *JAvascript Suite for Sparql Access* (Jassa)[18]. In the remainder of this section, we give an overview of Facete's components, which we partly published in [14].

4.1   User Interface

Facete is implemented as a Single Page Application (SPA) whose user interface comprises several UI components, which are depicted in Fig. 6 and explained in the following. In the top area, there are elements that enable the user to select a SPARQL endpoint and chose from one or more of its contained named graphs. The main panel is divided into three columns containing a set of widgets with the following functionality:

1. Selection. The first widget, labeled *Facet*, shows a facet tree that corresponds to the properties of all resources that match the set constraint. If there

---

[16] http://aksw.org/Projects/Facete
[17] http://angularjs.org/
[18] https://github.com/GeoKnow/Jassa-UI-Angular

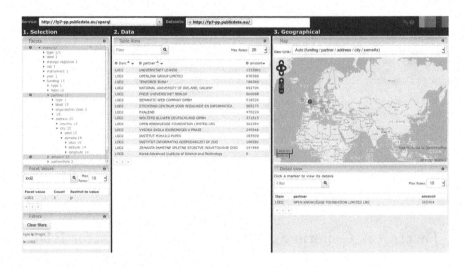

Fig. 6. Graphical user interface of facete

are no constraints, all resources that appear as a subject in the selected graphs are matched. Three actions can be performed for node in the facet tree. A click on the facet's name lists the facet's values in the *Facet Value* widget, where these values can be used for defining constraints. Clicking the caret symbol toggles the display of corresponding child facets. These are the properties of the selected facet's values. Lastly, a facet can be pinned as a column to the *Table View*. Note, that the root of the facet tree is formed by a facet labelled *Items*. This facet's values correspond to the set of resources in subject positions of the selected RDF graphs. The *Facet Values* widget enables a user to paginate through a selected facet's values and optionally filter these values by a search term. Furthermore, clicking the checkbox next to a value creates a constraint. The *Filters* widget lists all active constraints. Individual constraints can be removed by clicking their entry, whereas the *Clear Filters* button purges them all.

2. Data. The middle area contains the *Table View*, which lists a table whose content is based on resources that match the active constraints and the facets that were pinned as columns. Columns can be sorted by clicking the caret icons. Multiple orders are supported by holding the shift key down while clicking.

3. Geographical. The *Geo-Link* drop down menu enables the user to choose from property paths connecting the resources that match the constraints with those that can be shown on the map. By default, the option *automatic* is enabled, which always picks the shortest path among the found ones. The *Map* widget displays markers corresponding to the selected resources and the geo-link. Blue boxes indicate areas that contain too many markers to be shown at once. These boxes disappear when sufficiently zoomed in. Clicking a marker shows its details in the *Detail View*. The *Detail View* shows the excerpt of the *Table View* that corresponds to the selected marker(s).

4.2 Concepts

In this section we briefly outline the key concepts used in Facete, which are related to faceted search, detection of property paths that connect concepts and dealing with large amounts of spatial data.

4.2.1 Faceted Search

Facete's approach to faceted search based on the following concepts.

- A *SPARQL concept* is a pair comprising a SPARQL graph pattern and a variable thereof. As such, it intentionally describes a set of resources. For instance, the pair *({?s a Person}, ?s)* could be used to describe a set of people. SPARQL concepts are a key enabler for indirect faceted search as they can be used to represent virtually any set of resources (within the expressivity of SPARQL), such as the set of facets, the set of child facets, the set of facet values and the set of resources with geometric information.
- *Property Steps* are used to navigate from a set of resources to a related set of resources by following a specific property. A direction attribute determines whether to follow a property in forward or inverse direction. Hence, a destination SPARQL concept can be obtained from a given origin SPARQL concept and a property step.
- A *Property Path* is a sequence of property steps.
- *Constraint Specifications* express constraints via references to property paths. Constraint specifications are internally translated to corresponding SPARQL graph patterns.

4.2.2 Finding Connections between SPARQL Concepts

Depending on how a dataset was modeled, the spatial dimension may not be directly attached to instances of a certain type. In order to visualize the spatial dimension of such objects efficiently and intuitively we need an approach to find connecting property paths between two arbitrary SPARQL concepts efficiently. These paths can become relatively long, and naive path discovery approaches are not feasible. For example, in our RDFized version of the FP7 project funding dataset[19], projects are related to geometric information via paths of length 5.

Our approach is outlined as follows: because we are only interested in the detection of property paths, we pre-compute a *property join summary*. The basic SPARQL query for this purpose is:

```
1  CONSTRUCT
2    { ?p1 :joinsWith ?p2 }
3    {
4      { SELECT DISTINCT ?p1 ?p2 {
5          ?a ?p1 [ ?p2 ?b ]
6      } }
7    }
```

---

[19] http://fp7-pp.publicdata.eu/sparql

Conceptually, we could search for arbitrary complex paths, such as ones that include cyclic (same property followed multiple times in the same direction) and zig-zag (forward and backward on the same property traversals. However, for our use cases the restriction to directed acyclic paths leading from a *source concept* to a *target concept* was sufficient: we query the source concept for all of its properties *?p*, and conceptually add triples *(:source :joinsWith ?p)* to the join summary. Thereby *:source* is a distinguished resource representing the source concept. From a target concept's graph pattern, such as *(?s geo:long ?x ; geo:lat ?y, ?s)*, we can infer that we need to search for properties that according to the join summary are connected to both geo:long and geo:lat. As a consequence, we can query the joinsummary for a set of candidate target properties using:

```
1  SELECT DISTINCT ?p { ?p :joinsWith geo:long ; joinsWith geo:lat }
```

If the extensions of the source and target concepts have resources in common, this query's result set includes *:source* as a candidate.

We can now search for candidate paths on the join summary that connect *:source* with each of the candidate properties. For each candidate path we then fire an ASK query to check whether the given dataset contains an instance of it. Those paths for which actually data exists, are then listed in Facete's Geo-Link drop down box.

Note, that this approach is independent of any concrete vocabulary.

4.3   Display of Large Amounts of Geometries

Some spatial RDF datasets, such as DBpedia or Freebase, contain significantly more spatial information than can be reasonably retrieved and displayed on a map in a web application considering bandwidth and performance restrictions. Facete handles such cases using a quad tree data structure:

- Based on the users constraints on the facets and the geo-link, a corresponding SPARQL concept, named *geo-concept*, is created. The geo-concept specifies the set of resources to be shown on the map.
- A count of the number of instances matching the geo-concept is requested. If the count is below a configured threshold, all instances are retrieved at once and placed into the root node of the quad tree.
- If this count exceeds the threshold, the extent of the whole map is split recursively into four tiles of equal size. The recursion stops if either a maximum depth is reached, or if the tiles have reached a certain relative size when compared to the map viewport (e.g. when about 4 × 4 tiles are visible). For each tile, the geo-concept is then modified to only refer to resources within that tiles' bounding box. A tile's resources are only retrieved, if the new count is again below a configured threshold.
- Tiles that still contain too many geometries are rendered as boxes on the map.

An example of such display is shown in Fig. 7, which shows a subset of the approx. 20.000 resources with geo-positions in Germany. For each set of constraints, Facete creates a new quad tree that acts as a cache for the user's current configuration.

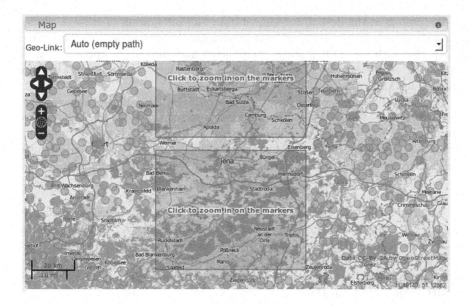

Fig. 7. Display of Freebase instances in Germany.

4.4 Related Work

The *RelFinder* system [6] is capable of finding property paths connecting a pair of *resources*, whereas Facete searches for paths between SPARQL *concepts*. Over the past decade, faceted search has become omnipresent, such as in web shop and content management systems. *Apache Solr*[20] is a popular system that offers extensive faceted search features, however, it does not offer native SPARQL support and thus requires pre-processing of RDF data. *Rhizomer* [1] and the *Virtuoso faceted browser*[21] support changing the focus from one set of resources to a related one (known as pivoting). However, with these systems, the user actually navigates between related list views of resources, whereas in Facete the user pins facets as new columns to the table view.

5   Conclusions and Future Work

In this chapter, we presented three tools as part of the LOD2 project that aim at facilitating the exploration of Linked Open Data. Rsine is a tool that sends notifications about changes in a RDF dataset. CubeViz is a data cube visualisation tool for statistical data. Facete is a faceted browser application with a focus on spartial data.

---

[20] http://lucene.apache.org/solr/

[21] http://virtuoso.openlinksw.com/dataspace/dav/wiki/Main/
VirtuosoFacetsWebService

We presented the design, implementation and integration of rsine, a service that notifies subscribers on specific changes in an RDF data set. We integrated the service with two LOD2 stack components and showed its applicability by supporting requirements for notifications in a thesaurus and metadata editing scenario at WKD.

Our immediate next steps are to evaluate the implemented thesaurus notifications in the context of a thesaurus development project at WKD. We are interested in the performance of our approach and the "usefulness" of the notifications, i.e., if and in what way they influence the quality of the created thesauri. We furthermore plan to set up multiple rsine instances in this environment to gain insights about how notifications can help when references between datasets on distinct servers are created, modified or deleted.

We presented the architecture, analysis components and visualization interfaces of CubeViz, a RDF Data Cube browser. In addition to the exploration of locally stored RDF data cubes it is possible to access remotely published ones using a combination of the SPARQL backend and the SPARQL services component. Such a setup was deployed on the European Commission's IT infrastructure as part of the European Data Portal[22].

There are further deployments of CubeViz made online such as Linked-Spending[23], which contain government spendings from all over the world represented and published as Linked Data (more than 2.4 million observations in 247 datasets). Using LinkedSpending, interested users can gather information about greek spending on police in certain regions in 2012 for instance (jump in using the button *Example Visualization 2* on the start page).

CubeViz is publicly available for download[24] and its latest releases can be evaluated using an online demonstrator[25]. CubeViz is under active development and will be further extended with new features such as drill-down functionality, additional interactive and customizable charts, further chart APIs such as the *Google Charts API*[26], aggregate functions and mashup features to compare observations from different domains.

Lastly, we gave an overview about Facete, a tool for browsing Linked Data in a domain-agnostic way with a focus on spatial data. Its major goal is to ease the navigation of RDF data in SPARQL endpoints using advanced faceted search techniques and - in addition - the provision of corresponding visualization widgets. Facete is published under the Apache 2.0, license and its development continues within the GeoKnow project[27]. Further information such as new releases, links to the sources, demos and documentation can be found on the project page[28].

---

[22] https://open-data.europa.eu/cubeviz/
[23] http://linkedspending.aksw.org/
[24] https://github.com/AKSW/CubeViz/
[25] http://cubeviz.aksw.org/
[26] https://developers.google.com/chart/
[27] http://geoknow.eu
[28] http://aksw.org/Projects/Facete

References

1. Brunetti, J.M., Gil, R., Garcia, R.: Facets and pivoting for flexible and usable linked data exploration. In: Interacting with Linked Data Workshop (ILD) (2012)
2. Cyganiak, R., Reynolds, D., Tennison, J.: The RDF data cube vocabulary. Technical report, W3C, 2013. http://www.w3.org/TR/vocab-data-cube/
3. Auer, S., Demter, J., Martin, M., Lehmann, J.: LODStats – an extensible framework for high-performance dataset analytics. In: ten Teije, A., Völker, J., Handschuh, S., Stuckenschmidt, H., d'Acquin, M., Nikolov, A., Aussenac-Gilles, N., Hernandez, N. (eds.) EKAW 2012. LNCS (LNAI), vol. 7603, pp. 353–362. Springer, Heidelberg (2012)
4. International Organization for Standardization. Statistical data and metadata exchange (SDMX). Technical report, Standard No. ISO/TS 17369:2005 (2005)
5. Harris, S., Seaborne, A.: SPARQL 1.1 Query Language - W3C Recommendation. Technical report, World Wide Web Consortium (W3C) (2013). http://www.w3.org/TR/sparql11-query/
6. Heim, P., Hellmann, S., Lehmann, J., Lohmann, S., Stegemann, T.: RelFinder: revealing relationships in RDF knowledge bases. In: Chua, T.-S., Kompatsiaris, Y., Mérialdo, B., Haas, W., Thallinger, G., Bailer, W. (eds.) SAMT 2009. LNCS, vol. 5887, pp. 182–187. Springer, Heidelberg (2009)
7. Heino, N., Dietzold, S., Martin, M., Auer, S.: Developing semantic web applications with the OntoWiki framework. In: Pellegrini, T., Auer, S., Tochtermann, K., Schaffert, S. (eds.) Networked Knowledge - Networked Media. SCI, vol. 221, pp. 61–77. Springer, Heidelberg (2009)
8. Mader, C., Haslhofer, B., Isaac, A.: Finding quality issues in SKOS vocabularies. In: Zaphiris, P., Buchanan, G., Rasmussen, E., Loizides, F. (eds.) TPDL 2012. LNCS, vol. 7489, pp. 222–233. Springer, Heidelberg (2012)
9. Mader, C., Wartena, C.: Supporting web vocabulary development by automated quality assessment: results of a case study in a teaching context. In: Workshop on Human-Semantic Web Interaction (HSWI14), CEUR Workshop Proceedings, May 2014
10. May, W., Alferes, J.J., Amador, R.: An ontology- and resources-based approach to evolution and reactivity in the semantic web. In: Meersman, R. (ed.) Coop-IS/DOA/ODBASE 2005. LNCS, vol. 3761, pp. 1553–1570. Springer, Heidelberg (2005)
11. United Nations: Guidelines for Statistical Metadata on the Internet. Technical report, Economic Commission for Europe (UNECE) (2000)
12. Management of Statistical Metadata at the OECD (2006)
13. Passant, A., Mendes, P.: sparqlPuSH: Proactive notification of data updates in RDF stores using PubSubHubbub. In: CEUR Workshop Proceedings ISSN 1613-0073, February 2011
14. Stadler, C., Martin, M., Auer, S.: Exploring the web of spatial data with facete. In: Companion proceedings of 23rd International World Wide Web Conference (WWW), pp. 175–178 (2014)

Supporting the Linked Data Life Cycle Using an Integrated Tool Stack

Bert Van Nuffelen[1]([✉]), Valentina Janev[2], Michael Martin[3], Vuk Mijovic[2],
and Sebastian Tramp[3]

[1] TenForce, Leuven, Belgium
bert.van.nuffelen@tenforce.com
[2] Institute Mihajlo Pupin, Pupin, Serbia
{valentina.janev,vuk.mijovic}@pupin.rs
[3] University of Leipzig, Leipzig, Germany
{martin,tramp}@informatik.uni-leipzig.de

Abstract. The core of a Linked Data application is the processing of the knowledge expressed as Linked Data. Therefore the creation, management, curation and publication of Linked Data are critical aspects for an application's success. For all of these aspects the LOD2 project provides components. These components have been collected and placed under one distribution umbrella: the LOD2 stack. In this chapter we will introduce this component stack. We will show how to get access; which component covers which aspect of the Linked Data life cycle and how using the stack eases the access to Linked Data management tools. Furthermore we will elaborate how the stack can be used to support a knowledge domain. The illustrated domain is statistical data.

1 Introduction

Publishing Linked Data requires the existence of management processes that ensure the quality. The management process passes through several stages; in the Linked Data life cycle the main stages are ordered in their typical application order. The starting point is very often the extraction stage in which data from the source format is turned into RDF. The extracted RDF formatted data must be stored in an appropriate storage medium, making the data available for further processing. At this moment the data is ready to be queried and can be manually updated to correct small mistakes. Within the linking stage the data is enriched by interconnecting the data with external data sources. These data linkages create new opportunities: the data can now be classified according to the external data; information that is spread over two entities can be fused together, ... All these data manipulations can be monitored with quality metrics. When the desired data quality is reached the data can be made public and be explored by end-user applications.

Of-course the world is ever changing and hence data will reflect this. Therefore, there is support for the evolution of the data from one structure into another.

S. Auer et al. (Eds.): Linked Open Data, LNCS 8661, pp. 108–129, 2014.
DOI: 10.1007/978-3-319-09846-3_6

For all these stages research institutes and companies around the world have created tools. At the start of the LOD2 project these tools were scattered around the Linked Data community. Specialists in the area shared lists of components in various degree of completeness. The LOD2 project had the ambition to start a platform in which all Linked Data components were collected. This common distribution platform was called the LOD2 stack, and will continue to exist after the LOD2 project has finished as the Linked Data stack[1]. Components in the stack are easy to install and directly usable. Moreover, they come with pre-configured setups that make the interplay between them easier. These additional features cannot be offered by the individual component owners but requires central coordination.

In the first part of this chapter, the LOD2 stack is elaborated in more detail. The second part is dedicated to the specialization of the LOD2 stack for statistical data. Indeed the LOD2 stack is in its own right is not dedicated towards a particular use case. For particular kinds of data, such as statistical data, the components of the stack can be further specialized and pre-configured to offer a much better dedicated end user support.

2   The LOD2 Linked Data Stack

The LOD2 Linked Data stack is a distribution platform for software components which support one or more aspects of the Linked Data life cycle. Each package contains a pre-configured component that on installation results in a ready-to-use application. The pre-configuration ensures that the deployed components are able to interact with each other. The system architecture of the deployed Linked data stack components is explained in Sect. 2.1. The subsequent sections provide more details on the distribution platform and what the requirements are for software to take part of it. Finally we provide an overview of the LOD2 stack contents in Sect. 2.5.

2.1   Building a Linked Data Application

The LOD2 stack facilitates the creation of Linked Data applications according to a prototypical system architecture. The system architecture is shown below in Fig. 1. From top to bottom, one has first the application layer with which the end-user is confronted. The applications are built with components from the component layer. These components communicate between each other and interact with the data in the data layer via the common data access layer.

The data access layer is build around the data representation framework RDF. The data is exchanged in RDF and retrieved with SPARQL queries from SPARQL end-points. All data format heterogeneity is hidden for the components by this layer. This yields an uniform data view easing the configuration of the data flow between the components. The RDF representation yields important

---

[1] http://stack.linkeddata.org

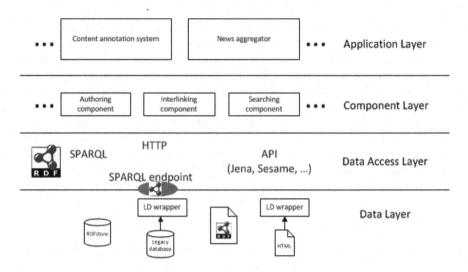

Fig. 1. Linked Data application system architecture

advantages making it suited for the role as common data representation formalism. It is a W3C standard, domain neutral, and it is web enabled: all identifiers are web addressable. And last but not least, data integration starts with just merging the data together in one store.

Matching the Linked Data life cycle presented in the introduction to the system architecture shows that the extraction and storage tools feature in the data layer and most of the other are part of the component layer.

An application end user will seldom be directly in touch with the underlying data layer. They are offered an application interface that shows the information in a domain adapted intuitive interface. Few of the LOD2 stack browsing and exploration components have been lifted and designed to this stage. Most of the stack components are designed for the (Linked Data) data manager. The components provide user interfaces that aid the data manager in its task. For instance, the SILK workbench is a user interface for creating linking specifications. This specification can then be used by the silk engine which might be embedded in a larger application. That is the task of the last targeted audience: the Linked Data application developer.

2.2 Becoming LOD2 Linked Data Stack Component

The system architecture defines minimal requirements for components to become part of the LOD2 stack, they are that

- Information is exchanged in RDF format
- Business information is requested through SPARQL endpoint access
- Updates are provided as SPARQL updates

A typical example is the SILK workbench. The business data is retrieved via querying SPARQL endpoints and the result (the link set) can be stored in a SPARQL endpoint that is open to updates. Of course these requirements do not hold for all communication channels of a component, for instance, extraction components such as D2R. Those obviously have to communicate with the original source of the information which is different than RDF, but the outcome is RDF.

A component is distributable via the LOD2 stack repository if it is provided as a Debian package that installs on Ubuntu 12.04 LTS. The Debian packaging system has been chosen because it is a well established software packaging system that is used by the popular Linux distribution Ubuntu. We decided for a reference OS release to ensure quality and reduce the maintenance efforts of the components. This choice does not limit the deployment of the software on other Linux distributions, whether they are Debian based or not. Using a tool called alien, debian packages can be installed on a RedHat distribution.

The above mentioned requirements ensure there is a common foundation between all components in the LOD2 stack. For application developers trained in the Linked Data domain the creation of an information flow is hence always possible. Because each data publishing editorial process is unique and the best solution depends on the data publishing organizations needs, the stack does not aim for a homogeneous LOD2 Linked Data publishing platform where all components are hidden behind a single consistent user interface. The goal is however on improving the information flow between components. In the first place, this is done via making sure that deployed components have access to each others output. Additionally, LOD2 has contributed supporting APIs and vocabularies to the component owners. If they extend their components with these, the data flow between the components will be further improved.

Using this approach, each component still has its individual identity but they are interoperable with each other.

2.3   LOD2 Stack Repository

In order to guarantee stability of the available component stack, a multi stage environment has been setup. There exist 3 stages currently:

- The developers' area: here the developers put their packages.
- The testing stage: this is a collection of LOD2 packages that are subject to integration tests. The goal is to detect with automatic testing problems in the installation of the packages.
- The stable stage: this is a collection of LOD2 packages that pass the tests.

The LOD2 stack managers are responsible for moving packages from the developers' area into the testing stage and then to the stable stage.

Orthogonally we have created 2 repositories that are OS-release dependent. These contain components that are dependent on the OS. The typical example is Virtuoso for which Ubuntu 12.04 64 bit builds are provided. Build and installation instructions are present to support more recent and other Linux distributions.

Developers have to contribute a Debian package with the correct LOD2 stack configuration. The rationale behind this choice for this approach is to distribute the knowledge on building packages to all partners, but more important to create awareness for software deployment. When the component owners are responsible for building the Debian packages they face the imperfections that make their software hard to deploy. That experience has as positive effect that deployment issues are tackled early on. All necessary information for the developers is collected in the contribution documentation[2].

The LOD2 stack repository distributes software components. However in addition to these components, there are more components or information sources valuable to the LOD2 stack available online. These come in two categories:

- software components which are only accessible online due to various reasons: special setup, license rules, etc. Examples are the Sindice search engine and PoolParty.
- information sources: for example dbpedia.org and vocabulary.wolterskluwer.de.

2.4 Installing the LOD2 Linked Data Stack

The installation of a local version of the LOD2 stack[3] is done in a few steps and are available online[4]. In short, the next steps must be executed:

1. Setup a Ubuntu 12.04 64 bit LTS system.
2. Download the repository package (of the stage of interest) and install it.
3. Update the local package cache.
4. Install the whole LOD2 stack or selected components.

If during the installation issues occur, support-stack@lod2.eu can be contacted for assistance. Background information and frequently occurring situations are documented at documentation wiki[5].

2.5 The LOD2 Linked Data Stack Release

In the following paragraphs all LOD2 stack components are summarized. First we list those that are available as Debian package, followed by those that are online available and finally we provide a table of online data sources that are of interest and have been supported by the LOD2 project.

2.5.1 Available as Debian Packages

Components colanut, limes (ULEI). LIMES is a link discovery framework for the Web of Data. It implements time-efficient approaches for large-scale link discovery based on the characteristics of metric spaces. The COLANUT (COmplex

---

[2] http://stack.linkeddata.org/how-to-contibute/
[3] http://stack.linkeddata.org
[4] http://wiki.lod2.eu/display/LOD2DOC/How+To+Start
[5] http://wiki.lod2.eu/display/LOD2DOC/Known+issues

Linking in A NUTshell) interface resides on top of LIMES and supports the user during the link specification process.
http://aksw.org/Projects/LIMES

Components *d2r, d2r-cordis* (UMA). D2R Server is a tool for publishing relational databases on the Semantic Web. It enables RDF and HTML browsers to navigate the content of the database, and allows applications to query the database using the SPARQL query language. The d2r-cordis package contains an example setup.
http://d2rq.org/d2r-server

Components *dbpedia-spotlight-gui, dbpedia-spotlight* (UMA/ULEI). DBpedia Spotlight aims to shed light on the Web of Documents. It recognizes and disambiguates DBpedia concepts/entities mentioned in natural language texts. There is an online instance that can be used for experimenting.
https://github.com/dbpedia-spotlight/dbpedia-spotlight/

Components *dl-learner-core, dl-learner-interfaces* (ULEI). The DL-Learner software learns concepts in Description Logics (DLs) from examples. Equivalently, it can be used to learn classes in OWL ontologies from selected objects. It extends Inductive Logic Programming to Descriptions Logics and the Semantic Web. The goal of DL-Learner is to provide a DL/OWL based machine learning tool to solve supervised learning tasks and support knowledge engineers in constructing knowledge and learning about the data they created.
http://dl-learner.org/

Component *libjs-rdfauthor* (ULEI). RDFauthor is an editing solution for distributed and syndicated structured content on the World Wide Web. The system is able to extract structured information from RDFa-enhanced websites and to create an edit form based on this data.
http://aksw.org/Projects/RDFauthor

Component *LODRefine* (Zemanta). Open Refine (http://openrefine.org/) extended with RDF (http://refine.deri.ie/) and Zemanta API (http://developer.zemanta.com) extensions.
http://code.zemanta.com/sparkica/

Component *lod2demo* (TenForce). The LOD2 demonstrator is a web application which brings together all LOD2 stack components in one interface. Components are loosely coupled through the Virtuoso store via which all information is exchanged. It also serves as the top level meta package in order to install the whole stack content on a machine. This is the top level meta package which installs the whole stack on a machine.
https://lod2-stack.googlecode.com/svn/trunk/lod2demo

Component *lod2-statistical-workbench* (TenForce/IMP). A web interface that aggregates several components of the stack organized in an intuitive way to support the specific business context of the statistical office. The workbench contains several dedicated extension for the manipulation of RDF data according to the

Data Cube vocabulary: validation, merging and slicing of cubes are supported. Also the workbench has been used to explore authentication via WebID and keeping track of the data manipulations via a provenance trail.
https://lod2-stack.googlecode.com/svn/trunk/lod2statworkbench

Component *lod2webapi* (TenForce). An REST API allowing efficient graph creation and deletion as well as regex based querying. It also support a central prefix management.
https://lod2-stack.googlecode.com/svn/trunk/lod2-webapi

Component *unifiedviews* (SWCG). UnifiedViews is Linked (Open) Data Management Suite to schedule and monitor required tasks (e.g. preform reoccurring extraction, transformation and load processes) for smooth and efficient Linked (Open) Data Management to support web-based Linked Open Data portals (LOD platforms) as well as sustainable Enterprise Linked Data integrations inside of organisations.
https://grips.semantic-web.at/display/UDDOC/Introduction

Components *ontowiki, ontowiki-common, ontowiki-mysql, ontowiki-virtuoso, owcli, liberfurt-php* (ULEI). OntoWiki is a tool providing support for agile, distributed knowledge engineering scenarios. OntoWiki facilitates the visual presentation of a knowledge base as an information map, with different views on instance data. It enables intuitive authoring of semantic content. It fosters social collaboration aspects by keeping track of changes, allowing to comment and discuss every single part of a knowledge base.
http://ontowiki.net

Component *ontowiki-cubeviz* (ULEI). CubeViz is a facetted browser for statistical data utilizing the RDF Data Cube vocabulary which is the state-of-the-art in representing statistical data in RDF. Based on the vocabulary and the encoded Data Cube, CubeViz is generating a facetted browsing widget that can be used to filter interactively observations to be visualized in charts. On the basis of the selected structure, CubeViz offer beneficiary chart types and options which can be selected by users.
http://aksw.org/Projects/CubeViz

Component *ontowiki-csv-import* (ULEI). Statistical data on the web is often published as Excel sheets. Although they have the advantage of being easily readable by humans, they cannot be queried efficiently. Also it is difficult to integrate with other datasets, which may be in different formats. To address those issues this component was developed, which focusses on conversion of multidimensional statistical data into RDF using the RDF Data Cube vocabulary.
https://github.com/AKSW/csvimport.ontowiki

Component *ore-ui* (ULEI). The ORE (Ontology Repair and Enrichment) tool allows for knowledge engineers to improve an OWL ontology by fixing inconsistencies and making suggestions for adding further axioms to it.
http://ore-tool.net/

Component *r2r* (UMA). R2R is a transformation framework. The R2R mapping API is now included directly into the LOD2 demonstrator application, allowing users to experience the full effect of the R2R semantic mapping language through a graphical user interface.

Component *rdf-dataset-integration* (ULEI). This tool allows the creation of debian packages for RDF datasets. Installing a created package will autoload the RDF dataset in the Virtuoso on the system.

Component *sieve* (UMA). Sieve is a Linked Data Quality Assessment and Fusion tool. It performs quality assessment and resolves conflicts in a task-specific way according to user configuration.
http://sieve.wbsg.de

Component *sigmaee* (DERI). Sigma EE is an entity search engine and browser for the Web of Data. Sig.ma EE is a standalone, deployable, customisable version of Sig.ma. Sig.ma EE is deployed as a web application and will perform on the fly data integration from both local data source and remote services (including Sindice.com).
http://sig.ma

Component *silk* (UMA). The Silk Linking Framework supports data publishers in setting explicit RDF links between data items within different data sources. Using the declarative Silk - Link Specification Language (Silk-LSL), developers can specify which types of RDF links should be discovered between data sources as well as which conditions data items must fulfil in order to be interlinked. These link conditions may combine various similarity metrics and can take the graph around a data item into account, which is addressed using an RDF path language.
http://wifo5-03.informatik.uni-mannheim.de/bizer/silk/

Component *silk-latc* (DERI). An improved version of SILK that has been used in the LATC project.

Component *siren* (DERI). SIREn is a Lucene/Solr extension for efficient schemaless semi-structured full-text search. SIREn is not a complete application by itself, but rather a code library and API that can easily be used to create a full-featured semi-structured search engine.
http://rdelbru.github.io/SIREn/

Component *sparqled* (DERI). SparQLed is an interactive SPARQL editor that provides context-aware recommendations, helping users in formulating complex SPARQL queries across multiple heterogeneous data sources.
http://sindicetech.com/sindice-suite/sparqled/

Component *sparqlify* (ULEI). Sparqlify is a SPARQL-SQL rewriter that enables one to define RDF views on relational databases and query them with SPARQL.
https://github.com/AKSW/Sparqlify

Component *sparqlproxy-php* (ULEI). A PHP forward proxy for remote access to SPARQL endpoints; forwards request/response headers and filters out non-SPARQL URL arguments.
https://github.com/AKSW/SparqlProxyPHP

Component *spatial-semantic-browser* (). The spatial semantic browser (recently labeled as Facete) project is comprised of a JavaScript library for faceted browsing of RDF data and an application for browsing geo-related RDF data. The application thereby offers filtering by facets, pivoting, and display of the data on a map.

Component *stanbol* (External - ULEI). Apache Stanbol's intended use is to extend traditional content management systems with semantic services.
https://stanbol.apache.org/

Component *valiant* (TenForce). Valiant is an command line tool that automates the extraction of RDF data from XML documents. Intended for bulk application on a large amount of XML documents.
https://github.com/tenforce/valiant

Component *virtuoso-opensource* (OGL). Virtuoso is a knowledge store and virtualization platform that transparently integrates Data, Services, and Business Processes across the enterprise. Its product architecture enables it to deliver traditionally distinct server functionality within a single system offering along the following lines: Data Management & Integration (SQL, XML and EII), Application Integration (Web Services & SOA), Process Management & Integration (BPEL), Distributed Collaborative Applications.
http://virtuoso.openlinksw.com/dataspace/dav/wiki/Main/

Components *virtuoso-vad-bpel, virtuoso-vad-conductor, virtuoso-vad-demo, virtuoso-vad-doc, virtuoso-vad-isparql, virtuoso-vad-ods, virtuoso-vad-rdfmappers, virtuoso-vad-sparqldemo, virtuoso-vad-syncml, virtuoso-vad-tutorial* (OGL). Virtuoso Application Distributions as debian packages, These VAD packages extend the functionality of Virtuoso, i.e. there is the web system admin interface (the conductor), the interactive SPARQL interface and many more.
http://virtuoso.openlinksw.com/dataspace/dav/wiki/Main/

Component *EDCAT* (TenForce). EDCAT is a service API for a DCAT based Linked Data catalogue. It provides a json compatible view with the DCAT W3C standard. The API is extendible via a plugin architecture. Its main purpose is to serve as an integration layer for to establish dataset catalogues inside organizations.
http://edcat.tenforce.com

Component *CKAN* (OKF). CKAN is a system for storing, cataloguing and visualising data or other "knowledge" resources. CKAN aims to make it easy to find, share and re-use open content and data, especially in ways that are machine automatable.
http://ckan.org

Component lod2stable-repository, lod2testing-repository. These packages
activate the repositories in order to get a coherent stack installation.
https://lod2-stack.googlecode.com/svn/trunk/lod2repository

2.5.2   Available as Online Component

Component Payola (UEP). Payola is a web application which lets you work
with graph data in a new way. You can visualize Linked Data using several
preinstalled plugins as graphs, tables, etc. Moreover, you can create an analysis
and run it against a set of SPARQL endpoints. Analysis results are processed
and visualized using the embedded visualization plugins.
http://www.payola.cz

Component PoolParty Thesaurus Manager (SWC). PoolParty is a thesaurus
management system and a SKOS editor for the Semantic Web including text
mining and linked data capabilities. The system helps to build and maintain
multilingual thesauri providing an easy-to-use interface. PoolParty server provides semantic services to integrate semantic search or recommender systems
into systems like CMS, DMS, CRM or Wikis.
http://poolparty.biz

Component PoolParty Extractor (SWC). The PoolParty Extractor (PPX)
offers an API providing text mining algorithms based on semantic knowledge
models. With the PoolParty Extractor you can analyse documents in an automated fashion, extracting meaningful phrases, named entities, categories or other
metadata. Different data or metadata schemas can be mapped to a SKOS thesaurus that is used as a unified semantic knowledge model.
http://lod2.poolparty.biz/extractor/testextractor

Component Sindice (DERI, OGL). Sindice is a state of the art infrastructure
to process, consolidate and query the Web of Data. Sindice collates these billions
of pieces of metadata into an coherent umbrella of functionalities and services.
http://sindice.com

2.5.3   Available Online Data Sources

Table 1 provides an overview of the main data sources to which LOD2 has contributed.

2.5.4   The LOD2 Stack Components Functional Areas Coverage

When distributing the components over the Linked Data Publishing cycle functionalities the following Fig. 2 is obtained. In this figure the component is associated with its main role in the data publishing cycle. In the middle are placed
the applications that are not dedicated to one area, such as the automatiza-
tion platform UnifiedViews, and the applications that exploit the LOD2 stack,
such as the lod2demo and LOD2 Statistical Workbench. Online components are

Table 1. Online Data Sources supported by LOD2

URL	SparqlEndpoint
Sindice (DERI, OGL)	
http://sindice.com	
CKAN Repositories (OKFN)	
http://publicdata.eu	http://publicdata.eu/sparql
Dbpedia (ULEI, SWC, OGL)	
http://dbpedia.org,	http://dbpedia.org/sparql
http://live.dbpedia.org,	
http://de.dbpedia.org	
LODcloud (OGL)	
http://lod.openlink.com	http://lod.openlink.com/ sparql
WebDataCommons RDFa, Microdata and Microformat data sets (UMA)	
http://webdatacommons.org/ structureddata/	http://webdatacommons. structureddata/
German Courts and Labor Law taxonomies (WKD, SWC)	
http://vocabulary.wolterskluwer.de/ arbeitsrecht.html	http://vocabulary. wolterskluwer.de/PoolParty/ sparql/arbeitsrecht
http://vocabulary.wolterskluwer.de/ courts.html	http://vocabulary. wolterskluwer.de/PoolParty/ sparql/court

marked with a globe icon. The cubed formatted components are dedicated components for the statistical domain. They are embedded in the LOD2 Statistical Workbench.

In this figure, we see that the current version of the stack has a high number of components geared towards the extraction, storage and querying parts. This can be explained by the large number of data formats that need to be transformed to RDF. Every component tackles a specific subset of these formats. Most of the other components contain a small selection of specialized tools for a specific task. In the search/browsing/exploration stage, every component has its own way of visualizing the data.

3   A Customized Linked Data Stack for Statistics

The work on the LOD2 Statistical Workbench was motivated by the need to support the process of publishing statistical data in the RDF format using

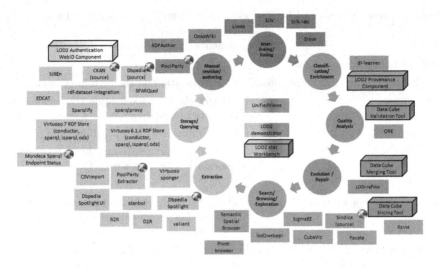

Fig. 2. Distribution of the LOD2 stack components w.r.t. Linked Data Publishing cycle

common vocabularies such as the RDF Data Cube[6]. The aim here was to provide support for performing different operations such as

- efficient transformation/conversion of traditional data stores (e.g. CSV, XML, relational databases) into linked, machine readable formats;
- building and querying triple stores containing RDF Data Cubes;
- validating RDF Data Cubes;
- interlinking and adding meaning to data;
- visualization and exploration of multi-dimensional RDF Data Cubes;
- publishing statistical data using a LOD publication strategy and respective metadata about the RDF data cube within a selected portal (i.e. a CKAN instance).

The potential benefits of converting statistical data into Linked Data format were studied through several scenarios for the National Statistical Office use case (cf. Table 2) [1].

3.1   Application Architecture and Scenarios

The LOD2 Statistical Workbench[7] implements the Linked Data application architecture sketched in Sect. 2. The workbench introduces a number of new components such as the *RDF Data Cube Validation tool*, the *RDF Data Cube Slicing tool* and the *RDF Data Cube Merging tool* dedicated for the statistical

---

[6] http://www.w3.org/TR/vocab-data-cube
[7] http://demo.lod2.eu/lod2statworkbench

Table 2. Potential goals and benefits of converting statistical data into Linked Data.

Scenario	Benefits/expected added value
Goal: *Metadata management*	
Code lists - creating and maintaining	Standardization on the metadata level: (a) will allow harmonization of specific concepts and terminology, (b) will improve interoperability and (c) will support multilinguality in statistical information systems across Europe
Goal: *Export*	
Export to different formats	Data exchange with other semantic tools, as well as other commonly used spreadsheet tool e.g. Microsoft Excel
Goal: *RDF Data Cube - Extraction, Validation and Initial Exploration*	
	Standardization of the extraction process
(a) CSV Data Extraction	CSV2DataCube
(b) XML Data Extraction	XML2DataCube
(c) SDMX-ML 2 RDF/XML	SDMX2RDFDataCube
Goal: *RDF Data Cube Quality Assessment (validation and analysis of integrity constraints)*	
Building well-formed RDF Data Cubes, where statistical data has been assigned an unique URI, meaning and links to similar data. This approach facilitates search and enables re-use of public statistical data	The well-formed RDF Data Cubes satisfy a number of integrity constraints and contain metadata thus enabling automation of different operations (exchange, linking, exploration)
Goal: *RDF Data Cube - Transformation, Exploratory Analysis and Visualization*	
(a) Merging RDF Data Cubes	Data fusion i.e. creation of a single dataset and different graphical charts that supports the exploratory analysis (e.g. indicator comparison)
(b) Slicing RDF Data Cubes	Facilitate creation of intersections in multidimensional data
(c) Visualization of RDF Data Cubes	Efficient analysis and search for trends in statistical data
Goal: *Interlinking*	
(a) Code lists - Interlinking	Assigning meaning, improved interoperability of data with similar governmental agencies
(b) CSV Data Extraction and Reconciliation with DBpedia	Assigning meaning
Goal: *Publishing*	
Publishing to CKAN	Increased transparency, improved accessibility of statistical data

domain. The workbench has also been augmented with extensions to explore other aspects: the *LOD2 authentication component*, the *LOD2 provenance component* and the *CKAN Publisher*.

In order to support the end-user, a new graphical user interface as been created wherein the LOD2 components are more intuitively organized for the statistical domain. There are grouped in the five topics: Manage Graph, Find more Data Online, Edit & Transform, Enrich Datacube, and Present & Publish.

Import features. The LOD2 Statistical Workbench is a framework for managing Linked Data stored in the RDF Data Cube format. Because statistical data is often provided in tabular format, it supports importing data from CSV. The CSV2RDF component allows the end users to transform tabular data from a CSV file into a multidimensional RDF Data Cube. Alternatively, LODRefine can be used. LODRefine is capable to import all kinds of structured formats including CSV, ODS and XSL(X) and transform them to RDF graphs based on arbitrary vocabularies.

Also the import from XML files is supported. The main international standard for exchanging statistical data is SDMX[8]. The users have the possibility to pass XML data as input to the XSLT processor and transform into RDF. The workbench provides ready to use XSLT scripts to deal with SDMX formatted data.

Additionally, using the *Find more Data Online* submenu, the user is able to find and import more data into the local RDF store using the respective tool of Statistical Workbench.

Semantic integration and storage. Linked Data applications are based on server platforms that enable RDF triple storage, semantic data integration and management, semantic interoperability based on W3C standards (XML, RDF, OWL, SOA, WSDL, etc). The Virtuoso Universal Server is used for this purpose in the LOD2 Statistical Workbench.

RDF Data Cube transformation features. Specialized components have been developed to support the most common operations for manipulating statistical data such as merging datasets, creating slices and data subsetting (Edit & Transform submenu). As each dataset defines components (e.g. dimensions used to describe the observations), the merging algorithm checks the adequacy of the input datasets for merging and compiles a new RDF Data Cube to be used for further exploration and analysis. Additionally, the slicing component can be used to group subsets of observations where one or more dimensions are fixed. This way, slices are given an identity (URI) so that they can be annotated or externally referenced, verbosity of the data set can be reduced because fixed dimensions need only be stated once, and consuming applications can be guided in how to present the data.

---

[8] http://sdmx.org

RDF Data Cube validation. The RDF Data Cube Validation tool [8] supports the identification of possibly not well-formed parts of an RDF Data Cube. The therein integrated analysis process consists mostly of integrity constraints rules represented as SPARQL queries as are defined in RDF Data Cube standard. The validation operation is applicable at several steps in the Linked Data publishing process e.g. on import/extraction/transformation from different sources or after fusion and creation of new RDF Data Cubes.

Authoring, querying and visualization. The OntoWiki authoring tool facilitates the authoring of rich semantic knowledge bases, by leveraging Semantic Wiki technology, the WYSIWYM paradigm (What You See Is What You Mean [3]) and distributed social, semantic collaboration and networking techniques. CubeViz, an extension of OntoWiki, is a facetted browser and visualization tool for statistical RDF data. It facilitates the discovery and exploration of RDF Data Cubes while hiding its complexity from users. In addition to using the browsing and authoring functionality of OntoWiki, advanced users are able to query the data directly (SPARQL) using one of the following offered SPARQL editors: OntoWiki query editor, Sindices SparQLed component and the Open-Link Virtuoso SPARQL editor.

Enrichment and interlinking. Linked Data publishing isn't just about putting data on the web, but also about creating links, so that a person or machine can explore the web of data. Therefore, the enrichment and interlinking features are very important as a pre-processing step in the integration and analysis of statistical data from multiple sources. LOD2 tools such as SILK and Limes facilitate mapping between knowledge bases, while LOD Open Refine can be used to enrich the data with descriptions from DBpedia or to reconcile with other information in the LOD cloud. PoolParty allows users to create their own high quality code lists and link the concepts therein to external sources as well. Once the code lists have been established, they can be reused as dimension values in Data Cubes or linked to Cubes that have been created separately.

Export and Linked Data publishing. The LOD2 Statistical Workbench export features are reachable via the Manage Graph and Present & Publish submenus. The Manage Graph option allows exporting of a graph with all its content in RDF/XML, RDF/JSON, Turtle, Notation 3. CubeViz supports subsetting of the data and extraction of a portion that is interesting for further analysis in CSV and RDF/XML format. The *CKAN Publisher* component aims at automating the upload and registration of new data with existing CKAN instances.

The use of the LOD2 Statistical Workbench for different data management operations is illustrated with online tutorials[9] for the scenarios summarized in Table 2.

---

[9] http://wiki.lod2.eu/display/LOD2DOC/LOD2+Statistical+Workbench

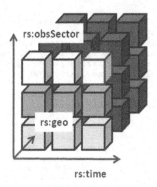

Fig. 3. RDF Data Cube - graphical representation

3.2   LOD2 Statistical Workbench in Use

This section provides some basic concepts of the Data Cube Vocabulary and how these were adapted in the Statistical Workbench, followed by some examples of using the workbench.

3.2.1   The RDF Data Cube Vocabulary

A statistical data set comprises a collection of observations (see Fig. 3) made at some points across some logical space. Using the RDF Data Cube vocabulary, a resource representing the entire data set is created and typed as qb:DataSet[10] and linked to the corresponding data structure definition via the qb:structure property.

The collection must be characterized by a set of dimensions (qb: DimensionProperty) that define what the observation applies to (e.g. time rs: time, observed sector rs:obsSector, country rs:geo)[11] along with metadata describing what has been measured (e.g. economic activity, prices) through measurements. Optionally, additional information can be provided on how the observation or cube was measured and how the observations are expressed through the use of attribute (qb:AttributeProperty) elements (e.g. units, multipliers, status).

The qb:dataSet property (see excerpt below) indicates that a specific qb:Observation instance is a part of a dataset. In this example, the primary measure, i.e. observation value (represented here via sdmx-measure:obsValue), is a plain decimal value. To define the units the observation in question is measured in, the sdmx-attribute:unitMeasure property which corresponds to the SDMX-COG concept of UNIT_MEASURE was used. In the example, the code MIO_NAT_RSD corresponds to millions of national currency (Serbian dinars). The values in the time and location dimensions (rs:geo and rs:time), indicate that the observation took place in the Republic of Serbia (geographic region code RS), and in 2003 (time code Y2003), respectively.

---

[10] qb is the prefix http://purl.org/linked-data/cube#.

[11] rs is the prefix http://elpo.stat.gov.rs/lod2/RS-DIC/rs/.

```
1   @prefix qb: <http://purl.org/linked-data/cube#> .
2   @prefix rs: <http://elpo.stat.gov.rs/lod2/RS-DIC/rs/> .
3   @prefix accounts: <http://elpo.stat.gov.rs/lod2/RS-DATA/NA/dsd/> .
4   @prefix time: <http://elpo.stat.gov.rs/lod2/RS-DIC/time/> .
5   @prefix geo: <http://elpo.stat.gov.rs/lod2/RS-DIC/geo/> .
6   @prefix measure: <http://elpo.stat.gov.rs/lod2/RS-DIC/esa95/> .
7
8   <http://elpo.stat.gov.rs/lod2/RS-DATA/NA/GDP_usage_Exports/data> a qb:DataSet ;
9     rdfs:label "GDP_usage_-_Exports"^^xsd:string ;
10    rdfs:comment "Source:_RZS_(http://www.stat.gov.rs/)" ;
11    qb:structure accounts:GDP_usage_Exports ;
12    dcterms:subject <http://purl.org/linked-data/sdmx/2009/subject/2.2>;
13    dc:publisher "Stat._Office_of_the_Republic_of_Serbia"^^xsd:string .
14
15  <http://elpo.stat.gov.rs/lod2/RS-DATA/NA/GDP_usage/data/obs46> a qb:Observation;
16    qb:dataSet <http://elpo.stat.gov.rs/lod2/RS-DATA/NA/GDP_usage/data> ;
17    sdmx-attribute:unitMeasure measure:MIO_NAT_RSD ;
18    sdmx-measure:obsValue "124309.7" ;
19    rs:obsSector <http://elpo.stat.gov.rs/lod2/RS-DIC/esa95/P31_S13>;
20    rs:geo geo:RS ;
21    rs:time time:Y2003.
```

Listing 1.1: RDF representation of an observation

Each data set has a set of structural metadata (see Table 3). These descriptions are referred to in SDMX and the RDF Data Cube Vocabulary as Data Structure Definitions (DSD). Such DSDs include information about how concepts are associated with the measures, dimensions, and attributes of a data cube along with information about the representation of data and related metadata, both identifying and descriptive (structural) in nature. DSDs also specify which code lists provide possible values for the dimensions, as well as the possible values for the attributes, either as code lists or as free text fields. A DSD can be used to describe time series data, cross-sectional and multidimensional table data. Because the specification of a DSD is independent of the actual data that the data cube is about, it is often possible to reuse a DSD over multiple data cubes.

3.2.2   Example 1: Quality Assessment of RDF Data Cubes

Prior to publishing the resulting RDF data on an existing data portal and thus enabling other users to download and exploit the data for various purposes, every dataset should be validated to ensure it conforms to the RDF Data Cube model.

Table 3. Example values for a Data Cube structure representing the Serbian economic statistics

Component property	Concept description	Identifier	Code list
Dimension	Geographical region	rs:geo	cl:geo
Dimension	Time	rs:time	cl:time
Dimension	Economic activity	rs:activityNACEr2	cl:nace_rev2
Attribute	Unit of measurement	sdmx-attribute:unitMeasure	cl:esa95-unit
Measure	Observed value	sdmx-measure:obsValue	

Fig. 4. RDF Data Cube - quality assessment

The data validation step is covered by the LOD2 stack, i.e. through the following software tools:

- The RDF Data Cube Validation Tool[12];
- CubeViz, a tool for visualization of RDF Data Cubes[13].

The RDF Data Cube Validation Tool aims at speeding-up the processing and publishing of Linked Data in RDF Data Cube format. Its main use is validating the integrity constraints defined in the RDF Data Cube specification. It works with the Virtuoso Universal Server as a backend and can be run from the LOD2 Statistical Workbench environment.

The main benefits of using this component are improved understanding of the RDF Data Cube vocabulary and automatic repair of identified errors. Figure 4 shows the component in action: the integrity constraints and their status are shown on the left side, while the results of analysis are shown on the right. A list of resources that violate the constraint, an explanation about the problem, and if possible, a quick solution to the problem is offered to the user. Once an RDF Data Cube satisfies the Data Cube integrity constraints, it can be visualized with CubeViz. More details can be found in the LOD2 Stack Documentation[14].

3.2.3   Example 2: Filtering, Visualization and Export of RDF Data Cubes

The facetted browser and visualization tool CubeViz can be used to filter observations to be visualized in charts interactively. Figure 5 shows an exploration session that comprises of the following steps:

---

[12] http://wiki.lod2.eu/display/LOD2DOC/RDF+Data+Cube+Quality+Assessment
[13] http://wiki.lod2.eu/display/LOD2DOC/Data+Subsetting+and+Export+Scenario
[14] http://wiki.lod2.eu/display/LOD2DOC/LOD2+Statistical+Workbench

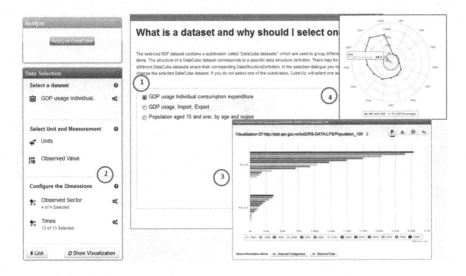

Fig. 5. RDF Data Cube - exploration and analysis

1. Select one out of the available datasets in the RDF graph;
2. Choose observations of interest by using a subset of the available dimensions;
3. Visualize the statistics by using slices, or
4. Visualize the statistics in two different measure values (millions of national currency and percentages).

3.2.4   Example 3: Merging RDF Data Cubes

Merging[15] is an operation of creating a new dataset (RDF Data Cube) that compiles observations from the original datasets (two or more), and additional resources (e.g. data structure definition, component specifications). In order to obtain meaningful charts the observed phenomena (i.e. serial data) have to be described on the same granularity level (e.g. year, country) and expressed in same units of measurement (e.g. euro, %). Therefore alignment of the code lists used in the input data is necessary before the merging operation is performed.

3.3   Towards a Broader Adoption

Linked Data principles have been introduced into a wide variety of application domains, e.g. publishing statistical data and interpretation of statistics [5], improving tourism experience [6], pharmaceutical R&D data sharing [7], crowdsourcing in emergency management [4], etc. A few years ago, our analysis of the adoption of Semantic Web technologies by enterprises [2] has shown that companies benefit from features that improve data sharing and re-use (57 %), improve searching (57 %), allow incremental modelling (26 %), explicit content

---

[15] http://wiki.lod2.eu/display/LOD2DOC/Eurostat+Merge+and+Enhance+Scenario

relation (24 %), identifying new relationships (17 %), dynamic content generation (14 %), personalization (10 %), open modeling (12 %), rapid response to change (10 %), reducing time to market (5 %), and automation (5 %). Of the features the LOD2 Statistical Workbench provides functionality improving the following areas: data share and re-use, improved search, explicit content relation, identifying new relationships, open model and automation. The LOD2 Statistical Workbench supports both publishers and consumers of Linked Data such as national statistical offices (institutes), national banks, publication offices, etc. Some of those collaborated with us as an early adopter of the approach.

3.3.1 Use Case 1: Digital Agenda Scoreboard

In the course of the LOD2 PUBLINK 2010 activities, the digital agenda scoreboard[16] has been created as the first web portal exploiting the RDF Data Cube. The Digital Agenda Scoreboard provides insight on how 'digital' Europa is. By using an early version of CubeViz the trends are visualized embedded in human readable scenario. Behind the scenes the data is provided and aggregated in a Virtuoso store according to the Data Cube vocabulary. This data is made available to the public in different formats including the RDF representation.

3.3.2 Use Case 2: Statistical Office of the Republic of Serbia (SORS)

In the course of the LOD2 PUBLINK 2011 activities, the SORS public data was integrated into the LOD cloud via the Serbian CKAN [1]. The Serbian CKAN is a metadata repository to be used for dissemination purposes by Serbian national institutions. Maintenance activities include identifying changes in the dissemination data (new public data, changes on metadata level) and fixing the mapping process (from XML to RDF) accordingly. The SORS is in the process of adopting the LOD2 Statistical Workbench[17] that will allow the users to automatically publish data (in the existing and new packages) to the Serbian CKAN.

3.3.3 Use Case 3: Business Registers Agency

In the course of the LOD2 PUBLINK 2012 activities, example data from the Regional Development Measures and Incentives Register was triplified using the LOD2 Statistical Workbench and registered with the Serbian CKAN. The data is reachable via the Serbian CKAN[18] and can be explored through a prototype application[19].

---

[16] http://digital-agenda-data.eu/
[17] http://lod2.stat.gov.rs/lod2statworkbench
[18] http://rs.ckan.net/dataset/apr-register-of-regional-development-measures-and
    -incentives
[19] http://rs.ckan.net/esta-ld/

3.3.4   Challenges Faced by Early Adopters

For each early adopter the publishing of the statistical data as Linked Data has influenced their data publishing process. The Linked Data vision impacts the publication process typically more deeply as it sees data from a more universal perspective and not as an isolated piece of information. When the statistical observations becomes real Linked Data, it means that also the dimensions have to become Linked Data, and this typically means that other organizations that maintain the dimensions have to be consulted.

Therefore in addition to our technological support in the identifying the set of applicable vocabularies and specifying the transformation flow to be setup, there has been an important activity in supporting the early adopters with their relationship with their data suppliers.

Over time the technological support has been improved. Whereas for the first case, the Digital Agenda Scoreboard, many of the transformation steps and data cleaning steps had to be done manually, they are for the more recent applications semi-automated.

Our approach to customize the LOD2 stack not only holds for the statistical domain, but can be applied other domains as well. For instance in the GeoKnow[20] project the GeoKnow Generator is being created for the support of geo-spatial Linked Data.

4   Conclusion

The LOD2 stack has successfully established a dissemination platform for Linked Data software. After the incubation period inside the LOD2 project the Linked Data community continues to be supported via http://stack.linkeddata.org. The success of the Linked Data stack is in the first place due to the quality and the progress of the software components it distributes. The inclusion of new and updated software is the oxygen that keeps the Linked Data stack alive. This oxygen will be provided by the core contributors as they keep on improving their components and are devoted to provide regular improvement releases to the stack.

The Statistical Workbench shows that starting from the LOD2 stack, the foundations are present to create applications tuned for a particular information domain. With the current state of the LOD2 stack, data managers can prototype the required data information streams. Although there is no uniform homogenous end-user interface, exactly this prototyping ability is crucial in bootstrapping the design of the desired end-user interfaces.

---

[20] http://geoknow.eu/

References

1. Janev, V., Milosevic, U., Spasic, M., Vranes, S., Milojkovic, J., Jirecek, B.: Integrating serbian public data into the LOD cloud. In: Ivanovic, M., Budimac, Z., Radovanovic, M. (eds.) BCI, pp. 94–99. ACM (2012)
2. Janev, V., Vranes, S.: Applicability assessment of semantic web technologies. Inf. Process. Manage. **47**(4), 507–517 (2011)
3. Khalili, A., Auer, S.: WYSIWYM authoring of structured content based on Schema.org. In: Lin, X., Manolopoulos, Y., Srivastava, D., Huang, G. (eds.) WISE 2013, Part II. LNCS, vol. 8181, pp. 425–438. Springer, Heidelberg (2013)
4. Ortmann, J., Limbu, M., Wang, D., Kauppinen, T.: Crowdsourcing linked open data for disaster management. In: Terra Cognita Workshop 2011 at ISWC2011. CEUR WS Proceedings (2011)
5. Paulheim, H.: Generating possible interpretations for statistics from linked open data. In: Simperl, E., Cimiano, P., Polleres, A., Corcho, O., Presutti, V. (eds.) ESWC 2012. LNCS, vol. 7295, pp. 560–574. Springer, Heidelberg (2012)
6. Sabou, M., Brasoveanu, A.M.P., Arsal, I.: Supporting tourism decision making with linked data. In: Presutti, V., Pinto, H.S. (eds.) I-SEMANTICS, pp. 201–204. ACM (2012)
7. Samwald, M., Jentzsch, A., Bouton, Ch., Kallesoe, C., Willighagen, E.L., Hajagos, J., Scott Marshall, M., Prud'hommeaux, E., Hassanzadeh, O., Pichler, E., Stephens, S.: Linked open drug data for pharmaceutical research and development. J. Cheminform. **3**, 19 (2011)
8. Mijovic, V., Janev, V., Vrane, S.: LOD2 tool for validating RDF data cube models. In: Conference Web Proceedings of the ICT Innovation Conference 2013 (2013)

Use Cases

LOD2 for Media and Publishing

Christian Dirschl[1](✉), Tassilo Pellegrini[2], Helmut Nagy[2], Katja Eck[1],
Bert Van Nuffelen[3], and Ivan Ermilov[4]

[1] Wolters Kluwer Deutschland GmbH, Unterschleißheim, Germany
cdirschl@wolterskluwer.de
[2] Semantic Web Company GmbH, Vienna, Austria
[3] TenForce, Leuven, Belgium
[4] Institute of Computer Science, Leipzig University, Leipzig, Germany

Abstract. It is the core business of the information industry, including traditional publishers and media agencies, to deal with content, data and information.
Therefore, the development and adaptation of Linked Data and Linked Open
Data technologies to this industry is a perfect fit. As a concrete example, the
processing of legal information at Wolters Kluwer as a global legal publisher
through the whole data life cycle is introduced. Further requirements, especially
in the field of governance, maintenance and licensing of data are developed in
detail. The partial implementation of this technology in the operational systems
of Wolters Kluwer shows the relevance and usefulness of this technology.

Keywords: Data transformation · Data enrichment · Metadata management ·
Linked data visualization · Linked data licensing · IPR · Wolters Kluwer ·
Media · Publishing · Legal domain

1 Introduction

1.1 Rationale for the Media and Publishing Use Case

The media and publishing use case within the LOD2 project[1] aims at enabling large-
scale interoperability of (legal) domain knowledge based on Linked Data. This is a
necessary precondition in the media industry to profit from the benefits of distributed
and heterogeneous information sources (DBpedia, EuroVoc) on the Semantic Web.
Hence, this use case aims at improving access to high-quality, machine-readable
datasets generated by publishing houses for their customers.

This attempt is accompanied by several challenges: Traditional official content such
as laws and regulations or court case proceedings are increasingly publicly available on
the web and are directly published by the respective issuing bodies. Social networks
and platforms, such as Wikipedia, aggregate professional knowledge and publish it at
no charge. At the same time e.g. news media generate large amounts of relevant
information about events and people that are complementary to conventional content of
specialized publishers, but hardly integrated (exception is e.g. integration between BBC
and DBpedia[2]). In addition, the amount of relevant information is still growing

---

[1] http://lod2.eu/Welcome.html, accessed May 10, 2014.
[2] Kobilarov et al. [7].

S. Auer et al. (Eds.): Linked Open Data, LNCS 8661, pp. 133–154, 2014.
DOI: 10.1007/978-3-319-09846-3_7

exponentially; this amount cannot be incorporated and structured by using traditional manual annotation mechanisms. Finally, the customer expects more and more exact and to-the-point information in her actual professional workflow that covers individual interests, personal preferences and one central trusted access to distributed data sources. Interests and preferences of a professional can even change over time and tasks to be completed.

From the perspective of Wolters Kluwer, the relevance of using schema-free data models like RDF and SKOS as well as accessing external content for their data-driven business is obvious.[3] By interlinking quality-approved proprietary data sources and "tapping" classification resources from the community and existing references in the LOD cloud, Wolters Kluwer is exploring diversification scenarios for existing assets as well as business opportunities under new licensing regimes. These efforts must lead to a win-win situation, where, on the one hand, additional revenues can be created by adding value to existing products and, on the other hand, customers of Wolters Kluwer and the public can benefit from well-licensed datasets, new tools and customized services to pursue their professional and personal goals.

The tasks within the use case can be organized according to three main areas:

- Making the Wolters Kluwer data available in a machine-readable form and then executing the interlinking and data enrichment tools of the LOD2 Stack on it.
- Creating a semantic knowledge layer based on this data and executing the editorial part of data management as well as general data visualization tools of the LOD2 Stack on it.
- Describing in more detail the business impact of this new kind of data in the media and publishing industry, especially with respect to expected hurdles in usage like governance and licensing issues.

1.2   Wolters Kluwer Company Profile

Wolters Kluwer Germany (WKD) is an information services company specializing in the legal, business and tax sectors. Wolters Kluwer provides pertinent information to professionals in the form of literature, software and services. Headquartered in Cologne, it has over 1,200 employees located at over 20 offices throughout Germany, and has been conducting business on the German market for over 25 years.

Wolters Kluwer Germany is part of the leading international information services company, Wolters Kluwer n.v., located in Alphen aan den Rijn (The Netherlands). The core market segments, targeting an audience of professional users, are legal, business, tax, accounting, corporate and finance services, and healthcare. Its shares are quoted on the Euronext Amsterdam (WKL), and are included in the AEX and the Euronext 100 indices. Wolters Kluwer has annual sales of €3.56 billion (2013), employs approximately 19,000 people worldwide and operates in over 40 countries throughout Europe, North America, the Asia Pacific region and in Latin America.

---

[3] For more detailed information see [5].

1.3   Data Transformation, Interlinking and Enrichment

This task has two main goals. The first goal is to adopt and deploy the LOD2 Stack[4] to the datasets of Wolters Kluwer. These datasets cover all document types being normally used in legal publishing (laws and regulations, court decisions, legal commentary, handbooks and journals). The documents cover all main legal fields of law like labor law, criminal law, construction law, administration law, tax law, etc. The datasets also cover existing legal taxonomies and thesauri, covering each a specific field of law, e.g. labor law, family law or social law. The overall amount of data (e.g. 600.000 court decisions) is large enough to make sure that the realistic operational tasks of a publisher can be executed with the data format and tools developed within the LOD2 project to support the respective use case. The datasets were analyzed according to various dimensions, e.g. actors, origin, geographical coverage, temporal coverage, type of data etc. relevant to the domain of legal information. Within the LOD2 project, all datasets were made available in formats adhering to open-standards, in particular RDF and Linked Data. Note that the datasets already existed in XML format at the start of the project and were transformed to RDF via XSLT script. The second goal is to automatically interlink and semantically enrich the Wolters Kluwer datasets. In order to achieve this, we leveraged the results from the LOD2 research work packages 3 and 4 (Chaps. 3 and 4) on the automated merging and linking of related concepts defined according to different ontologies using proprietary and open tools. Data from external sources (German National Library[5], DBpedia, STW[6], TheSoz[7] & EuroVoc[8]) were used to enrich the Wolters Kluwer datasets to leverage their semantic connectivity and expressiveness beyond the state of the art. This effort resulted in operational improvements at Wolters Kluwer Germany (WKG) as well as added-value for WKG customers. WKG was expecting that high current internal (manual) efforts concerning taxonomy and thesaurus development and maintenance would partly be substituted by integrating external LOD sources. This held also true for specific metadata like geographical information, detailed information about organizations and typical legal content itself from public issuing bodies. The internal workflow at WKG would therefore be enhanced as automated alerting (e.g. push notifications, see Chap. 5) could be executed to inform internal editors of data changes based on the underlying interlinked data. This would be a major gain as this process is currently labor intensive as it requires editors to physically monitor changes to content.

1.4   Editorial Data Interfaces and Visualization Tools

This task provided the main functionality for publishing, searching, browsing and exploring interlinked legal information. This included querying and facet-based

---

[4] See Chap. 6 and http://stack.linkeddata.org/, accessed May 10, 2014.

[5] http://www.dnb.de/DE/Standardisierung/GND/gnd_node.html, accessed June 10, 2014.

[6] http://zbw.eu/stw/versions/latest/about, accessed June 10, 2014.

[7] http://www.gesis.org/en/services/research/thesauri-und-klassifikationen/social-science-thesaurus/, accessed June 10, 2014.

[8] http://eurovoc.europa.eu/, accessed June 10, 2014.

browsing of dataset metadata along various dimensions (dataset type, spatial/temporal coverage, origin etc.), as well as authoring of new metadata and data. It also investigated issues, such as access control and user rights management, to enable customized access levels for various user roles and clients. Additionally, different visualizations of e.g. geo location and statistical information were implemented (see LOD2 work package 5, Chap. 5).

1.5 Business Impact and Relevant Pre-conditions for Success

This task investigated into Intellectual Property Rights (IPR) management (licensing and management of usage rights) as well as business value of interoperable metadata. While traditional regimes, especially in the private sector, mostly rely on a Strong-IPR philosophy, by which the use and commercial exploitation of metadata is strictly regulated and governed, interoperable metadata requires more flexible licensing arrangements that take advantage of openness- and commons-based approaches. While the continuum between and the interplay of strong and light intellectual property rights for interoperable metadata is still a young and unexplored research field, it is the licensing strategy that defines the legal framework in which asset diversification and value creation takes place. The application of the uniform data model of RDF to metadata enables syntactic and semantic interoperability and leverages the network characteristics of metadata. While the lack of a uniform data model leads to proprietary lock-ins with respect to metadata assets like schemata, vocabularies, ontologies, indices, queries etc., interoperable metadata transcend these boundaries and open up possibilities for asset creation under the circumstances of economies of scale and positive feedback (Metcalfe's Law) as well as the social dynamics behind it (Reed's Law). Diversification for interoperable metadata can be looked at from a resource-based and a market-based point of view. The resource-based approach investigates how economically valuable resources are created and commercially exploited. The market-based approach looks at new customers and market segments that can be entered and secured.

2   Processing Data

The core challenge in this use case was to develop the (legal) data ecosystem by using the tools from the LOD2 Stack. Since the whole Semantic Web paradigm was new to WKD, we chose an iterative approach to learn and to optimize and smoothen the workflows and processes that come with it [4].

In order to focus on the highlights, we will not report on this iterative part here, but more on the results of every task. First, we built a knowledge framework based on the information we already stored in the XML documents. This led to an initial version of the knowledge graph describing our domain. We then executed LOD2 Stack tools [1] on this graph in order to enrich this information using data extraction technologies as well as executing data curation for cleansing; and linking tools for ingesting knowledge from external sources. Finally, we added a visualization layer (i) to support the editorial team in metadata management and (ii) to help our customers with visualizations supporting data analytics capabilities (see also [8]).

2.1   Transformation from XML to RDF

One major goal of the "Media and publishing" use case was to develop a stable transformation process for the WKG XML data. The development of the mapping schema from XML to RDF was based on the provided WKG DTD – so that the ontology was chosen to express the WKG data. The development of the schema for the transformation has been done in the following steps:

- Define vocabularies used for the WKD RDF schema (see Table 1)
- Define the URI pattern used for the WKD RDF schema
- Mapping definition
- Develop the XSLT style sheet based on the vocabularies and the URI patterns

In addition, a WKD schema description (http://schema.wolterskluwer.de) was developed, extending the used vocabularies to cover specific classes and properties. For the transformation of the WKD XML data to RDF various URI patterns had to be developed to cover the various types of data/information created:

- Resources (The transformed documents and document parts themselves)
  e.g. labor protection law http://resource.wolterskluwer.de/legislation/bd_arbschg
- Vocabularies (used to harmonize parts of the used metadata e.g. taxonomies, authors, organizations, etc.)
  e.g. labor law thesaurus http://vocabulary.wolterskluwer.de/kwd/Arbeitsschutz
- WKD Schema Vocabulary (Specific properties defined for the mapping schema)
  e.g. keyword http://schema.wolterskluwer.de/Keyword

The mappings between the WKD DTD and the WKD schema were implemented as XSLT functions. The WKD XML data was then transformed into RDF triples by applying the functions related to the relevant XML elements. Note that the output of the transformation was using the RDF/XML serialization.

Table 1. Schemas that have been evaluated and are used in the WKD RDF schema (applied vocabularies)

Vocabulary	Prefix	Namespace
BIBO	bibo	http://purl.org/ontology/bibo/
Dublin core	dc	http://purl.org/dc/elements/1.1/
Dublin core terms	dcterms	http://purl.org/dc/terms/
FOAF	foaf	http://xmlns.com/foaf/0.1/
Metalex	metalex	http://www.metalex.eu/metalex/2008-05-02#
OWL	owl	http://www.w3.org/2002/07/owl#
RDF	rdf	http://www.w3.org/1999/02/22-rdf-syntax-ns#
RDF schema	rdfs	http://www.w3.org/2000/01/rdf-schema#
SKOS	skos	http://www.w3.org/2004/02/skos/core#
XHTML vocabulary	xhtml	http://www.w3.org/1999/xhtml/vocab#

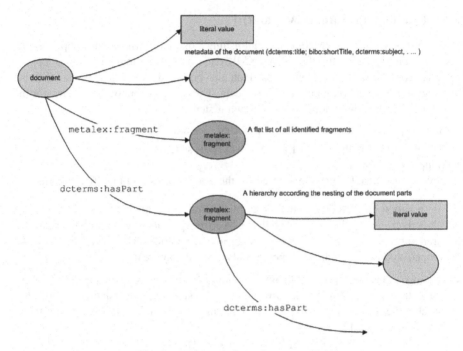

Fig. 1. RDF graph for a document URI

The transformation resulted in a number of triples, stored in a named graph per document (see Fig. 1). In this way, a provenance relationship between the existence of the triple, the XSLT template and the original XML document was created. If either the XSLT template or the XML document was updated, then the set of triples to be updated was uniquely identified with the graph name.

Valiant[9], a command line processing tool written in JAVA supporting XSLT2.0, has been developed for the transformation process within the work package . As a first step, Virtuoso Sponger Cartridge was explored, as Virtuoso[10] was part of the LOD2 Stack, but this track was abandoned due to the lack of support for XSLT 2.0. For the management of the taxonomies and vocabularies PoolParty[11] was used. Additionally, Venrich was developed to support the batch process for the alignment of the document metadata and the vocabularies and taxonomies. All the data was stored in Virtuoso.

The initial transformation resulted in:

- 785,959 documents transformed to RDF graphs with a total of 46,651,884 triples
- several taxonomies and vocabularies that have been created based on the data

---

[9] https://github.com/bertvannuffelen/valiant, accessed June 10, 2014.

[10] http://virtuoso.openlinksw.com/, accessed June 10, 2014.

[11] http://www.poolparty.biz/, accessed June 10, 2014.

Additionally, two of the developed vocabularies have been released as linked open data under an open source license by WKG[12],[13].

2.2   Metadata Management Process

In the past, publishers have focused their content management systems around printed products: books, leaflets, journals, etc. A document centric approach, in which metadata and content are combined in one document, is well suited. Electronic publishing offers new opportunities, but also provides challenges for existing content management systems. For instance, it has changed the way people find information: instead of following the imposed structure and taking advantage of the printed index and the footnote system, electronic publishing allows jumping arbitrary through the publication following more closely a person's processes of thought. Without quality metadata this is unrealizable.

Having quality data is crucial for a publisher's business. Incomplete, erroneous or inaccurate information reduce the customers trust in the data, and hence in the publishing body. Consequently a large amount of effort in this work package was around improving and controlling the quality of the data. We will elaborate how the Linked Data representation of the extracted metadata is an enabler in the data quality processes.

The editorial process of a publisher like Wolters Kluwer Germany is today driven by 3 key stakeholders:

- The content editor creates the content: comments on law or jurisdictions, news, etc. Often the content editor is not part of the publisher organization, but an expert in the field who is using the publisher's dissemination channels to reach its audience. In the Use case contents are also partly harvested from legal institutions.
- The metadata editor manages the metadata of the content provided by the content editor.
- The taxonomist is responsible for the coherency and completeness of the controlled vocabularies used to create the metadata.

While applying the Linked Data paradigm on the editorial process a fourth role has emerged:

- the enrichment manager is a role which naturally emerges from the Linked Data paradigm. She is responsible for selecting external data sources that are thrust worthy and which contain data that provides added value to the content.

These stakeholders interact with each other via the content management system of the publisher (Fig. 2). The prototypical interaction pattern is the following. The content editor uploads a (new) version of a document. Via automated extractions, metadata is added. Inside the publishers organization the metadata editor is validating and

---

[12] See http://vocabulary.wolterskluwer.de/, accessed June 10, 2014.

[13] See further information about this in 3 Licensing Semantic Metadata and Deliverable 7.1.1 http://static.lod2.eu/Deliverables/Deliverable-7.1.1.pdf.

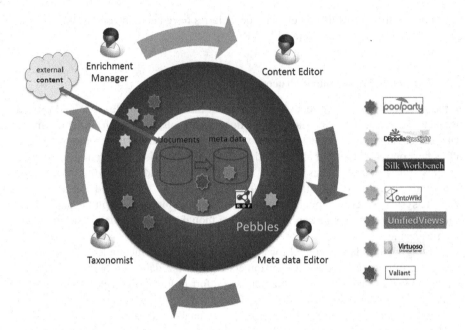

Fig. 2. Metadata management workflow

augmenting the attached metadata to make sure the document is ready for publication. In that process the metadata editor is using the controlled vocabularies that the taxonomist is maintaining. Controlled vocabularies need constant curation (responsibility of the taxonomist) in order to meet the ever changing world.

To explore how Linked Data can transform and support the metadata quality management and editorial process, a dedicated LOD2 Stack instance was setup. Since metadata quality is the center of the problem statement, the central component is formed by an adapted version of Ontowiki[14], called Pebbles. Pebbles supports the editing of the metadata independently of the content, and it is aimed for the metadata editors. For the taxonomists, software support is given by the PoolParty suite. And finally the enrichment manager is supported by a whole arsenal of tools of which Silk[15] and LOD Management Suite[16] – also called UnifiedViews (with the automated annotation processes for DBpedia Spotlight[17] and PoolParty Extractor[18]) - are the most notable.

Pebbles, a Metadata Editor
The user is welcomed in Pebbles with a dashboard overview showing the most recent updated documents and the documents with the most outstanding issues.

---

[14] http://aksw.org/Projects/OntoWiki.html, accessed June 10, 2014.

[15] http://wifo5-03.informatik.uni-mannheim.de/bizer/silk/, accessed June 10, 2014.

[16] https://grips.semantic-web.at/display/public/LDM/Introduction, accessed June 10, 2014.

[17] https://github.com/dbpedia-spotlight/dbpedia-spotlight/wiki, accessed June 10, 2014.

[18] http://www.poolparty.biz/portfolio-item/poolparty-extractor/, accessed June 10, 2014.

Such dashboard view aids to focus on the most important items, but also it reflects the users' current state of work. After the user selects a document, Pebbles shows the document view on which the textual document content is shown together with its metadata. It is important that the metadata editor sees the document content in order to being able to validate the correctness of the associated metadata. Here the metadata can be updated, but also new metadata properties can be added according to the WKD schema. New properties can be added by hand, or result from the suggestions that are associated with the document (Fig. 3).

A suggestion is an association of some value with the document that has been added via an external process. This external process is controlled by the enrichment manager. The enrichment manager uses a linking environment (e.g. Silk) or an annotation engine (e.g. DBpedia Spotlight) to create these associations. At this point in time the enrichment manager has two options: either she directly adds the resulting associations to the metadata store, or the associations are reviewed through the quality assurance process. The quality assurance process is performed by the metadata editor by accepting/rejecting suggestions in the Pebbles environment. As the metadata editor that has the ownership of the documents metadata, she is the right person to make that decision. In case of the acceptance of a concept, the associated default metadata property can also be updated. This creates flexibility in the process: the enrichment manager can suggest new associations without deciding upfront the property which is handy in the case an annotation engine is being used. Such annotation engines often return related concepts belonging to a wide variety of domains (persons, countries, laws, …) It is however advised for the smoothness of the process to make the properties as concrete as possible.

The provided collection of documents by Wolters Kluwer forms an interconnected network. Journal articles refer to laws and court cases, and so on. In a document centric environment, these links are typically stored inside the document container. It is easy given a document to follow the outgoing references, whereas the reverse search (i.e. finding all documents that refer the current document) is much harder. Applying this

Fig. 3. Pebbles document metadata view

search on data in a RDF store simply requires inverting patterns in the SPARQL query. The non-directionality of the RDF graph model allows creating quickly any exploration path that is desired. Often exploration paths are quite generic: for instance to show the list of documents that belong to a particular document category is very similar to showing the list of documents for an author. By configuring the tree navigation widget with the values for a taxonomy, Pebbles offers a faceted approach to explore documents. The usability of the faceted browsing is determined by the quality of the taxonomies being used and the quality of the metadata that are tagging the documents.

Issues Identified in Existing Metadata, Based on Developed Vocabularies
During transformation of WKD data to RDF, several metadata properties were defined as having skos:Concepts as their range. The rationale behind that was that this data may be organized and managed in a next step in taxonomies or thesauri. In a second iteration after processing all the data, missing concepts have been detected and were added to the vocabularies.

During the review of the generated data, besides missing mappings to taxonomies the following issues in the existing metadata transformed to RDF were found:

- Transformation errors (e.g. concept generated with "" labels): To avoid this, the schema transformation has to be adapted to ignore empty metadata entries.
- Wrong Metadata (e.g. job titles or page numbers instead of organization name concerning the organizations taxonomy): This needs to be cleaned up manually. Rules can be provided to detect such kind of data during transformation; and the same rules could be applied to exclude this data from display in the metadata editor (Pebbles). Since this data can also be managed (changed/edited/deleted) in Pebbles, no additional efforts for a rule based cleaning have been made.
- Same concepts with different label: We decided that automatic mapping of metadata representing the same concepts (e.g. different spelling for persons, see Table 2 for different reasons) could not be done during schema transformation, because no quality assurance could be provided that way. So an interface for disambiguation of concepts based on label similarity was developed to provide a semi-automatic way of cleaning up those concepts.

Notification Service
We developed a scenario, where several vocabularies were developed and partly published as Linked Open Data (labor law thesaurus and courts thesaurus) with PoolParty. Furthermore, Pebbles was developed as an environment designed to manage RDF metadata for the WKD documents. To stay up-to-date with the latest changes in these datasets, the resource subscription and notification service (rsine[19], published under an open-source license at GitHub) was developed, allowing dataset curators to subscribe for specific changes that they are interested in and to get a notification as soon as such changes occur.

---

[19] https://github.com/rsine/rsine, accessed June 10, 2014.

Table 2. Possible issues for different author names

Confusions	First version	Second version	Third version
Family name change after marriage	Gritt Diercks	Gritt Dierks-Oppler	–
	Andrea Banse	Andrea Schnellbacher geb. Banse	Andrea Schnellbacher
Second forename	Bernd Schneider	Bernd Peter Schneider	–
Initials	Detlev Müllerhoff	D.Müllerhoff	–
Typos	Cornelius Prittwitz	Cornelins Prittwitz	–
Punctuation	Hans-Dieter Becker	Hans Dieter Becker	–
Different writings	Detlev Burhoff	Detlef Burhoff	–
Different characters	Østerborg	Österborg	Osterborg

Rsine is a service that tracks RDF triple changes in a triple store and creates a history of changes in a standardized format by using the change set ontology[20]. Users wanting to receive notifications can express the kind of changes they are interested in via SPARQL queries. These queries are sent to rsine, encapsulated in a subscription document that can also contain further information such as how the notification message should be formatted. Notifications were sent via mail.

The implemented scenarios focused on the following three main use cases:

- vocabulary management
- vocabulary quality
- metadata management

For all main use cases, several scenarios[21] have been implemented.

2.3   Enrichment of WKD Data

In a first step, the enrichment of WKD Data has been applied to the vocabularies published by WKD. The WKD Arbeitsrechtsthesaurus (labor law thesaurus) was linked (skos:exactMatch) with DBpedia[22], STW[23], Thesoz[24] and Eurovoc[25]. The WKD

---

[20] http://vocab.org/changeset/schema.html, accessed June 10, 2014.

[21] Scenarios are listed in Deliverable 5.3.2.

[22] http://de.dbpedia.org/, accessed June 10, 2014.

[23] Thesaurus for economics of the Leibniz Information Centre for Economics http://zbw.eu/stw/versions/latest/about, accessed June 10, 2014.

[24] Social science thesaurus of the Leibniz Institute of Social Sciences, http://www.gesis.org/en/services/research/thesauri-und-klassifikationen/social-science-thesaurus/, accessed April 18, 2014.

[25] Multilingual thesaurus of the European Union, http://eurovoc.europa.eu/, accessed June 15, 2014.

Table 3. Data added to the concepts of the WKD vocabulary

		DBpedia	STW	TheSoz	EuroVoc
skos:altLabel	Alternative wording		X	X	X
skos:scopeNote	Note		X	X	X
dbpedia-owl:abstract	Abstract/short definition	X			
dcterms:subject	Subject	X			
rdfs:label	Wording	X			
foaf:page	Related pages	X			
dbpedia-owl: thumbnail	Picture	X			
geo:long	Longitude	X			
geo:lat	Latitude	X			

Gerichtsthesaurus (courts thesaurus) was linked to DBpedia. In addition to linking to the respective sources, the WKD vocabularies have been enriched by including data from the respective sources (see Table 3). The provenance of the included data has been preserved, storing the added data in separate graphs.

The mapping to those resources was based on the similarity of concept labels and has been done in a semi-automatic process using Silk. Figure 4 shows the evaluation workspace where the user can check and accept or decline the suggested links. The enrichment with additional data as shown in Table 3 has been done automatically using the LOD Management Suite.

The published vocabularies are publicly available under CC BY 3.0. The frontend uses the data from the external datasets to enhance the user experience. For instance, the geographic location of courts can be leveraged to be displayed on a map (Fig. 5). The map is also available on the detail pages of the courts, where images, showing from DBpedia are also displayed, showing mostly the court building.

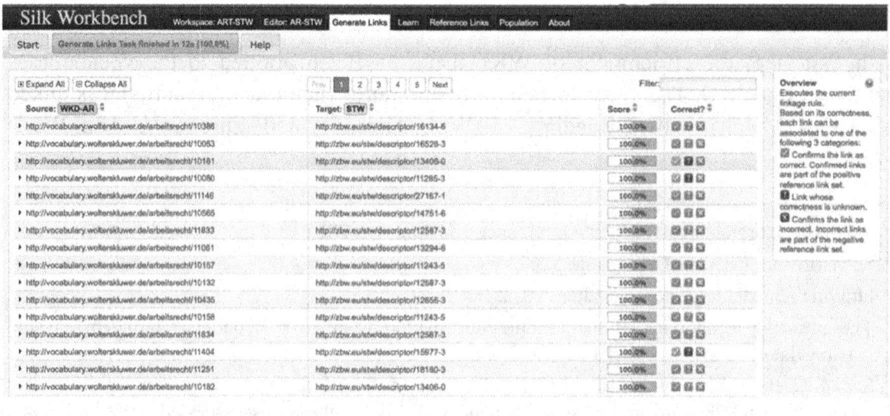

Fig. 4. Mapping results in Silk

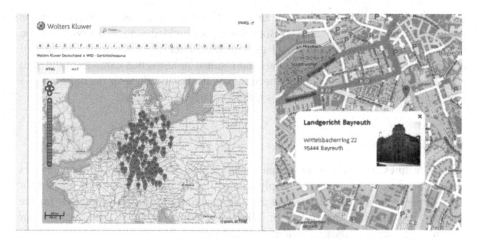

Fig. 5. Court maps of courts within Germany and a specific court

In a second step, WKD document data has been enriched by linking to external resources. Legislations were matched (skos:exactMatch) with DBpedia information – data coming from Wikipedia info boxes (especially scope and practice area) could be used to enrich the documents further. Authors were linked to persons in the GND[26] dataset (Integrated Authority File of the German National Library) – links to these external sources are included in Pebbles. The GND dataset contains more metadata about authors than WKD does collect. Both mappings to DBpedia and GND were done using Silk (Table 4). A third enrichment project took place with the EU Publication Office to match documents from the EU Cellar platform with documents from Pebbles.

Entity Extraction was another approach to enrich the metadata of documents. It was tested randomly with two tools: DBpedia Spotlight and the PoolParty Extractor.

Table 4. Overview of WKD concept linking to external and internal sources

Links to external/internal sources	Links
Courts thesaurus to DBpedia	997
Extended version of courts thesaurus	–
Labor law thesaurus to DBpedia	776
Labor law thesaurus to Thesoz	443
Labor law thesaurus to STW	289
Labor law thesaurus to EuroVoc	247
Legislations to DBpedia	155
Authors to GND	941
WKD Labor Law Thesaurus to WKD subjects	70

---

[26] http://www.dnb.de/DE/Standardisierung/GND/gnd_node.html, accessed June 10, 2014.

Spotlight uses DBpedia concepts as an extraction base, whereas PoolParty uses the predefined controlled vocabularies. Both solutions provided a good overview on the topics and main issues of the tested documents. Nonetheless, the main problem of ambiguity appeared in both approaches and resulted in terms that came from different contexts (e.g. "deadline" that could mean the application deadline or the deadline of a labor agreement and therefore address different areas of labor law).

2.4 Visualization

Special features and visualization functionalities are crucial as part of the activities related to the publishing content supply chain. Visualizations are not only created for the internal management of data, but also for enabling product developments for the customers of information services of WKD. Therefore, we investigated options for presenting the created data in an appealing manner.

The visualization of controlled vocabularies provides different interfaces depending on the dataset. For instance, courts are visualized in form of a map in the Linked Data frontend[27], where the geographical information is used either to visualize courts as pins on a map of Germany or a local map presenting the geolocation information for each individual court (see Fig. 5).

For the labor law thesaurus we chose the visualization in form of a semantic network. Concepts are shown with related concepts within the same context of labor law (Fig. 6).

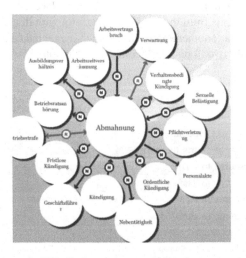

Fig. 6. Semantic net of labor law

---

[27] At http://lod2.wolterskluwer.de/, accessed May 10, 2014.

The visualization of overall datasets is possible with CubeViz[28] and gives an insight to the amount of available data for specific document types, practice areas, time frames and courts (Fig. 7).

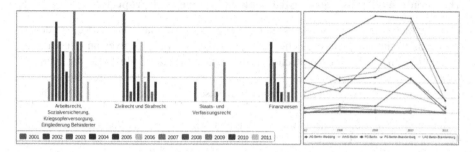

Fig. 7. Laws of specific practice areas per year; jurisdictions per court per year

Visualizing the data has proven to be an important step to give the user deeper understanding of the underlying data and to provide contextual information that can give new insights.

3   Licensing Semantic Metadata

Data is not an easy subject to talk about, especially when doing it from an economic perspective. From all intangible assets imaginable, data is a highly controversial one, given that its economic characteristics are hard to describe and even more difficult to protect. But to own, to control, and to share data one needs to define policies that describe the conditions under which data can be (re-)used in various contexts and for various purposes. Licensing is one such policy that allows us to define data as an economic good. Accordingly, data licensing is crucial in the development of data-driven businesses as it defines the properties of data in a generic economic sense in the dichotomies of scarcity-abundance, private-public and rivaling-complementary. Licenses are an enabler and a barrier for economic transactions. They set the boundaries in which economic actions take place and they define the legitimate or illegitimate usage of data for commercial or non-commercial purposes.

Beside licensing, technology as a constructivist framework for the creation and utilization of data plays an important role. Technology defines the good characteristics of data. According to this premise, it makes a difference whether data is generated manually or algorithmically; or optimized for syndication or storage within a silo etc. Technology influences the context in which data is being generated and utilized, thus changing the hermeneutic conditions under which data is being defined. It makes a difference, whether data is being treated as a solitary thing or linked for purposes of knowledge discovery and targeted insights. Hence it is crucial to gain a good

---

[28] http://aksw.org/Projects/CubeViz.html, accessed June 10, 2014.

understanding of the technology with which data has been generated to make economic sense out of it.

3.1 Traditional Protection Instruments for Intellectual Property

Semantic metadata is a fairly new kind of intellectual asset that is still subject to debate – concerning the adequate protection instruments [12]. Table 5 gives an overview on the applicability of various protection instruments. The table illustrates the complex nature of semantic metadata as intellectual property. Various instruments can be applied to various assets; while copyright, database right and competition right are the most relevant ones.

Copyright basically protects the creative and original nature of a literary work and gives its holder the exclusive legal right to reproduce, publish, sell, or distribute the matter and form of the work. Hence, any literary work that can claim a sufficient degree of originality can be protected by copyright.

Database Right protects a collection of independent works, data or other materials, which have been created with considerable financial investment, are arranged in a systematic or methodological way and are individually accessible by electronic or other means. Databases are also protected as literary works and need to have a sufficient degree of originality that requires a substantial amount of investment.

An Unfair Practices Act protects rights holders against certain trade practices, which are considered unfair in terms of misappropriation, advertising, sales pricing or damages to reputation. Especially the first aspect is relevant to semantic metadata, which actually occurs, when data is being reused without appropriate compensation i.e. in terms of attribution or financial return.

Patenting protects the inventory aspects of a novel technical artefact. Hence it does not directly impact the protection of semantic metadata as – at least in Europe – patents can just be acquired for hardware-related inventions. But as soon as semantic metadata becomes an indispensable subject of a methodology that generates physical effects, has a sufficient level of inventiveness and can be exploited commercially, these components can be protected under Patent Law.

Table 5. IPR instruments for semantic metadata [9]

	Copyright	Database right	Unfair practice	Patents
Documents	YES	YES	YES	NO
Dataset	NO	YES	PARTLY	NO
Description	YES	NO	YES	NO
Identifier	NO	NO	NO	NO
Name space	YES	YES	YES	NO
Vocabulary	PARTLY	YES	YES	NO
Classification	PARTLY	PARTLY	PARTLY	NO
Ontology	PARTLY	YES	YES	PARTLY
Rules	PARTLY	YES	YES	PARTLY

This overview conceals the fact that there exist regional differences in the practical application of IPR instruments. These differences and specificities of so called IPR regimes make the licensing of Linked Data a complex and sometimes confusing issue. I.e. while in the USA data is generally protected under the US copyright law[29], the European Union additionally provides the instrument of Database Right[30] to fill certain gaps between the various national copyrights of the EU member states. Additionally while the US Patent Act[31] allows the patenting of software, which also includes collections of data as output of an algorithmic process; this is formally forbidden in Europe under Article 52 of the European Patent Convention[32].

This situation has long been scrutinized by critics of traditional IPR practices. On the one hand, the differences between the various regional regimes lead to judicial uncertainty. On the other hand, the overlapping and complementary protection instruments tend to favor an "overprotection" of intellectual assets that stifle competition and innovation and prevent the development of business models and new ways of value creation (i.e. [2, 3, 6, 11]).

As a reaction to these structural externalities of the traditional IPR system, new licensing instruments have emerged over the past few years that deliberately focus on the creative and self-governed re-purposing of intellectual property with the aim to foster innovation, collaborative creation of value and finally the public domain. These so called commons-based instruments – well known under Creative Commons and lately Open Data Commons – play an important role in the commercial and non-commercial appropriation of Linked Data and are an important part of a Linked Data licensing policy. Additionally, we will discuss the purpose of so called "community norms" as a third important component in Linked Data licensing policy.

3.2   Licensing Policies for Linked Data

The open and non-proprietary nature of Linked Data design principles allow to easily share and reuse data for collaborative purposes. This also offers new opportunities for data publishers to diversify their assets and nurture new forms of value creation (i.e. by extending the production environment to open or closed collaborative settings) or unlock new revenue channels (i.e. by establishing highly customizable data syndication services on top of fine granular accounting services based on SPARQL).

To meet these requirements, commons-based licensing approaches like Creative Commons[33] or Open Data Commons[34] have gained popularity over the last few years, allowing maximum re-usability while providing a framework for protection against unfair usage practices and rights infringements. Nevertheless, to meet the requirements

---

[29] See http://www.copyright.gov/title17/, accessed July 10, 2013.

[30] See http://eurlex.europa.eu/LexUriServ/LexUriServ.do?uri=CELEX:31996L0009:EN:HTML, accessed July 10, 2013.

[31] See http://www.law.cornell.edu/patent/patent.overview.html, accessed July 10, 2013.

[32] See http://www.epo.org/law-practice/legal-texts/html/epc/2010/e/ma1.html, accessed July 10, 2013.

[33] See http://creativecommons.org/, visited April 22, 2012.

[34] See http://opendatacommons.org/, visited April 22, 2012.

of the various asset types, a Linked Data licensing strategy should make a deliberate distinction between the database and the content stored in it (see Table 5). This is necessary as content and databases are distinct subjects of protection in intellectual property law and therefore require different treatment and protection instruments. An appropriate commons-based protection strategy for a data provider could look as follows:

The contents of a linked dataset, which are comprised of the terms, definitions and its ontological structure, are protected by a CC-By v3.0 License[35], which allows the commercial and non-commercial reuse of any published artefact as long as the owner is mentioned.

The underlying database, which is comprised of all independent elements and works that are arranged in a systématic or methodological way and are accessible by electronic or other means, are protected by a ODC-By v1.0 License[36], which also allows the commercial and non-commercial reuse of any published artefact as long as the owner is mentioned.

Additionally to these two aspects, the licensing strategy also should incorporate a Linking Policy Community Norm, which explicitly defines the expectations of the rights holder towards good conduct when links are made to the various artefacts provided in the dataset.[37] This norm should provide administrative information (i.e. creator, publisher, license and rights); structural information about the dataset (i.e. version number, quantity of attributes, types of relations) and recommendations for interlinking (i.e. preferred vocabulary to secure semantic consistency).

All in all the three elements of a commons-based licensing policy – the CC-By v3.0 License, the ODC-By v1.0 License and the Community Norm – provide a secure and resilient judicial framework to protect against the unfair appropriation of open datasets.

3.3   Rights Expression Languages for Linked Data Licenses

The basic idea of Linked Data is to create an environment where information can flow freely and can be repurposed in multiple ways, not necessarily evident at the time of content creation. This holds true for open and closed settings alike. Hence a clear machine-readable explication of prohibits and permits associated with the usage rights of linked datasets is a necessary precondition to realize the promises of the Linked Data vision.

Open Digital Rights Language (ODRL): With the emergence and mass adoption of Digital Rights Management Systems since the end of the 1990s, several attempts have taken place to define machine-readable standards for the expression of rights over digital assets. One of these endeavors was ODRL, an XML vocabulary to express rights, rules, and conditions – including permissions, prohibitions, obligations, and

---

[35] See http://creativecommons.org/licenses/by/3.0/, visited April 20, 2012.

[36] See http://opendatacommons.org/category/odc-by/, visited April 20, 2012.

[37] See for example the community norm provided by the Leibniz Information Centre for Economics: http://zbw.eu/stw/versions/8.08/mapping/gnd/, accessed April 20, 2012.

assertions – for interacting with online content.[38] The corresponding ODRL Standards Group[39], a member of the World Wide Web (W3C) Community and Business Groups[40] since 2011, acts as an international initiative to define the specifications for expressing policy information over digital content residing on the Open Web Platform (OWP)[41].

ODRL utilizes an Entity-Attribute-Value Model to express a policy about rights and restrictions associated with a digital artefact. The legal information about allowed actions with a media asset (i.e. copying, sharing, modifying, attributing etc.) can be expressed within the ODRL vocabulary. Hence ODRL basically provides a machine-readable policy framework that supports the flexible and fine-granular definition of usage rights within dynamic usage settings like the web and other multi-channel environments. In 2013, the International Press and Telecommunications Council (IPTC) adopted ODRL as the basis for its Rights Markup Language (RightsML)[42,43]. Still in an experimental phase, the RightsML has mainly been applied to specify rights and restrictions with respect to photos[44], but its application goes beyond this specific asset type.

Besides ODRL, the Creative Commons Community has developed *Creative Commons Rights Expression Language*[45] (CCREL) to represent the various CC licenses in a machine-readable format. CCREL is the product of an informal W3C working group that issued its specifications in 2008. Since then, CCREL is being recommended by the Creative Commons Foundation as a standard for the machine-readable provision of Creative Commons licensing information to the public. Although never acknowledged as an official W3C recommendation, CCREL has evolved into a de facto standard for the special domain of Creative Commons Licenses and is expected to spread with the increasing need to provide explicit licensing information for automated processing on the web.

CCREL basically complements the ODRL vocabulary. It provides a condensed and hierarchically ordered set of properties that define the actions allowed with certain licenses. These properties can be seamlessly integrated into the ODRL vocabulary and allow to define fine-grained usage policies and constraints associated with a certain asset that falls into the legal domain of Creative Commons.

Generally it is important to mention that a combination of ODRL and CCREL is not obligatory to provide machine-readable licensing information on the web. The semantic expressivity of CCREL is sufficient to simply annotate existing assets with licensing information for automated processing. But in case of very complex and

---

[38] A comparable endeavour to create a data model for machine-readable statements on IPR in e-commerce transactions can be traced back to the year 1999. For details see [10].

[39] http://www.w3.oeg/cumunity/odrl/, accessed June 17, 2013.

[40] http://www.w3.org/community/, accessed June 17, 2013.

[41] http://www.w3.org/wiki/Open_Web_Platform, accessed June 17, 2013.

[42] http://dev.iptc.org/RightsML, accessed June 17, 2013.

[43] http://dev.iptc.org/RightsML-Introduction-to-ODRL, accessed July 1, 2013.

[44] http://dev.iptc.org/RightsML-10-Implementation-Examples, accessed June 17, 2013.

[45] http://www.w3.org/Submission/CCREL/, accessed July 1, 2013.

differentiated usage scenarios, a combination of ODRL and CCREL will be necessary, as ODRL provides the necessary semantic expressivity to define fine-granular usage policies associated with a certain asset that goes beyond the simple explication of licensing information, i.e. for the purposes of Digital Rights Management.

Beside Creative Commons, which is basically an extension of copyright, the *Open Data Commons* initiative[46] has started to provide legal tools for the protection of commons-licensed data assets. This is necessary as diverging regional judicial regimes require different IPR instruments to fully protect the various assets involved in the digital processing of information. For instance, data sources are protected by copyright in the USA, while in the European Union the protection of data sources is additionally complemented by so called database rights as defined in the Database Directive (96/9/EC)[47]. Hence to fully protect datasets in the European Union, it is actually necessary to provide legal information on various asset types from which certain parts can be licensed under Creative Commons, while others require Open Data Commons.

In contrast to ODRL and CCREL, the Open Data Commons initiative has not yet provided a REL of its own and it is to question whether this is necessary as licenses of Open Data Commons can be easily integrated in the vocabulary of other RELs.

4 Conclusion

The "Media and Publishing" use case has shown – based on real requirements from a global information service provider – that the expected added value to legal products and company processes can be achieved when using Linked Data and the accompanying Semantic Web technologies.

As a major outcome of this project, some tools from the LOD2 Stack like PoolParty and Virtuoso are already implemented and used in the operational systems of WKD. In that sense, the LOD2 Stack has shown its value for enterprises even before the project terminated.

The steps taken, described in this chapter, are most likely representative for many use case scenarios where Linked Data comes into play. First, existing internal and external data must be transformed into standard formats like RDF and SKOS. Then tools need to be utilized for further enrichment and linking and the resulting enhanced domain knowledge network needs to be further maintained and its content translated into functionalities in products[48]. This also covers different areas of visualization, which we investigated. Finally, governance and licensing of data need to be properly addressed, which is still at the end of the project a major issue. Potential business impact could be shown, but when the data is not usable in professional environments, it will not be taken up in the end.

---

[46] http://opendatacommons.org/, accessed July 1, 2013.

[47] http://eurlex.europa.eu/LexUriServ/LexUriServ.do?uri=CELEX:31996L0009:EN:HTML, accessed July 4, 2013.

[48] https://www.jurion.de, accessed June 10, 2014.

However, the steps taken are not at all easy. Already during transformation, the paradigm shift from a content to a data centric point of view raised a lot of questions and issues around quality, especially around normalization and granularity of information. This included the generation and maintenance of valid and stable identifiers. This challenge continued during enrichment phase, where the importance of identifiable and comparable contexts became obvious in order to link things properly and not to compare apples and oranges. During visualization activities, an important aspect, which was new to us in its consequence, was the need for consistent and complete data, which is normally not available when coming from a content based approach. So actually, the process that we faced was not only a technical and data driven one, it also changed our mindset when looking at data and its importance for our future business. In this respect, an important aspect we were not able to cover in this chapter is that of new business models based on Linked Data. Detailed information will be available at the end of the project at the project website.

All the major cornerstones for success mentioned above need to be further elaborated in the future.

Wolters Kluwer will actively participate in further research projects to make more data – and more clean (!) data – publicly available; to add more sophisticated tools to the open source tool stack of LOD2; and to address the licensing challenge within a growing community of data providers and customers of this data. First conversations with public information providers (e.g. with the Publications Office of the European Union or the German National Library) indicate common interests across and beyond traditional company boundaries.

References

1. Auer, S., Bühmann, L., Dirschl, C., Erling, O., Hausenblas, M., Isele, R., Lehmann, J., Martin, M., Mendes, P.N., van Nuffelen, B., Stadler, C., Tramp, S., Williams, H.: Managing the life-cycle of linked data with the LOD2 stack. In: Cudré-Mauroux, P., Heflin, J., Sirin, E., Tudorache, T., Euzenat, J., Hauswirth, M., Parreira, J.X., Hendler, J., Schreiber, G., Bernstein, A., Blomqvist, E. (eds.) ISWC 2012, Part II. LNCS, vol. 7650, pp. 1–16. Springer, Heidelberg (2012)
2. Barton, J.H.: Adapting the intellectual property system to new technologies. In: Wallerstein, M.B., Mogee, M.E., Schoen, R.A. (eds.) Global Dimensions of Intellectual Property Rights in Science and Technology, pp. 256–283. National Academic Press, Washington (1993)
3. Bessen, J., Meurer, M.: Patent Failure: How Judges Bureaucrats and Lawyers Put Innovators at Risk. Princeton University Press, Princeton (2008)
4. Dirschl, C., Eck, K., Lehmann, J., Bühmann, L., Auer, S.: Facilitating data-flows at a global publisher using the LOD2 stack. Submitted to the Semant. Web J.
5. Hondros, C.: Standardizing legal content with OWL and RDF. In: Wood, D. (ed.) Linking Enterprise Data, pp. 221–240. Springer, New York (2010)

 6. Klemens, B.: Math You can't Use: Patents, Copyright and Software. Brookings Institution Press, Washington (2006)
 7. Kobilarov, G., Scott, T., Raimond, Y., Oliver, S., Sizemore, C., Smethurst, M., Bizer, C., Lee, R.: Media meets semantic web – how the BBC uses DBpedia and linked data to make connections. In: Aroyo, L., Traverso, P., Ciravegna, F., Cimiano, P., Heath, T., Hyvönen, E., Mizoguchi, R., Oren, E., Sabou, M., Simperl, E. (eds.) ESWC 2009. LNCS, vol. 5554, pp. 723–737. Springer, Heidelberg (2009)
 8. Lee, S., Kim, P., Seo, D., Kim, J., Lee, J., Jung, H., Dirschl, C.: Multi-faceted navigation of legal documents. In: 2011 International Conference on and 4th International Conference on Cyber, Physical and Social Computing (2011)
 9. Pellegrini, T.: Linked data licensing – Datenlizenzierung unter netzökonomischen Bedingungen. In: Schweighofer, E., Kummer, F., Hötzendorfer, W. (Hg.) Transparenz. Tagungsband des 17. Internationalen Rechtsinformatik Symposium IRIS 2014. Wien: Verlag der Österreichischen Computergesellschaft, S. 159–168 (2014)
10. Rust, G., Bide, M.: The <indecs> metadata framework - principles, model and data dictionary. http://www.doi.org/topics/indecs/indecs_framework_2000.pdf (2000). Accessed 18 July 2013
11. Sedlmaier, Roman: Die Patentierbarkeit von Computerprogrammen und ihre Folgeprobleme. Herbert Utz Verlag, München (2004)
12. Sonntag, M.: Rechtsschutz für Ontologien. In: Schweighofer, E., Liebwald, D., Drachsler, M., Geist, A. (eds.) e-Staat und e-Wirtschaft aus rechtlicher Sicht, pp. 418–425. Richard Boorberg Verlag, Stuttgart (2006)

Building Enterprise Ready Applications
Using Linked Open Data

Amar-Djalil Mezaour[1]([⊠]), Bert Van Nuffelen[2], and Christian Blaschke[3]

[1] Dassault Systemes, Vélizy-Villacoublay, France
amardjalil.mezaour@3ds.com
[2] Tenforce, Leuven, Belgium
bert.van.nuffelen@tenforce.com
[3] SWCG, Vienna, Austria
blaschkec@semantic-web.at

Abstract. Exploiting open data in the web community is an established movement that is growing these recent years. Government public data is probably the most common and visible part of the later phenomena. What about companies and business data? Even if the kickoff was slow, forward-thinking companies and businesses are embracing semantic technologies to manage their corporate information. The availability of various sources, be they internal or external, the maturity of semantic standards and frameworks, the emergence of big data technologies for managing huge volumes of data have fostered the companies to migrate their internal information systems from traditional silos of corporate data into semantic business data hubs. In other words, the shift from conventional enterprise information management into Linked Opened Data compliant paradigm is a strong trend in enterprise roadmaps. This chapter discusses a set of guidelines and best practices that eases this migration within the context of a corporate application.

1 Introduction

Linked Data, Open Data and Linked Open Data (LOD) are three concepts that are very popular nowadays in the semantic community. Various initiatives, like openspending.org, are gaining ground to promote the openness of data for more transparency of institutions. But what is the difference between these three concepts?

Linked Data refers to the way of structuring the data and creates relationships between them. Open Data similar to open-source, opens content to make it available to citizens, developers, etc. for use with as limited restrictions as possible (legal, technological, financial, license). Linked Open Data, that we refer to as LOD, is the combination of both: to structure data and to make it available for others to be reused.

The LOD paradigm democratized the approach of opening data sources and interlinking content from various locations to express semantic connections like similarity or equivalence relationships for example. In business environment,

S. Auer et al. (Eds.): Linked Open Data, LNCS 8661, pp. 155–174, 2014.
DOI: 10.1007/978-3-319-09846-3_8

data interlinking practice is highly recommended for lowering technological and cost barriers of data aggregation processes. In fact, semantic links between data nuggets from separate corporate sources, be they internal or external, facilitate the reconciliation processes between data references, enhance semantic enrichment procedures of data like for example propagating annotations from similar references to incomplete data, etc.

In the context of enterprises, the LOD paradigm opens new scientific and technical challenges to answer emerging semantic requirements in business data integration. The impact of LOD in enterprises can be measured by the deep change that such an approach brings in strategic enterprise processes like domain data workflows. In fact, semantic enrichment and data interlinking contribute to optimize business data lifecycle as they shorten the data integration time and cost. Moreover, when data is semantically managed from its source, i.e. from its acquisition or creation, less time and efforts are required to process and integrate it in business applications. This semantic management implies a set of procedures and techniques like data identification as resources using URIs, metadata annotations using W3C standards, interlink with other data preferably from authority sources or domain taxonomies, etc.

On the other hand, LOD techniques foster the creation of advanced data applications and services by mashing up various heterogeneous content and data:

- from internal sources like CRM, ERP, DBMS, filesystems;
- from external sources like emails, web sources, social networks, forums.

As a consequence, new perspectives are open to offer innovative channels to consume, exploit and monetize business data and assets. To understand the rationale behind this new perspectives, Fig. 1 depicts a generic enterprise semantic data lifecycle from the acquisition to the final consumption.

Fig. 1. Data workflow in enterprise application

2   The Landscape of Enterprise and Corporate Data Today

Data integration and the efficient use of the available information in a business context are major challenges. A typical enterprise has critical applications from different vendors running on various technologies, platforms and communicating via different routes and protocols within and outside an Enterprise. These applications create disparate data sources, data silos and introduce enormous costs. To manage this complexity, an enterprise IT eco-system is viewed as a set of interconnected (or partially connected) applications managing different processes of the enterprise, where separation of the applications often means replication of the same data in different forms. Each process manipulates different kinds of data and produces new data in a structured or unstructured fashion as it is depicted in Fig. 2.

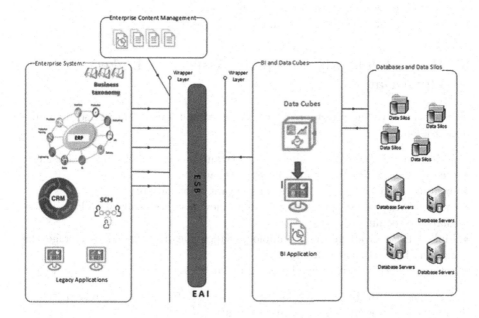

Fig. 2. Classical Enterprise Information System

Existing technological approaches such as Enterprise Application Integration (EAI) create middleware between all these diverse information sources making use of several architectural models with examples being Event Driven Architecture (EDA) or Service Oriented Architecture (SOA) which are usually implemented with web services and SOAP. Common approaches in the enterprises typically include Data Warehousing and Master Data Management.

Simple XML messages and other B2B standards ensure the "flow" of information across internal systems in an easy-to-use and efficient manner. In some cases this is enough but, for example, with a portfolio of over 30,000 offered products and services it is not possible to describe complex components with a handful of simple XML elements. There is a clear need for providing clear definitions or semantics to the data to facilitate integration at the data layer.

However, integration in the data layer is far from being a straightforward task and the Linked Data paradigm provides a solution to some of the common problems in data integration. The two technological approaches, i.e. EAI and LOD, are not contradictory but rather complementary. SOA architecture deployed in an EAI approach works with service oriented whereas LOD works with hyperlinked resources (data, data sets, documents, ...). Note that SOA architecture needs many custom services where LOD uses only a few services (SPARQL, REST) and hyperlinking with the referenced resources. Both approaches have complementary standardization efforts (on metadata vs. services) which makes them better suited for different tasks. EAI-SOA approach is well suited for well-defined tasks on well-defined service data whereas LOD is more targeted for innovative tasks involving semantics (integrations, mappings, reporting, etc.).

3   Why Should My Company Assets Go Linked Open Data?

The benefit of the adoption of Linked Data technologies in enterprises is multi-dimensional:

- address the problem of data heterogeneity and integration within the business;
- create value chains inside and across companies;
- meaning on data enables search for relevant information;
- increase value of existing data and create new insights using BI and predictive analytics techniques;
- Linked Data is an add-on technology which means no need to change the existing infrastructure and models;
- get a competitive advantage by being an earlier adaptor of LOD technologies.

These benefits are better detailed in Fig. 3 taken from Deloitte report "Open data: Driving growth, ingenuity and innovation"[1].

4   LOD Enterprise Architectures

When adopting LOD principles, the Classical Enterprise IT Architecture (Fig. 2) is enhanced for working over the Internet with means to overcome the technical barriers of the format and semantic differences of exchanged and manipulated data. This generates a data processing workflow that is described in the following three figures:

1. Figure 4 evolves the legacy or classic architecture by replacing the Enterprise Software Bus (ESB) with Linked Open Data protocols for data published on an external server.

---

[1] http://www.deloitte.com/assets/Dcom-UnitedKingdom/
Local%20Assets/Documents/Market%20insights/Deloitte%20Analytics/
uk-insights-deloitte-analytics-open-data-june-2012.pdf

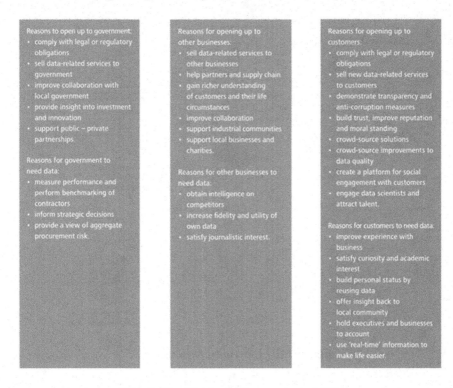

Fig. 3. Benefits for businesses to go LOD

2. Figure 5 evolves the legacy or classic architecture by replacing the Enterprise Software Bus with Linked Open Data protocols among the enterprise LOD publishing servers.
3. Figure 6 zooms-in on a publishing workflow, a transformation pipeline that is added on top of the legacy enterprise services (CRM, ERP, . . .). Some legacy systems may evolve and upgrade to include LOD publishing or they may provide feeds into the LOD publishing workflow.

4.1   LOD Enterprise Architecture with a Publishing Workflow

Figure 4 illustrates the LOD Enterprise architecture where the middleware framework (ESB) of the Classical IT architecture (Fig. 2) is replaced with the LOD cloud. This architecture shows two types of data publishing, with the enterprise putting their RDF data on an external LOD server (server 5 in Fig. 4) according to one of two scenarios:

1. An RDF data set is produced from various data sources and subsystems (box 1 in Fig. 4) and is transferred to an external central LOD server.
2. Metadata is added to a classic web site using semantic metadata annotations (*e.g.* RDFa, Schema.org) on the HTML pages (box 3 in Fig. 4). An LOD server

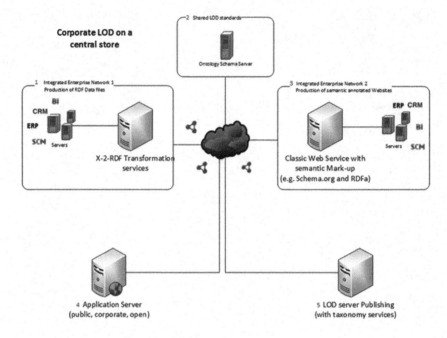

Fig. 4. LOD Enterprise Architecture

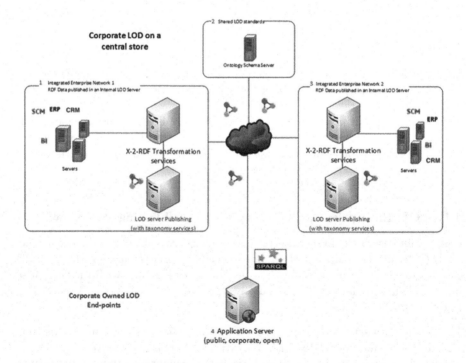

Fig. 5. LOD Enterprise Integration Architecture

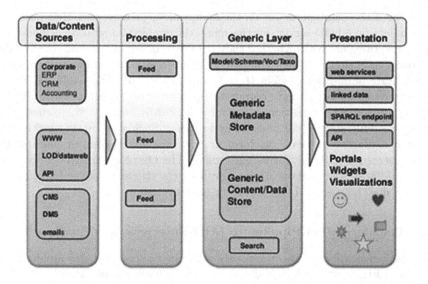

Fig. 6. Transformation pipeline

extracts this metadata, organizes it and makes it accessible as a central service (box 4 in Fig. 4).

The Ontology Schema Server (box 2 in Fig. 4) hosts the used ontologies capturing the semantics of the Linked Open Data. It may be standard (preferred) or custom designed. Other application services or platforms (server 4 in Fig. 4) may use the central LOD services to build specific calculations and reports. Business niches or completely new business opportunities can be created with visualizations and aggregations of data.

Example
A head-hunter can crawl job postings and match with CVs. Aggregations of offered vacancies in real-estates can create new insights. Search engines may use the data for advanced searching while portals[2] can harvest data sets from other portals and publish them from a single point of access in a LOD server (server 5 in Fig. 4).

4.2   LOD Enterprise Architecture Integration

In the previous LOD Enterprise Architecture (Fig. 4 on p. 160) the business operations are described where Linked Data were produced or semantic annotations were made to the corporate content. The data produced (or extracted from crawling through websites) was not published by the enterprise but was made available to the community. Any external LOD server could be used for the publishing of the data, depending on the needs and requirements of the re-users.

---

[2] Such as ODP: http://open-data.europa.eu/en/data/

In Fig. 5 the highlight is put on the operation of an enterprise that publishes its own data on a LOD server. Furthermore, the enabled integration is illustrated between various networks whether they belong to different branches of the same enterprise or entirely different companies. Figure 5 on p. 160 shows two company owned LOD publishing services (box 1 and 3 in Fig. 5). The published RDF is put on the company owned (corporate or enterprise) server platform. Other application services or platforms (server 4 in Fig. 5) may use the owned LOD services to build specific calculations and reports. Such application services may be on a dedicated external platform or they may be on one or more of the corporate owned LOD platforms/end-points. The Ontology Schema Server (box 2 in Fig. 5) hosts the used ontologies capturing the semantics of the Linked Open Data. It may be standard (preferred) or custom designed.

4.3 Transformation Pipeline to LOD Enterprise Architecture

The implementation of the previously described types of LOD architectures (shown in Figs. 4 and 5) is based on a transformation pipeline that is added on top of the legacy enterprise services (e.g. CRM, ERP, etc.). The pipeline includes:

1. Identification of the types of data which are available, i.e. separate data into public and private and define access security strategy, identify data sources, design retrieval procedures, setting data versions, provide data provenance;
2. Modelling with domain-specific vocabularies;
3. Designing the URI Strategy for accessing the information, i.e. how the model and associated data should be accessed;
4. Publishing the data which includes extraction as RDF, storage and querying;
5. Interlinking with other data.

5   Best Practices

5.1 Data Sources Identification

Corporate information can be defined as the data that is used and shared by the different employees, departments, processes (IT or not) of a company. Depending on the information security policy, corporate data can be accessed, processed and published via different business applications of the enterprise IT system. Note that it may be spread across different locations (internal departments and entities, regional or cross countries subsidiaries, etc.).

When integrating LOD technologies into an existing enterprise IT system or application, the first recommendation is to perform an audit on the different business data sources used by the company. This audit should include the following elements:

- Classification of business data sources according to their importance to the operation of strategic business processes.

- Cartography of data workflow between the identified data sources to discover missing, redundant or incomplete information exchanged, the type of data (structured, unstructured), etc.
- Mapping table between native business data formats and the corresponding standard formats (preferably W3C RDF like formats) and the impact from shifting from the native to the standard format.

This audit allows the data architects to better understand the corporate applications' functioning and help them evaluating the cost of integrating LOD technology. According to the required effort and cost, the first best practice consists on migrating as much as possible native formats to standards, preferably RDF-like W3C standards when possible. This considerably eases the publishing, annotation and interlinking of business data.

To comply with the openness criterion of LOD paradigm, publishing data is a major recommendation in the "LODification" process of corporate data. To do so, a licensing scheme must be released to define how the opened data can be reused and exploited by third-party users, applications and services. Considering the company interest, a compromise must be found to open as much data as possible and maintaining a good balance between keeping strategic enterprise data confidential, like the know-how for example, and the rest of data open. Lot of reusable licensing schemes can be considered.

Last but not least, the opened data license scheme must guarantee the reuse principle of data by third-party applications with as few technical, financial and legal restrictions as possible. One way of achieving these goals is to provide rich metadata descriptions of the opened data with appropriate vocabularies, like DCAT[3], VoID[4], DublinCore[5], etc. To make the opened and published data understandable and retrievable, the metadata description must provide key elements like the copyright and associated license, update frequency of data, publication formats, data provenance, data version, textual description of the data set, contact point when necessary to report inconsistencies or errors for example, etc.

5.2 Modelling for the Specific Domain

In order to transform the existing model of an enterprise to a more interoperable schema, best practices focus on the use of common vocabularies. Using terms of existing vocabularies is easier for the publisher and contributes a lot in the re-use and the seamless information exchange of enterprise data.

As a first step, the inherent structure of the legacy data has to be analysed. If no specified hierarchy exists, it can often be created based on expert knowledge of the data. If such an organization of the data is not possible, then only a list of concepts, basically a glossary, can be constructed. Depending on the complexity

---

[3] http://www.w3.org/TR/vocab-dcat/

[4] http://www.w3.org/TR/void/

[5] http://dublincore.org/

of the data and how the entities are related, different data schemas can be used to express them.

5.3 Migration of Legacy Vocabularies

The migration of an existing vocabulary to an RDF scheme varies in complexity from case to case, but there are some steps that are common in most situations. Transforming enterprise data to RDF requires:

- Translating between the source model and the RDF model is a complex task with many alternative mappings. To reduce problems, the simplest solution that preserves the intended semantics should be used.
- The basic entity of RDF is a resource and all resources have to have a unique identifier, a URI in this case. If the data itself does not provide identifiers that can be converted to URIs, then a strategy has to be developed for creating URI for all the resources that are to be generated (see Sect. 5.4).
- Preserve original naming as much as possible. Preserving the original naming of entities results in clearer and traceable conversions. Prefix duplicate property names with the name of the source entity to make them unique.
- Use XML support for data-typing. Simple built-in XML Schema datatypes such as xsd:date and xsd:integer are useful to supply schemas with information on property ranges.
- The meaning of a class or property can be explicated by adding an "`rdfs:comment`", preferably containing a definition from the original documentation. If documentation is available online, "`rdfs:seeAlso`" or "`rdfs:isDefinedBy`" statements can be used to link to the original documentation and/or definition.

Domain specific data, can be modelled with vocabularies like Org[6] or GoodRelations[7]. Only when existing vocabularies do not cover ones needs new schemas should be developed. Data sets that will be published on the web should be described with metadata vocabularies such as VoiD, so that people can learn what the data is about from just looking at its content.

Where suitable vocabularies to describe the business data do not exist, one possibility is to develop a SKOS thesaurus instead of an RDFS model (e.g. taxonomies, organizations, document types). This approach is easier to follow for organisations new to RDF. Tools such as PoolParty[8] exist and support users in such a task. The most recent international standard regarding thesaurus development is the ISO 25964[9]. This standard provides detailed guidelines and best practices that interested readers should consider.

Once the data is in this format it can be loaded in a triple store like Virtuoso and published internally or on the web.

---

[6] http://www.w3.org/TR/2014/REC-vocab-org-20140116/
[7] http://www.heppnetz.de/projects/goodrelations/
[8] http://www.poolparty.biz
[9] http://www.niso.org/schemas/iso25964/

5.4   Definition of the URI Strategy

To meet high quality standards for managing business data, a company must define a persistent data representation policy for identifying each data item from the enterprise data universe. Such a policy must include the addressing schemes for locating data resources within the enterprise space. An URI[10] is a relevant mechanism for defining a global representation scheme of the enterprise business data space.

Identification of Business Items as Resources Referenced by URIs
The first recommendation in building a coherent and persistent representation policy is to identify business data items as resources, which can be individually referenced. To conform to the LOD principles, URIs should be used as the identification mechanism for referencing the business information resources.

Use HTTP/DNS Based URIs
A URI is a mechanism that can be used for identifying different objects and concepts. Some of these objects and concepts may have a physical existence like books for example with ISBN, web page with URL locations. Other concepts are abstract and represent conceptual things like ontology concepts or data items. Different schemes of URIs exist for representing a resource: URIs based on DNS (Domain Name Server) names, ARK (Archival Resource Key) and URIs based on names and IDs like ISBN (International Standard Book Number), DOI (Digital Object Identifiers), Barcodes, etc. Some of the schemes described above can be inadequate to implement basic Linked Open Data features like publishing, referencing and interlinking. Therefore, it is strongly recommended to use URIs based on HTTP protocol and DNS names (like URLs and ARK) to ensure visibility, accessibility and reuse of business items in external applications and to third party users.

Use De-referenceable URIs
Human users associate mechanically HTTP based URIs to URLs and expect to have a web page when pasting a URI into a browser address bar. Unfortunately, the association of a URI to a web page is not always true and automatic. For some businesses, such a situation may generate confusion and frustration. To avoid such misunderstanding, it is highly recommended to provide means to have "dereferenceable" and resolvable URIs, *i.e.* URIs that return meaningful responses when pasted into a browser's address bar. A typical meaningful response could be an HTML page containing a complete or partial description, including the properties of the corresponding resource.

Separate Resource and Resource Representation
Making business items accessible and dereferenceable through the HTTP protocol may generate a conceptual confusion between the resource itself and the document describing it (the HTML answer for example when requesting the resource over HTTP). The resource itself as a business data item should be identified by

---

[10] Uniform Resource Identifier: RFC3986 http://tools.ietf.org/html/rfc3986

a URI that is different from the possible representations that one could generate to describe the resource (an HTML, RDF, XML or JSON description document, a document in a given language, a document using a given technology: PHP, HTML, etc.). W3C proposes two technical solutions to avoid the previous confusion: use of hash URIs and use of 303 URIs:

- Hash URIs - This solution consists in using fragment URIs to reference a non-document business resource. A fragment URI is a URI that separates the resource identifier part from the DNS server path location part using the hash symbol '#'. For example, a book reference 2-253-09634-2 in a library business application could be dissociated from its description using a hash URI as follows: http://www.mylibrary.com/books/about#2-253-09634-2. With this example, the library can manage a repository of books in one single big RDF file containing all the books references and their properties. When accessing 2-253-09634-2 book, a selection query can be applied on that RDF document to extract the RDF fragment corresponding to 2-253-09634-2 triples. The HTTP server managing the de-referencement of URIs will apply business specific rules to render the RDF fragment in the desired technology (as JSON, HTML, XML, etc.).
- 303 URIs - This solution consists in implementing a redirection mechanism represented by the HTTP response code 303 to indicate that the resource has been identified and the server is redirecting the request to the appropriate description option. In the example of the library, the URI could be http://www.mylibrary.com/books/2-253-09634-2. The HTTP server will answer to the request of that URI by a redirect (HTTP code 303) to a new location; let's say http://www.library.com/books/2-253-09634-2.about.html, to provide the description of the requested resource.

Both techniques have advantages and drawbacks as discussed by Sir Tim Berners Lee here: http://www.w3.org/Provider/Style/URI. Whereas hash URI technique may look restrictive due to the same root part URI (before the hash) for different resources, the 303 URI technique introduces latency in requests due to the redirection mechanism.

Design Cool URIs
On the conceptual design side of URIs, Sir Tim Berners Lee proposes the notion of Cool URIs to guarantee that URIs are maintainable, persistent and simple (see http://www.w3.org/TR/cooluris/). To ensure sustainable URIs, it is important to design a "cool" URI scheme that doesn't change over time. To do so one has to follow these basic rules, resumed in Fig. 7:

- Make the URI independent from the underlying technology used to generate or describe the resource. This means avoid extensions such as .php, .cgi and .html in the URI path. To know what to return when a resource is requested (without any extension), it is recommended to implement a content negotiation mechanism in the HTTP server that is able to outstream the appropriate content.

- Make also the URI independent of the physical location of the file describing the resource. Never forget that physical locations are subject to change.
- Make sure that resource metadata are not included in the URI because of their evolution over time. In other words, one has to not encode the following in the URI the authorship, the status of the resource (final, old, latest, etc.), the access rights (public, private, etc.) since this may change over time.

Fig. 7. URI Design rules

Opaque vs. Non opaque URIs
Designing mnemonic and readable URIs for identifying business resources can help human users to get preliminary knowledge on the targeted item. However, from a business point of view, this readability may have side effects if it also reveals an internal organisation system structure. Non Opaque URI may reveal conceptual structure but never should reveal physical or logical data structures. In fact, third party users or external applications can attempt to hack the URI scheme, reverse engineer all business resources and abuse the access to some strategic assets. When there are security risks, it is recommended to use opaque URIs instead of readable ones. An opaque URI is a URI conforming to a scheme that satisfies the following conditions:

- Addressable and accessible resources should be referenced by identifiers instead of human readable labels.

- The resource URI should not contain explicit path hierarchy that can be hacked to retrieve sibling resources for example.
- The URI content should not provide means to gain information on the referenced resource, i.e., a third party client cannot analyse the URI string to extract useful knowledge on the resource.

For non-opaque URI, only the first constraint is not followed.

5.5   Publishing

Publishing procedures in Linked Data follows the identification of data sources and the modelling phase and actually refers to the description of the data as RDF and the storing and serving of the data. A variety of tools have been created to assist the different aspects of this phase from different vendors and include a variety of features. According to the needs of each specific business case and the nature of the original enterprise data, shorter publishing patterns can be created.

5.5.1   Publishing Pattern for Relational Data

Relational databases (RDB) are the core asset in the existing state-of-art of data management and will remain a prevalent source of data in enterprises. Therefore the interest of the research community[11,12] has gathered around the development of mapping approaches and techniques in moving from RDB to RDF data. These approaches will enable businesses to:

- Integrate their RDB with another structured source in RDB, XLS, CSV, etc. (or unstructured HTML, PDF, etc.) source, so they must convert RDB to RDF and assume any other structured (or unstructured) source can also be in RDF.
- Integrate their RDB with existing RDF on the web (Linked Data), so they must convert to RDF and then be able to link and integrate.
- Make their RDB data to be available for SPARQL or other RDF-based querying, and/or for others to integrate with other data sources (structured, RDF, unstructured).

Two key points should be taken into consideration and addressed within the enterprise (see Fig. 8):

Definition of the Mapping Language from RDB2RDF

Automatic mappings provided by tools such as D2R[13] and Virtuoso RDF Views provide a good starting point especially in cases when there is no existing Domain Ontology to map the relational schema to. However, most commonly the manual definition of the mappings is necessary to allow users to declare domain-semantics in the mapping configuration and take advantage of the integration

---

[11] http://www.w3.org/2011/10/rdb2rdf-charter.html

[12] http://www.w3.org/DesignIssues/RDB-RDF.html

[13] http://d2rq.org/d2r-server

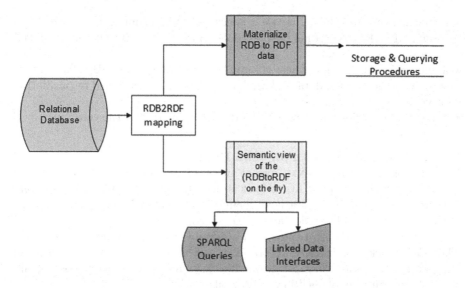

Fig. 8. RDB2RDF publishing pattern

and linking facilities of Linked Data. R2RML[14], a W3C recommendation language for expressing such customized mappings, is supported from several tools including Virtuoso RDF Views and D2R.

Materializing the Data

A common feature of RDB2RDF tools is the ability to create a "semantic view" of the contents of the relational database. In these cases, an RDF version of the database is produced so that content can be provided through a SPARQL endpoint and a Linked Data interface that works directly on top of the source relational database, creating a virtual "view" of the database. Such a "semantic view" guarantees up-to-date access to the source business data, which is particularly important when the data is frequently updated. In contrast, generating and storing RDF requires synchronization whenever either the source data model, the target RDF model, or the mapping logic between them changes. However, if business decisions and planning require running complicated graph queries, maintaining a separate RDF store becomes more competitive and should be taken under consideration.

5.5.2   Publishing Pattern for Excel/CSV Data

When the original data reside in Excel or CSV format, describing them with RDF would be a first step of a publishing pattern while hosting and serving it on the Web follows. LODRefine is a stack component, well-suited to automating and easing the "RDFizing" procedure. Usage brings direct added business value:

• powerful cleaning capabilities on the original business data.

---

[14] http://www.w3.org/TR/r2rml/

- reconciliation capabilities, in case it is needed, to find similar data in the LOD cloud and make the original business data compatible with well-known Linked Data sources.
- augmenting capabilities, where columns can be added from DBpedia or other sources to the original data set based on the previous mentioned reconciliation services.
- extraction facilities when entities reside inside the text of the cells.

5.5.3   Publishing Pattern for XML Data

When the original data is in XML format an XSLT transformation to transform the XML document into a set of RDF triples is the appropriate solution. The original files will not change; rather a new document is created based on the content of the existing one. The basic idea is that specific structures are recognized and they are transformed into triples with a certain resource, predicate and value. The LOD2 stack supports XML to RDF/XML XSLT transformations. The resulting triples are saved as an RDF/XML graph/file that can follow the same hosting and serving procedures explained in the previous section.

5.5.4   Publishing Pattern for Unstructured Data

Despite the evolution of complex storage facilities, the enterprise environment is still a major repository paradigm for unstructured and semi-structured content. Basic corporate information and knowledge is stored in a variety of formats such as PDF, text files, e-mails, classic or semantic annotated websites, may come from Web 2.0 applications like social networks or may need to be acquired from specific web API's like Geonames[15], Freebase[16] etc. Linked Data extraction and instance data generation tools maps the extracted data to appropriate ontologies en route to produce RDF data and facilitate the consolidation of enterprise information. A prominent example of a tool from the LOD2 stack that facilitate the transformation of such types of data to RDF graphs is Virtuoso Sponger.

Virtuoso Sponger[17] is a Linked Data middleware that generates Linked Data from a big variety of non-structured formats. Its basic functionality is based on Cartridges, that each one provides data extraction from various data source and mapping capabilities to existing ontologies. The data sources can be in RDFa format[18], GRDDL[19], Microsoft Documents, and Microformats[20] or can be specific vendor data sources and others provided by API's. The Cartridges are highly customizable so to enable generation of structured Linked Data from virtually any resource type, rather than limiting users to resource types supported by the default Sponger Cartridge collection bundled as part of the Virtuoso Sponger.

---

[15] http://www.geonames.org/

[16] http://www.freebase.com/

[17] http://virtuoso.openlinksw.com/dataspace/doc/dav/wiki/Main/VirtSponger

[18] http://rdfa.info

[19] http://www.w3.org/TR/grddl/

[20] http://microformats.org/

The PoolParty Thesaurus Server[21] is used to create thesauri and other controlled vocabularies and offers the possibility to instantly publish them and display their concepts as HTML while additionally providing machine-readable RDF versions via content negotiation. This means that anyone using PoolParty can become a W3C standards compliant Linked Data publisher without having to know anything about Semantic Web technicalities. The design of all pages on the Linked Data front-end can be controlled by the developer who can use his own style sheets and create views on the data with velocity templates.

DBpedia Spotlight[22] is a tool for automatically annotating mentions of DBpedia resources in text, providing a solution for linking unstructured information sources to the Linked Open Data cloud through DBpedia. DBpedia Spotlight recognizes that names of concepts or entities have been mentioned. Besides common entity classes such as people, locations and organisations, DBpedia Spotlight also spots concepts from any of the 320 classes in the DBpedia Ontology. The tool currently specializes in English language, the support for other languages is currently being tested, and it is provided as an open source web service.

Stanbol[23] is another tool for extracting information from CMS or other web application with the use of a Restful API and represents it as RDF. Both Dbpedia Spotlight and Stanbol support NIF implementation (NIF will soon become a W3C recommendation) to standardise the output RDF aiming on achieving interoperability between Natural Language Processing (NLP) tools, language resources and annotations.

5.5.5 Hosting and Serving

The publishing phase usually involves the following steps:

1. storing the data in a Triple Store,
2. make them available from a SPARQL endpoint,
3. make their URIs dereferenceable so that people and machines can look them up though the Web, and
4. provide them as an RDF dump so that data can easily be re-used.

The first three steps can be fully addressed with a LOD2 stack component called Virtuoso, while uploading the RDF file to CKAN[24] would be the procedure to make the RDF public.

OpenLink Virtuoso Universal Server is a hybrid architecture that can run as storage for multiple data models, such as relational data, RDF, XML, and text documents. Virtuoso supports a repository management interface and faceted browsing of the data. It can run as a Web Document server, Linked Data server and Web Application server. The open source version of Virtuoso is included in the LOD2 stack and is widely used for uploading data in its Quad store, it

---

[21] http://www.poolparty.biz
[22] https://github.com/dbpedia-spotlight/dbpedia-spotlight/wiki
[23] http://stanbol.apache.org/
[24] http://ckan.org/

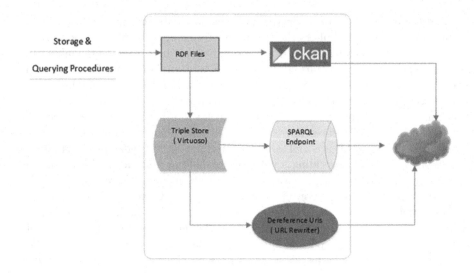

Fig. 9. Publishing pattern for registering data sets

offers a SPARQL endpoint and a mechanism called URL-Rewriter to make URIs dereferenceable.

According to the fourth step, sharing the data in a well-known open datahub such as CKAN will facilitate their discovery from other businesses and data publishers. The functionality of CKAN is based on packages where data sets can be uploaded. CKAN enables also updates, keeps track of changes, versions and author information. It is advised as good practice to accompany the data sets with information files (e.g. VOID file) that contain relevant metadata (Figs. 9, 10).

5.6 Interlinking - The Creation of 5-Star Business Data

5-Star business data[25] refers to Linked Open Data, the 5 stars being:

1. data available on the web with an open-data license,
2. the data is available in a machine readable form,
3. the machine readable data is in a non-proprietary form (e.g. CSV),
4. machine readable, non-proprietary using open standards to point to things,
5. all the above, linked with other data providing context.

To get the full benefits of linked data with the discovery of relevant new data and interlinking with it, requires the 5th star, but that does not mean that benefits are not derived from the Linked Data approach before that point is reached. A good starting point can be business registers such as Opencorporates[26] or

---

[25] http://5stardata.info/
[26] https://opencorporates.com/

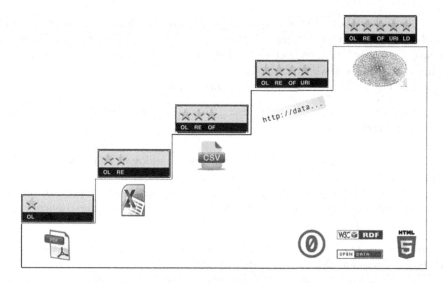

Fig. 10. 5 star data

UK Companies House[27] that contain the metadata description of other companies. The discovery of more related business data can further be facilitated with Linked Data browsers and search engines like SigmaEE[28]. However, the implementation of interlinking between different data sources is not always a straightforward procedure. The discovery of joint points and the creation of explicit RDF links between the data in an automated way can be supported with tools both included in the Interlinking/Fusion LOD2 life cycle.

The process that is referred to as interlinking is the main idea behind the Web of Data and leads to the discovery of new knowledge and their combinations in unforeseen ways. Tools such as SILK[29] offer a variety of metrics, transformation functions and aggregation operators to determine the similarity of the compared RDF properties or resources. It operates directly on SPARQL endpoints or RDF files and offers a convenient user interface namely Silk Workbench.

5.7   Vocabulary Mapping

Sometimes, an enterprise may need to develop a proprietary ontology when applying Linked Data principles. Mapping the terms that were used for publishing the triples with terms in existing vocabularies will facilitate the use of the enterprise data from third-party applications. A tool that supports this kind of mapping is R2R[30].

---

[27] http://www.companieshouse.gov.uk/
[28] http://sig.ma
[29] http://lod2.eu/Project/Silk.html
[30] http://wifo5-03.informatik.uni-mannheim.de/bizer/r2r/

R2R searches the Web for mappings and apply the discovered mappings to translate Web data to the application's target vocabulary. Currently it provides a convenient user interface that facilitates the user in a graphical way to select input data from a SPARQL endpoint as well as from RDF dumps, create the mappings and write them back to endpoints or RDF files.

6   Conclusion

In this chapter, we discussed the best practices to deploy in an enterprise application to ensure a full LOD paradigm compliant semantic dataflow. We also saw that deploying LOD tools and procedures does not necessary requires to start the IT design from scratch but can be deployed on top of existing applications. This guarantees low cost deployment and integration.

Lifting Open Data Portals to the Data Web

Sander van der Waal[1][✉], Krzysztof Węcel[2][✉], Ivan Ermilov[3],
Valentina Janev[4], Uroš Milošević[4], and Mark Wainwright[1]

[1] Open Knowledge Foundation, Cambridge, UK
{sander.vanderwaal,mark.wainwright}@okfn.org
[2] I2G, Poznań, Poland
krzysztof.wecel@i2g.pl
[3] University of Leipzig, Leipzig, Germany
iermilov@informatik.uni-leipzig.de
[4] Institute Mihajlo Pupin, Belgrade, Serbia
{valentina.janev,uros.milosevic}@pupin.rs

Abstract. Recently, a large number of open data repositories, catalogs
and portals have been emerging in the scientific and government realms.
In this chapter, we characterise this newly emerging class of information systems. We describe the key functionality of open data portals,
present a conceptual model and showcase the pan-European data portal
PublicData.eu as a prominent example. Using examples from Serbia and
Poland, we present an approach for lifting the often semantically shallow
datasets registered at such data portals to Linked Data in order to make
data portals the backbone of a distributed global data warehouse for our
information society on the Web.

1 Public Data and Data Portals

Although there are many different sources of data, government data is particularly important because of its scale, breadth, and status as the canonical source
of information on a wide range of subjects. Governments gather data in many
areas: demographics, elections, government budgets and spending, various types
of geospatial data, environmental data, transport and planning, etc. While the
data is gathered to support the functions of government, it is increasingly recognised that by publishing government data under permissive open licences (with
due precautions to avoid publishing sensitive or personal data), huge amounts
of value can be unlocked.

The growth of open government data has been particularly striking in Europe.
The EU recognised its advantages very early, and issued the PSI (Public Sector
Information) Directive in December 2003. This encouraged governments to make
their data available, without restrictions on its use. However, though forward-
looking at the time, the directive did allow for charging for use of data, provided
that the charges did not exceed those calculated on a cost-recovery basis. It therefore did not require what would now be considered 'open' data. The Directive
was revised in 2013, bringing more public bodies within scope and encouraging

S. Auer et al. (Eds.): Linked Open Data, LNCS 8661, pp. 175–195, 2014.
DOI: 10.1007/978-3-319-09846-3_9

free or marginal-cost, rather than recovery-cost, pricing – reflecting what was by then already practice in many EU states. A study in 2011 for the EU estimated the economic value of releasing public sector data throughout the EU at between 30–140 billion EUR.

Except the economical importance, there are additional issues concerning public data that we briefly characterise below: discoverability, harvesting, interoperability, and community engagement.

Discoverability. One of the first problems to be solved when working with any data is where to find it. In using data, one needs exactly the right dataset – with the right variables, for the right year, the right area, etc. – and web search engines, while excellent at finding documents relevant to a given term, do not have enough metadata to find datasets like this, particularly since their main use case is for finding web pages rather than data. There is little point in publishing data if no-one can find it, so how are governments to make their data 'discoverable'? One possibility would be to link it from an on-line tree-structured directory, but such structures are hard to design and maintain, difficult to extend, and do not really solve the problem of making nodes findable when there is a very large number of them (governments typically have at least tens of thousands of datasets).

To solve this problem of discoverability, in the last few years, an increasing number of governments have set up data portals, specialised sites where a publishing interface allows datasets to be uploaded and equipped with high-quality metadata. Using this metadata, users can then quickly find the data they need with searching and filtering features. One good example is the European Open Data portal[1], which is developed by LOD2 partners, using LOD2 stack tools. Numerous countries, including a good number of EU member states, have followed, along with some local (e.g. city) governments.

Harvesting. Many of these portals use CKAN[2], a free, open-source data portal platform developed and maintained by Open Knowledge. As a result they have a standard powerful API, which raises the possibility of combining their catalogues to create a single Europe-wide entry point for finding and using public data. This has been done as part of the LOD2 project: the result is PublicData.eu[3], a data portal also powered by CKAN which uses the platform's 'harvesting' mechanism to copy metadata records of many thousands of datasets from government data portals in over a dozen countries, with new ones added when they become available. Some other portals are also harvested (e.g. city level portals or community-run catalogues of available government data). Sites are regularly polled for changes, ensuring that the aggregate catalogue at PublicData.eu stays roughly in sync with the original catalogues. The PublicData.eu portal is described in more detail in Sect. 2.

---

[1] http://open-data.europa.eu

[2] http://ckan.org

[3] http://publicdata.eu

Interoperability. Non-CKAN portals can also be harvested if they provide a sufficiently powerful API, but for each different platform, some custom code must be written to link the platform's API to CKAN's harvesting mechanism. A few such sites are included in those harvested by PublicData.eu, but rather than writing endless pieces of code for custom harvesting, effort has instead been directed to working towards defining a standard simple interface which different data catalogues can use to expose their metadata for harvesting. This work in progress can be seen at http://spec.datacatalogs.org.

Community Engagement. If governments want to realise the potential benefits of open data, it is not enough just to publish data and make it discoverable. Even the most discoverable data will not be actually discovered if no-one knows that it exists. It is therefore recognised that best practice in data publishing includes an element of 'community engagement': not just waiting for potential users to find data, but identifying possible re-users, awareness raising, and encouraging re-use.

2   Using PublicData.eu

2.1   Data Publishing

Since PublicData.eu harvests datasets from national portals, it is not used directly by civil servants to publish data. Rather, an entire portal, such as the Romanian portal data.gov.ro, is added to PublicData.eu as a 'harvest source', after which it will automatically be regularly polled for updates. If the portal being added is CKAN-based, then the process of setting up harvesting for it takes only a few minutes. However, it is worth briefly explaining the process of publishing data on a source portals. Government employees have individual accounts with authorisations depending on their department. A web user interface guides an authorised user through the process of publishing data, either uploading or linking to the data itself and adding metadata such as title, description, keywords, licence, etc., which enable users to find and identify it. A published dataset may have a number of data files and displays the publishing department as well as the other added metadata. For most common data formats (including CSV, XLS, PDF, GeoJSON and others), users can not only see the metadata but also preview the data in tables, maps and charts before deciding to download it. The process described is for using a CKAN portal, but other data portals will have similar functionality.

Importantly, publishers are not constrained to publish only linked data, or only data in a particular format. While publication of linked data may be desirable, it is far more desirable for data to be published than to be not published. Pragmatically, this often means governments making data available in whatever form they have. One of the ways in which PublicData.eu adds value to published data is with a feature (described in more detail in Sect. 3) to lift data in the simple CSV spreadsheet format into linked data's native RDF. Two projects by governments to publish well-modelled, high-quality linked data are also described later in this chapter.

2.2   Data Consumption

Users on PublicData.eu can search for data from any of the harvested portals[4]. A search is made by specifying particular words or terms. CKAN searches for matching terms anywhere in a metadata record, including for example the description, and returns results (datasets) ordered by relevance or date modified. The user can add filters to the search to find only datasets from particular countries, or with particular tags or available file formats. A top-level set of nine topic areas (Finance & Budgeting, Transport, Environment, etc.) is also displayed and can be used for filtering search results. As with the source portals described above, they can preview the data in various ways before deciding to download it. Users can search, preview and download without registering, but registering enables a user to follow particular datasets or topics, being notified when the dataset changes or when new datasets are published.

The user interface of CKAN has been translated into a wide range of languages, and users can choose the language in which they interact with the site.

Like all CKAN instances, PublicData.eu can be accessed via an RPC-style API[5], as well as via the web interface. Metadata for each dataset is also available as linked data, in N3 or RDF-XML format[6]. It is also possible to get a dump of the entire catalogue as linked data. As mentioned above, the site also includes a feature for lifting data published in CSV spreadsheets to RDF.

3   Semantic Lifting of CSV to RDF

3.1   Lifting the Tabular Data

Integrating and analysing large amounts of data plays an increasingly important role in today's society. Often, however, new discoveries and insights can only be attained by integrating information from dispersed sources, which requires considerable amounts of time and can be error prone if information is stored in heterogeneous representations.

The Semantic Web and Linked Data communities are advocating the use of RDF and Linked Data as a standardized data publication format facilitating data integration and visualization. Despite its unquestionable advantages, only a tiny fraction of open data is currently available as RDF. At the Pan-European data portal PublicData.eu, which aggregates dataset descriptions from numerous other European data portals, only 1,790 out of more than 49,000 datasets (i.e. just 4 %) were available as RDF. This can be mostly attributed to the fact, that publishing data as RDF requires additional effort in particular with regard to identifier creation, vocabulary design, reuse and mapping.

---

[4] As of June 2014, there was 1 pan-European, 13 national level, 15 regional data portals, where some of the national portals where community-supported.

[5] http://docs.ckan.org/en/latest/api/index.html

[6] For example http://publicdata.eu/dataset/chemical-water-quality-by-distance-1990 to2006.rdf.

Various tools and projects (e.g. Any23, Triplify, Tabels, Open Refine) have been launched aiming at facilitating the lifting of tabular data to reach semantically structured and interlinked data. However, none of these tools supported a truly incremental, pay-as-you-go data publication and mapping strategy, which enabled effort sharing between data owners and consumers. The lack of such an architecture of participation with regard to the mapping and transformation of tabular data to semantically richer representations hampers the creation of an ecosystem for open data publishing and reuse. In order to realize such an ecosystem, we have to enable a large number of potential stakeholders to effectively and efficiently collaborate in the data lifting process. Small contributions (such as fine-tuning of a mapping configuration or the mapping of an individual column) should be possible and render an instant benefit for the respective stakeholder. The sum of many such small contributions should result in a comprehensive Open Knowledge space, where datasets are increasingly semantically structured and interlinked.

The approach presented in this section supports a truly incremental, pay-as-you-go data publication, mapping and visualization strategy, which enables effort sharing between data owners, community experts and consumers. The transformation mappings are crowd-sourced using a Semantic MediaWiki[7] and thus allow incremental quality improvement. The transformation process links related tabular data together and thus enables the navigation between heterogeneous sources. For visualization, we integrate CubeViz for statistical data and Facete for spatial data, which provide the users with the ability to perform simple data exploration tasks on the transformed tabular data. The application of our approach to the PublicData.eu portal results in 15,000 transformed datasets amounting to 7.3 Billion triples[8], thus adding a sizeable part to the Web of Data.

3.2 Tabular Data in PublicData.eu

At the time of writing (May 2014) PublicData.eu comprised 20,396 datasets. Each dataset can comprise several data resources and there are overall 60,000+ data resources available at PublicData.eu. These include metadata such as categories, groups, license, geographical coverage and format. Comprehensive statistics gathered from the PublicData.eu are described in [3].

A large part of the datasets at PublicData.eu (approx. 37 %) are in tabular format, such as, for example, CSV, TSV, XLS, XLSX. These formats do not preserve much of the domain semantics and structure. Also, tabular data represented in the above mentioned formats can be syntactically quite heterogeneous and leaves many semantic ambiguities open, which make interpreting, integrating and visualizing the data difficult. In order to support the exploitation of tabular data, it is necessary to transform the data to standardized formats facilitating the semantic description, linking and integration, such as RDF.

---

[7] http://wiki.publicdata.eu/

[8] The dynamic dump is available at http://datahub.io/dataset/publicdata-eu-rdf-data.

Other formats represented on the PublicData.eu portal comprise: 42 of the datasets have no format specified, 15 % are human-readable representations (i.e. HTML, PDF, TXT, DOC), the other 6 % are geographical data, XML documents, archives as well as various proprietary formats. Thus for a large fraction (i.e. 42 %) of the datasets a manual annotation effort is required, and at the time of writing they can not be converted automatically due to the absence of the format descriptions. Discussion of the conversion of human-readable datasets (i.e. 15 %) to RDF is out of scope of this book. The known fact is that such conversion has been proven to be time-consuming and error-prone. The other 6 % of the datasets are tackled partially in other projects, for instance, GeoKnow project[9] is aimed at converting geographical data to RDF, whereas statistical data from XML documents are converted within Linked SDMX project[10].

3.3   User-Driven Conversion Framework

The completely automatic RDF transformation as well as the detection and correction of tabular data problems is not feasible. In [3] we devised an approach where the effort is shared between machines and human users. Our mapping authoring environment is based on the popular MediaWiki system. The resulting mapping wiki located at wiki.publicdata.eu operates together with Public-Data.eu and helps users to map and convert tabular data to RDF in a meaningful way. To leverage the wisdom of the crowd, mappings are created automatically first and can then be revised by human users. Thus, users improve mappings by correcting errors of the automatic conversion and the cumbersome process of creating mappings from scratch can be avoided in most cases. An overview of the entire application is depicted in Fig. 1.

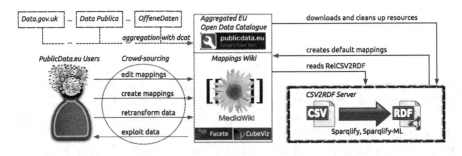

Fig. 1. Architecture of our CSV2RDF extension for PublicData.eu.

Our application continuously crawls CSV resources from PublicData.eu and validates them. Around 20 % of CSV resources are filtered out, mostly because of response timeouts, server errors or missing files. After the validation default

---

[9] http://geoknow.eu
[10] http://csarven.ca/linked-sdmx-data

mappings are created and resources are converted to RDF. In order to obtain an RDF graph from a table T we essentially use the table as class approach [1], which generates triples as follows: subjects are generated by prefixing each row's ID (in the case of CSV files this by default is the line number) with the corresponding CSV resource URL. The headings become properties in the ontology namespace. The cell values then become the objects. Note that we avoid inferring classes from the CSV file names, as the file names often turned out to be simply labels rather than meaningful type names.

Conversion to RDF is performed by the Sparqlify-CSV. Although the Sparqlify-ML syntax should not pose any problems to users familiar with SPARQL, it is too complicated for novice users and therefore less suitable for crowd-sourcing. To lower the barrier, we define a simplified mapping format, which releases users from dealing with the Sparqlify-ML syntax. Our format is based on MediaWiki templates and thus seamlessly integrates with MediaWiki. To define mappings we created a template called RelCSV2RDF. The complete description for the template is available on the mapping wiki.

At the end of the transformation a page is created for each resource on the mappings wiki at wiki.publicdata.eu. The resource page comprises links to the corresponding resource and dataset on PublicData.eu as well as one or several mappings and visualization links. Each mapping is rendered using the RelCSV2RDF template into a human-readable description of the parameters including links for transformation rerun and RDF download.

Sharing the effort between the human users and machines is never a simple task. The trade-off between human involvement and machine automatic processing should be balanced in a way, that the most precision is achieved with the least time expense from the user side. After automatic mapping generation and resource conversion, user is supposed to find the relevant RDF schema for the given CSV table with third-party tools such as LOV search engine. This task required the background knowledge in the field of Semantic Web, that is the knowledge about existence of specific RDF processing tools. To eliminate this requirement we developed special interface for the finding relevant properties for linking table schema to existing RDF terms.

Additionally, the mapping wiki uses the Semantic MediaWiki [4] (SMW) extension, which enables semantic annotations and embedding of search queries over these annotations within wiki pages. The RelCSV2RDF template utilizes SMW and automatically attaches semantic links (using has_property) from mappings to respective property pages. This allows users to navigate between dataset resources which use the same properties, so that dataset resources are connected through the properties used in their mappings.

3.4 Conversion Results

We downloaded and cleaned 15,551 CSV files, that consume in total 62 GB of disk space. The vast majority (i.e. 85 %) of the published datasets have a size less than 100 kB. A small amount of the resources at PublicData.eu (i.e. 14.5 %) are between 100 kB and 50 MB. Only 44 resources (i.e. 0.5 %) are large and very large files above 50 MB, with the largest file comprising 3.3 GB. As a result, the largest 41 out of the 9,370 converted RDF resources account for 7.2 (i.e. 98.5 %) out of overall 7.3 billion triples.

The results of the transformation process are summarized in Table 1. Our efficient Sparqlify RDB2RDF transformation engine is capable to process CSV files and generate approx. 4.000 triples per second on a quad core 2.2 GHz machine. As a result, we can process CSV files up to a file size of 50 MB within a minute. This enables us to re-transform the vast majority of CSV files on demand, once a user revised a mapping. For files larger than 50 MB, the transformation is currently queued and processed in batch mode.

Table 1. Transformation results summary

CSV res. converted	9,370	Avg. no. properties per entity	47
CSV res. volume	33 GB	Generated default mappings	9,370
No. generated triples	7.3 billions	Overall properties	80,676
No. entity descriptions	154 millions	Distinct properties	13,490

4   Statistical Data in Serbia

The National Statistical Office is a special professional organisation in the system of state administration that performs expert tasks related to: organisation and conduction of statistical surveys, preparing and adopting unique statistical standards; cooperation with international organisations in order to provide standardisation and data comparability (e.g. EUROSTAT[11]), establishment and maintenance of the system of national accounts, cooperation and expert coordination with bodies and organisations that are in charge of carrying out the statistical surveys, as well as other tasks stipulated by the law.

National statistical offices across the world already possess an abundance of structured data, both in their databases and files in various formats, but lack the means for exposing, sharing, and interlinking this data on the Semantic Web. Statistical data underpins many of the mash-ups and visualisations we see on the Web, while also being the foundations for policy prediction, planning and adjustments. Making this data available as Linked Open Data would allow for easy enrichment, advanced data manipulation and mashups, as well as effortless publishing and discovery. More specifically, publishing statistical data using RDF comes with the following benefits:

- The individual observations, and groups of observations, become (web) addressable, allowing for third party annotations and linking (e.g. a report can reference the specific figures it is based on, allowing for fine grained provenance trace-back).

---

[11] http://ec.europa.eu/eurostat

- In RDF, the fact that the data is decoupled from the layout means the layout has no effect on the interpretation of the data, unlike the table approach, where the layout has significant influence on the way the information can be read and interpreted.
- As RDF does not rely on the data being properly laid out, this separation makes it possible to re-contextualize the dataset by embedding or integrating it with another dataset. This further extends to combination between statistical and non-statistical sets within the Linked Data web.
- Datasets can be manipulated in new ways, due to the fine grained representation enabled by the Linked Data approach.
- For publishers who currently only administer static files, Linked Data offers a flexible, non-proprietary, machine readable means of publication that supports an out-of-the-box web API for programmatic access.

4.1   Relevant Standards

We can think of the statistical dataset as a multi-dimensional space, or hypercube, indexed by those dimensions. This space is commonly referred to as a *cube* for short; though the name should not be taken literally, it is not meant to imply that there are exactly three dimensions (there can be more or fewer), nor that all the dimensions are somehow similar in size.

The Statistical Data and Metadata eXchange (SDMX)[12] is an ISO standard used by the U.S. Federal Reserve Board, the European Central Bank, Eurostat, the WHO, the IMF, and the World Bank. The United Nations and the Organization for Economic Cooperation and Development expect the national statistics offices across the world to use SDMX to allow aggregation across national boundaries. However, the fact that the concepts, code lists, datasets, and observations are not named with URIs or routinely exposed to browsers and other web-crawlers, makes SDMX not web-friendly, which, in turn, makes it more difficult for third parties to annotate, reference, and discover that statistical data.

The Data Cube RDF vocabulary[13] is a core foundation, focused purely on the publication of multi-dimensional data on the Web. It supports extension vocabularies to enable publication of other aspects of statistical data flows. As this cube model is very general, Data Cube can also be used for other datasets (e.g. survey data, spreadsheets and OLAP data cubes).

SDMX-RDF is an RDF vocabulary that provides a layer on top of Data Cube to describe domain semantics, dataset's metadata, and other crucial information needed in the process of statistical data exchange. More specifically, it defines classes and predicates to represent statistical data within RDF, compatible with the SDMX information model.

---

[12] http://sdmx.org

[13] http://www.w3.org/TR/vocab-data-cube/

4.2   Working with Statistical Linked Data

Within LOD2 a specialized version of the Stack – the *Statistical Workbench* – has been developed to support the need of experts that work with statistical data. Figure 2 shows the main menu of the software environment where the operations are organized into five subgroups called Manage Graph, Find more Data Online, Edit & Transform, Enrich Datacube, and Present & Publish respectively. Once the graph is uploaded into the RDF store, it can be further investigated with the Validation Tool, or with the OntoWiki semantic browser. The validation component checks if the supplied graph is valid according to the integrity constraints defined in the RDF Data Cube specification. Each constraint in the document is expressed as narrative prose, and where possible, SPARQL ASK queries are provided. These queries return true if the graph contains one or more Data Cube instances which violate the corresponding constraint. If the graph contains a well-formed RDF Data Cube, it can be visualized with the CubeViz tool.

Fig. 2. LOD2 Statistical Workbench

4.3   Serbian Statistical Office Use Case

The information published by the Statistical Office of the Republic of Serbia (SORS)[14] on monthly, quarterly and yearly basis is mostly available as open, downloadable, free of charge documents in PDF format, while raw data with short and long-term indicators is organized in a central statistics publication database. The SORS publication list includes press releases, a monthly statistical bulletin, statistical yearbook, working documents, methodologies and standards, trends, etc. Serbia's national statistical office has shown strong interest in being able to publish statistical data in a web-friendly format to enable it to be linked and combined with related information. A number of envisioned main actors,

---

[14] http://www.stat.gov.rs

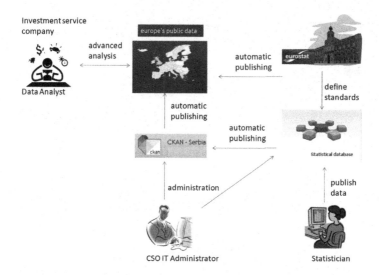

Fig. 3. Simplified workflow for an end-user case

and a sample scenario, were used to elaborate the requirements for the Linked Open Data tools to be included in the Statistical Workbench.

The SORS data publishing process with the Linked Open Data extension is shown in Fig. 3. The data prepared by a Statistician are published through the SORS Dissemination database. Using the LOD2 Statistical Workbench, reports can be transformed into a machine processable format and published to a local governmental portal (e.g. the Serbian CKAN). The IT Administrator maintains the necessary infrastructure for storing and publishing statistical data in different formats (Excel, XML, RDF). Public data are retrieved by a Data analyst that wants to use the data in his research.

An in-depth analysis of the SORS dissemination database has shown that there are a number of standard dimensions that are used to select and retrieve information. The Linked Data principles suggest modeling these dimensions as code lists in accordance with the recommendation for publishing RDF data using the RDF Data Cube vocabulary. In order to formalize the conceptualisation of each of the domains in question, the Simple Knowledge Organisation System (SKOS) was used. The concepts are represented as skos:Concept and grouped in concept schemes that serve as code lists (skos:ConceptScheme) the dataset dimensions draw on to describe the data (Fig. 4).

As the direct central database access is restricted, all input data is provided as XML files. The SORS statistical data in XML form is passed as input to the Statistical Workbench's built-in XSLT (Extensible Stylesheet Language Transformations) processor and transformed into RDF using the aforementioned vocabularies and concept schemes. Listing 1 shows an example RDF/XML code snippet from a transformed dataset.

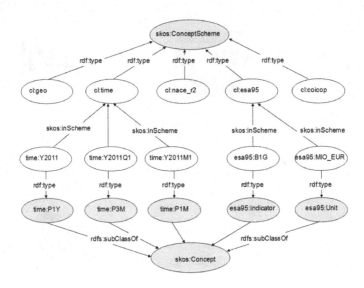

Fig. 4. Representing SORS code lists

Listing 1. Sample observation from a SORS dataset in RDF/XML syntax

```
<qb:Observation rdf:about="RS-DATA/NA/GVA/data#obs978">
 <qb:dataSet rdf:resource="RS-DATA/NA/GVA/data"/>
  <sdmx-attribute:unitMeasure
              rdf:resource="RS-DIC/esa95-unit#MIO_NAT"/>
  <rs:geo rdf:resource="RS-DIC/geo#RS"/>
  <rs:time rdf:resource="RS-DIC/time#Y2001Q3"/>
  <sdmx-measure:obsValue>183802.6</sdmx-measure:obsValue>
</qb:Observation>
```

The above example describes the setup, the overall process and the outcome of the use case. It shows how (local) raw statistical data can be moved to (globally visible) rich collections of interrelated statistical datasets. A future-proof novel method is used for data representation, compatible with international statistical standards. The resulting data relies on both international and domestic code lists, allowing for easy comparison, interlinking, discovery and merging across different datasets. Finally, the results are cataloged in a local metadata repository, and periodical harvesting at an international level is scheduled, thereby increasing transparency and improving public service delivery, while enriching the Linked Data Cloud.

5   Multidimensional Economy Data in Poland

The Polish Ministry of Economy (MoE) publishes various types of yearly, quarterly, monthly and daily economical analyses, based on the data coming from the Ministry of Finance, Central Statistical Office, Warsaw Stock Exchange,

Ministry's own data and other governmental agencies resources. There are also other larger data sets made available either on-line or for download which could be made more easily processable without human intervention. The data as of today is being published in the formats and presentation forms intended for direct consumption by humans, but with very limited possibilities for automated processing or analysis conducted by custom software. Within the LOD2 project the data was lifted to the semantic level.

5.1 Polish Open Economy Data

The primary source of data, subject to publication using the LOD2 tools, was the warehouse for macroeconomic information, namely the INSIGOS database. The data stored by INSIGOS, concerns the Polish economy as well as the international trade of Poland (import and export). The INSIGOS database was built using the internal database of the MoE, namely the Business Information Knowledge Base, maintained since 2001.

The INSIGOS contains the following datasets:

- HZ/GEO – foreign trade broken down by countries
- HZ/CN – foreign trade broken down by type of goods traded, as reported using the Common Nomenclature codes (CN)
- POLGOS – several economic indicators broken down by type of activity, as reported by companies in Poland using F-01 statistical form, using PKD – Polish Classification of Activities. POLGOS was later divided into POLGOS/PKD2004 and POLGOS/PKD2007, because there was no simple way to convert the data to one of the classifications.

5.2 Modelling Multidimensional Data with Data Cube Vocabulary

The most important artefacts that we used from RDF Data Cube Vocabulary include: qb:DimensionProperty, qb:ComponentSpecification, qb:DataSet and qb:DataStructureDefinition. The model prepared for INSIGOS HZ module is presented in Fig. 5.

In INSIGOS HZ module there are only two indicators: *import* and *export*. SKOS concept scheme was created to facilitate the use of measures in dimensions and then in observations. The name of the skos:ConceptScheme is HZ and it was assigned by qb:CodedProperty. Both measure properties were defined according to pattern presented in Listing 2.

Listing 2. Sample measure property from INSIGOS HZ/GEO dataset in turtle

```
<http://data.i2g.pl/insigos/properties/import>
  a qb:MeasureProperty, skos:Concept ;
  skos:prefLabel "Import"@pl ; skos:prefLabel "Import"@en ;
  rdfs:range xsd:decimal ;
  dcterms:source <https://insigos.mg.gov.pl/DaneHZFiltr.aspx> ;
  dcterms:publisher "Polish_Ministry_of_Economy"@en ;
  dcterms:publisher "Ministerstwo_Gospodarki"@pl .
```

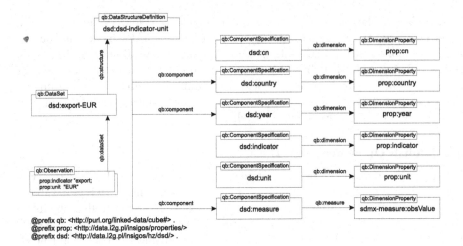

@prefix qb: <http://purl.org/linked-data/cube#> .
@prefix prop: <http://data.i2g.pl/insigos/properties/>
@prefix dsd: <http://data.i2g.pl/insigos/hz/dsd/> .

Fig. 5. INSIGOS HZ modelled in Data Cube vocabulary

5.3   Slices Generation

After conversion of source data to data cube we still have just detailed data. In order to show some useful statistics, and in particular to visualise in CubeViz, we need to provide slices and aggregations. Such artefacts need to be modelled and included along with RDF data.

In order to generate slices we provided a Python script for materialisation of datasets. It first queries for a list of dimensions enumerated in data structure definition (DSD). Then, all elements (members) of dimensions are retrieved. We assume that slice contains two dimensions (for use in two-dimensional charts), therefore pairwise combination of all dimensions is generated. Finally, respective links between observations, datasets and slices are generated.[15]

Listing 3 presents relevant parts of our generated data. In this example, a *slicekey* with fixed dimensions for indicator and unit is defined – `slicekey-indicator-unit`. Using this structure, several slices are generated, one for each combination of free variables. One of them is the slice with values fixed on 'export' (*indicator*) and 'EUR' (*unit*) – `export-EUR`. The last line by `qb:observation` contains ellipsis because there are in fact 1330 observations attached.

---

[15] A mechanism should be introduced to allow querying for observations instead of explicit assignments. Currently, such assignments require materialisation of a big number of additional triples, which makes solution questionable in enterprise data warehouse settings when considering the volume of data.

Listing 3. Data cube slices in INSIGOS data

```
@prefix dsd: <http://data.i2g.pl/insigos/hz/dsd/> .
dsd:dsd a qb:DataStructureDefinition ;
   rdfs:label "Complete_DSD_for_indicator-unit"@en ;
   qb:component dsd:year, dsd:unit, dsd:indicator, dsd:country,
      dsd:measure ;
   qb:sliceKey dsd:slicekey-indicator-unit .
dsd:slicekey-indicator-unit a qb:SliceKey ;
   rdfs:label "slicekey_by_indicator-unit"@en ;
   qb:componentProperty
      <http://data.i2g.pl/insigos/properties/year>,
      <http://data.i2g.pl/insigos/properties/country> .
dsd:dataset a qb:DataSet ;
   rdfs:label "Dataset_with_all_dimensions"@en ;
   qb:structure dsd:dsd;
   qb:slice dsd:slice-export-EUR .
dsd:slice-export-EUR a qb:Slice ;
   rdfs:label "export_-_EUR" ;
   qb:sliceStructure dsd:slicekey-indicator-unit ;
   qb:observation
      <http://data.i2g.pl/insigos/hz/geo/export/AD/2006/EUR>, ...
```

5.4   Aggregations

Aggregations are commonly used in reporting using multidimensional data. The most prominent example is a data warehouse with OLAP cubes. Aggregations are selected and calculated in such a way that speeded up reporting is possible. By analogy, aggregations may be deemed also useful for cubes defined as linked data.

In our case aggregation is necessary for drill-down operations. For example, daily data can be aggregated on a monthly basis to better observe a phenomenon. Also, we can display data in yearly sums, and allow drill-down to be even more precise. SPARQL is capable of calculating sums on-the-fly, but it takes time and sometimes time-out is reached.[16] Materialisation is then necessary for quicker operations.

Our first idea was to prepare aggregations using Python script, similar to slicing. That would require too much querying and would be inefficient. In the end, we found a way to implement the method for aggregation as a set of SPARQL queries.

One of the issues was generation of URIs for new observations as aggregation is in fact a new observation – the same dimensions but values are on higher level, e.g. month → year. For INSIGOS/POLGOS observations we have defined a pattern for identifiers. We used the capabilities of Virtuoso to generate identifiers directly in SPARQL.

---

[16] For example, a query calculating the value of public procurement contracts by voivodeships takes 100 seconds, which is outside of acceptable response times.

Before aggregation is done, a correct hierarchy should be prepared. The prerequisite for the script is that dimensions are represented as SKOS concept scheme, and elements of dimension are organised in hierarchy with *skos:narrower* property.

6   Exploration and Visualisation of Converted Data

In the following we describe two scenarios to showcase benefits of the presented framework. The first one is about statistical data discovery using CubeViz. The second scenario is about discovering geospatial information by the use of Facete.

6.1   Statistical Data Exploration

CubeViz, the RDF Data Cube browser, depicted in Fig. 6 allows to explore data described by RDF Data Cube vocabulary [2]. CubeViz generates facets according to the RDF Data Cube vocabulary artefacts such as Data Cube DataSet, Data Cube Slice, a specific measure and attribute (unit) property and a set of dimension elements that are part of the dimensions.

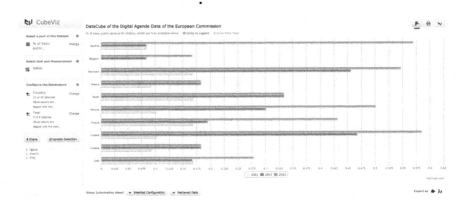

Fig. 6. Screenshot of CubeViz with faceted data selection and chart visualization component.

Based on the selected facets, CubeViz retrieves data from a triplestore and suggests possible visualizations to the user. Users or domain experts are able to select different types of charts such as a bar chart, pie chart, line chart and polar chart that are offered depending on the selected amount of dimensions and respective elements.

6.2   Geospatial Data Discovery

Facete, depicted in Fig. 7, is a novel web application for generic faceted browsing of data that is accessible via SPARQL endpoints. Users are empowered to create custom data tables from a set of resources by linking their (possibly nested) properties to table columns. A faceted filtering component allows one to restrict the resources to only those that match the desired constraints, effectively filtering the rows of the corresponding data table. Facete is capable of detecting sequences of properties connecting the customized set of resources with those that are suitable for map display, and will automatically show markers for the shortest connection it found on the map, while offering all further connections in a drop down list. Facete demonstrates, that meaningful exploration of a spatial dataset can be achieved by merely passing the URL of a SPARQL service to a suitable web application, thus clearly highlighting the benefit of the RDF transformation.

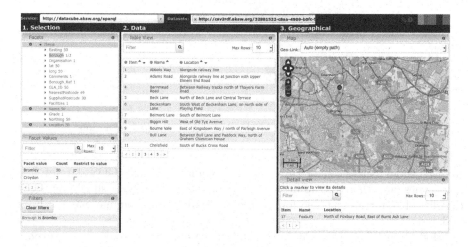

Fig. 7. Screenshot of Facete showing data about allotments in South East London.

6.3 Drill-Down Choropleth Maps

Import and export statistics of Poland collected in INSIGOS HZ/GEO dataset are best visualised on the globe. The globe itself is part of D3 library[17]. Some work was, however, necessary in order to allow display of data from triple store. Several parameters are defined in the graphical interface, and based on it SPARQL queries are prepared. Then, the legend is defined in such a way that colours are more or less equally distributed. Normally the numbers for import and export are subject to power law, therefore the legend scale cannot be linear. The map is coloured according to values assigned to selected countries. A sample map is presented in Fig. 8 shows 20 countries with the greatest value of export in 2012 expressed in PLN (Polish currency), with the unit being millions.

Not only technical communication with Virtuoso had to be solved. We first needed to integrate data on semantic level, i.e. map of the world in D3 had

---

[17] Data-Driven Documents, D3.js, http://d3js.org/.

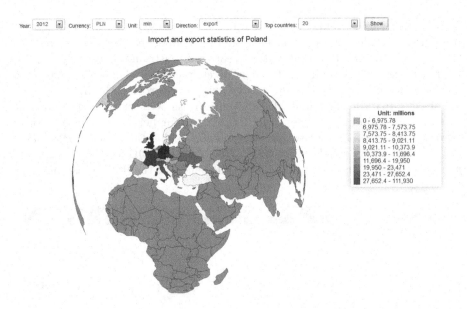

Fig. 8. Export statistics of Poland in 2012 presented on a globe

country codes consisting of three letters. Countries in INSIGOS dataset had just names, and therefore additional mapping was necessary. It should be noted that list of countries changed for the period analysed but the map has not been updated.

More popular is visualisation of data on the country level. For this purpose we need a map of country available in SVG and compatible with D3 library. It can also be derived from open data. For example, a map of Poland has been prepared based on OpenStreetMap and administrative division included there.

On the map of Poland we visualise data concerning public contracts. Several measures can be visualised like: number of contractors, number of contracts or value of contracts. All measures are sliced by geographical dimensions reflecting administrative division of Poland. There are 16 voivodeships (*województwo*) and 380 districts (*powiat*) in Poland. Showing 380 entities on the map is not very useful for interpretation. Therefore we have applied the drill-down approach. First, a user is presented with a map of the whole Poland with 16 voivodeships. Then, after clicking on selected region, the user goes to detailed map of districts in a given region. There is also another administrative level – county (*gmina*) – which can be included when needed. Analogous maps can be prepared for other countries as well.

6.4   Drill-Down Tables

In terms of the drill-down functionality, we need to remember that datasets can be aggregated on various level of detail and very often they are offered as the same package. Geography is not the only dimension. There are several others that cannot be visualised within the map, hence the need to develop a drill-down table. Some examples include (in the case of Polish data): time dimension; Polish classification of activities (PKD, NACE): sections and chapters; common nomenclature (CN): several levels; various economic indicators in energy-related data (e.g. production total → from renewable sources → from solar plants).

Due to required integration with triple store we prepared our own drill-down table from scratch. The prerequisite is that the dimension to be used for drill-down is described as SKOS concept scheme. It is an industry standard and allows to represent hierarchies conveniently. It has also mechanism for labels in various languages. Alternative labels make mapping to this headers more flexible when heterogeneous sources are considered. All vocabularies, including time dimension, were prepared with this prerequisite in mind.

There are in fact three queries necessary to prepare a drill-down table. The approach is thus similar to multidimensional queries against OLAP cubes in MDX[18]. First, we need to get headers of rows and columns, then data itself. Not only labels for headers are necessary but also interdependencies between headers and their level. When a drill-down table is first loaded, rows and columns are collapsed, so that only most aggregated data is shown. It is then possible to click on the respective row or column marked with 'plus' sign to expand one level. Figure 9 presents expanded columns.

Year	Income						Import	Expenditure
		Production altogether	Proffesional power plants	Industrial thermal-electric power stations	Independent power plants	(consumption)	
2007	167109	159348	148977	7666	2705	7761	167109
2008	163975	155494	144774	7937	2783	8481	163975
2009	158612.778204	151210.163204	140312.696	6560.414	4337.053204	7402.615	158612.778204
2010	161332.618	155038.723	143294.293	7267.168	4477.262	6293.895	161332.618

Fig. 9. Drill-down table with expanded columns

7 Conclusions and Future Work

Opening up governmental data requires two elements: discoverability – where more data portals are available, harvesting is used to gather data; and quality machine readable data – where data can be trusted. LOD2 tools support development of these functionalities.

We have addressed the general challenge where data currently being published is in formats and presentation forms intended for direct consumption by humans, but with limited possibilities for automated processing or analysis

---

[18] MultiDimensional eXpressions, a query and manipulation language for OLAP databases.

conducted by a custom software. As one of the important issues for data discoverability we have identified the need for providing data catalogues. CKAN is a reference solution in this area but it requires further extensions. Working implementations include: http://publicdata.eu and http://open-data.europa.eu. The quality of data has been demonstrated by providing Polish and Serbian data first automatically converted and then carefully improved.

One of the missing features is cross-language searching. Although the user interface can be used in multiple languages, metadata for datasets can of course be read only in the language in which it was input. A limitation of search on PublicData.eu is that as the source catalogues are naturally in different languages, a single search term in any given language will usually not find all the relevant datasets.

For wider adoption of CKAN we also need better metadata management. The current harvesting arrangement does not preserve all the original metadata. In particular, even where the harvest source is CKAN-based and datasets have identifiable publishing departments, this information is not preserved in the record on PublicData.eu. Adding this information to the harvesting system would enable users on PublicData.eu to 'follow' individual departments and see dashboard notifications when departments published new or updated data. An example of an alternative harvesting process (built on top of LOD2 stack tools) that preserves the original metadata is available at http://data.opendatasupport.eu.

Several other tools, not mentioned in the chapter, have been particularly useful for making data accessible for machines: Virtuoso, Ontowiki (with CubeViz plug-in), SILK, Open Refine and PoolParty. Various datasets have been elaborated in detail manually, particularly those using the RDF Data Cube vocabulary. Some examples include: national accounts, foreign trade, energy-related, and public procurement data. We have increased the openness of the data by preparing respective vocabularies and providing linking to other data sources available on the Web.

A significant amount of time was absorbed by data quality issues. Even though data was available in 'machine processable' XML, it were users who entered incorrect data. These are, however, typical problems of integration projects and should not under any circumstances be considered to be related to the linked data paradigm. On the contrary, applying tools that we had at our disposal allowed to spot quality problems even faster than we would have been able to otherwise.

References

1. Berners-Lee, T.: Relational databases on the semantic web, 09 1998. Design Issues. http://www.w3.org/DesignIssues/RDB-RDF.html
2. Cyganiak, R., Reynolds, D., Tennison, J.: The RDF Data Cube vocabulary. Technical report, W3C (2013)
3. Ermilov, I., Auer, S., Stadler, C.: Csv2rdf: user-driven csv to rdf mass conversion framework. In: ISEM '13, 04–06 September 2013, Graz, Austria (2013)
4. Krötzsch, M., Vrandecic, D., Völkel, M., Haller, H., Studer, R.: Semantic Wikipedia. J. Web Semant. **5**, 251–261 (2007)

Linked Open Data for Public Procurement

Vojtěch Svátek[1]([✉]), Jindřich Mynarz[1], Krzysztof Węcel[2], Jakub Klímek[3], Tomáš Knap[4], and Martin Nečaský[5]

[1] University of Economics, Prague, Czech Republic
{Svatek,jindrich.mynarz}@vse.cz
[2] I2G, Poznań, Poland
krzysztof.wecel@i2g.pl
[3] Czech Technical University and University of Economics, Prague, Czech Republic
[4] Charles University and University of Economics, Prague, Czech Republic
[5] Charles University, Prague, Czech Republic
{klimek,knap,necasky}@ksi.mff.cuni.cz

Abstract. Public procurement is an area that could largely benefit from linked open data technology. The respective use case of the LOD2 project covered several aspects of applying linked data on public contracts: ontological modeling of relevant concepts (Public Contracts Ontology), data extraction from existing semi-structured and structured sources, support for matchmaking the demand and supply on the procurement market, and aggregate analytics. The last two, end-user oriented, functionalities are framed by a specifically designed (prototype) web application.

1 Public Procurement Domain

Among the various types of information produced by governmental institutions as open data, as obliged by the law, are descriptions of *public contracts*, both at the level of *requests for tenders* (RFT, also 'calls for bids' or the like)—open invitations of suppliers to respond to a defined need (usually involving precise parameters of the required product/s or service/s)—and at the level of *awarded contract* (revealing the identity of the contractor and the final price). The whole process is typically denoted as public/government *procurement*. The domain of public procurement forms a fundamental part of modern economies, as it typically accounts for tens of percents of gross domestic product.[1] Consequently, due to the volume of spending flows in public procurement it is a domain where innovation can have significant impact. Open disclosure of public procurement data also improves the transparency of spending in the public sector.[2]

An interesting aspect of public contracts from the point of view of the semantic web is the fact that they unify two different spheres: that of *public* needs and that of *commercial* offers. They thus represent an ideal meeting place for data models, methodologies and information sources that have been (often) independently designed within the two sectors. Furthermore, the complex life cycle of

---

[1] For example, as of 2010 it makes up for 17.3 % of the EU's GDP [8].
[2] See, e.g., http://stopsecretcontracts.org/.

S. Auer et al. (Eds.): Linked Open Data, LNCS 8661, pp. 196–213, 2014.
DOI: 10.1007/978-3-319-09846-3_10

public contracts gives ample space for applying diverse methods of data analytics, ranging from simple aggregate statistics to analyses over complex alignments of individual items. On the other hand, using linked data technology is beneficial for the public contract area since it allows, among other, to increase interoperability across various formats and applications, and even across human language barriers, since linked data identifiers and vocabularies are language-independent.

As three major views of the e-procurement domain we can see those of *domain concepts*, *data* and *user scenarios*. Plausible and comprehensive *conceptualization* of the domain is a prerequisite for correct design of computerized support as well as for ensuring data interoperability. Management of the large amounts of *data* produced in the procurement domain has to take into account its varying provenance and possibility of duplicities and random errors. Finally, the activities of *users*, i.e., both contract authorities and bidders/suppliers, along the different phases of the public contract lifecycle, have to be distinguished. Linked data technology provides a rich inventory of tools and techniques supporting these views. The last, user-oriented view is least specific of the three; typically, the user front-end does not differ much from other types of (web-based) applications, except that some functionality, such as autocompletion of user input, exhibits online integration to external linked data repositories.

Public procurement domain has already been addressed by projects stemming from the semantic web field. The most notable ones are probably LOTED[3] and MOLDEAS [1]. LOTED focused on extraction of data from a single procurement source, simple statistical aggregations over a SPARQL endpoint and, most recently, legal ontology modeling [5]. MOLDEAS, in turn, primarily addressed the matchmaking task, using sophisticated computational techniques such as spreading activation [2] and RDFized classifications. However, the effort undertaken in the LOD2 project is unique by systematically addressing many phases of procurement linked data processing (from domain modeling through multi-way data extraction, transformation and interlinking, to matchmaking and analytics) as well as both EU-level and national sources with diverse structure.

The chapter structure follows the above views of public procurement. First, the *Public Contract Ontology* (PCO) is presented, as a backbone of the subsequent efforts. Then we review the original public contract data sources that have been addressed in our project, and describe the process of their *extraction*, *cleaning* and *linking*. Finally, the end user's view, in different business scenarios, supported by a *Public Contract Filing Application* (PCFA for short) is presented. It is further divided into the *matchmaking* functionality and the *analytic* functionality (the full integration of the latter only being in progress at the time of writing the chapter).

2   Public Contracts Ontology

The ontology developed within the use case covers information related to public contracts that is published by contracting authorities during the procurement

---
[3] http://loted.eu/

process. We built the ontology on the basis of analysis of the existing public procurement portals (especially TED[4] as the European one, but also national ones) and information published by contracting authorities on these portals. We did not consider all information but primarily the information relevant for matching public contracts with potential suppliers. Therefore, for the most part we consider the information that is produced in the tendering phase (description of the public contract, received tenders and the eventually accepted tender). From the evaluation phase we consider the actual final price for the contract, as its modeling is identical to that of estimated (in the contract notice) as well as agreed price; no further complexity is thus added to the ontology by including it.

2.1 Ontologies Reused by the PCO

Reusing existing, established ontologies when building one's own ontology is crucial for achieving interoperability on the semantic web, since applications capable of working with the original ontologies can then also process the reused elements (and even their derivatives, such as subclasses and subproperties) in the new ontology as well. The PCO reuses the following models:

- GoodRelations Ontology[5] (gr prefix) – to model organizations and price specifications
- VCard Ontology[6] (vcard prefix) – to express contact information
- Payments Ontology[7] (payment prefix) – to express subsidies
- Dublin Core[8] (dcterms prefix) – to express descriptive metadata (e.g., title, description)
- Simple Knowledge Organization System (SKOS)[9] (skos prefix) – to express code lists and classifications
- Friend-of-a-friend Ontology (FOAF)[10] (foaf prefix) – to express agents, especially persons and relationships between them
- schema.org[11] (s prefix) – to express locations and other generic kinds of entities
- Asset Description Metadata Schema (ADMS)[12] (adms prefix) – to express identifiers.

---

[4] http://ted.europa.eu/TED/
[5] http://purl.org/goodrelations/v1#
[6] http://www.w3.org/2006/vcard/ns#
[7] http://reference.data.gov.uk/def/payment#
[8] http://purl.org/dc/terms/
[9] http://www.w3.org/2004/02/skos/core#
[10] http://xmlns.com/foaf/0.1/
[11] http://schema.org/
[12] http://www.w3.org/ns/adms#

2.2   Core Concepts of the PCO

Figure 1 depicts the ontology in the form of a UML class diagram. The core concept of the ontology is that of *public contract* represented by the class pc:Contract. We understand a public contract as a single object that groups pieces of information related to the contract. These pieces of information gradually arise during the public procurement process. They are published by contracting authorities on various public procurement portals in the form of different kinds of notification documents, e.g., *call for tenders* (sometimes also called *contract notice*), *contract award notice, contract cancellation notice*, or the like. Another important concept of the ontology are *business entities*, i.e., in this context, contracting authorities and suppliers. Business entities are not represented via a new class in the ontology; we rather reuse the class gr:BusinessEntity from the GoodRelations ontology.

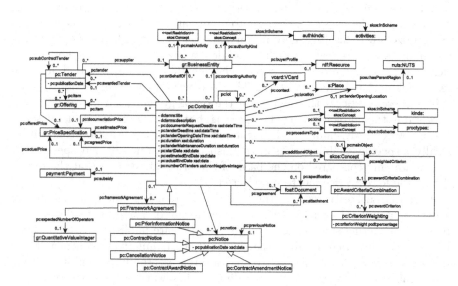

Fig. 1. Public Contracts Ontology – UML class diagram

2.2.1   Tendering Phase Modeling

In this phase the contracting authority publishes initial information about a public contract. This includes basic information, e.g., contract title, description, and the reference number assigned to the contract by the authority (which is usually unique only in the scope of the authority itself). If the contract is too large or too complex, the authority can split it into two or more sub-contracts, which are called *lots*. Each lot is a contract on its own but it is a part of its parent contract. In the ontology, lots are represented using the class pc:Contract. A lot is associated with its superior contract via the property pc:lot.

The authority also publishes basic information about itself, e.g., its legal name, official number or contact information. An important piece of information is the so-called *buyer profile*, which is a web page where the contracting authority publishes information about its public contracts.

Moreover, the authority publishes various requirements and restrictions on the contract. The restrictions include the specification of the kind and objective areas of the contract (Supplies, Works and Services), deadline for tenders, time to realize the contract (in a form of estimated end date or required duration in days or months), estimated price and non-structured specification documents. The objective areas restrict potential suppliers to only those operating in the objective areas. The authority also specifies the procedure by which an awarded tender will be selected from the received tenders. We consider the following procedure types in the core, which are primarily defined by the EU legislation but can be applied world-wide: Open, Restricted, Accelerated Restricted, Negotiated, Accelerated Negotiated, and Competitive Dialogue.

The requirements include two kinds of information. First, the authority specifies the items (i.e., products or services) that constitute the contract. The ontology reuses the class gr:Offering to represent items. Basically, the items are characterized by their name, description and price, but other kinds of characteristics can be used as well, which we however do not cover in the domain model (e.g., references to various product or service classification schemes). Second, it specifies a combination of award criteria. The class pc:AwardCriteriaCombination is the representation of this feature in the ontology. For each award criterion, expressed in the ontology using class pc:WeightedCriterion, a textual description (or, we can say, name) and weight percentage of the criterion is specified. Usually, a specific combination is distinguished. For instance, it may specify that tenders are only compared on the basis of the price offered and that the tender offering the lowest price has to be selected.

After the authority receives the tenders, it publishes either the number of tenders or details of each particular tender received. For each tender, details about the tendering supplier and the offered price are published. A tender may also comprise information about particular items (similarly to contract items, i.e. products or services) offered. Tenders are represented in the ontology using a class called pc:Tender. Then, according to the award criteria, the authority selects and awards the best tender. In this stage, the authority publishes the date of the award and marks the selected tender as the awarded tender.

During the tendering phase, the contract can be cancelled by the authority. If so, the authority publishes the date of cancellation.

2.2.2   Pre-realization, Realization and Evaluation Phase Modeling

In the pre-realization phase, the contracting authority signs an agreement with the supplier and publishes the agreement on the Web. The agreement is a non-structured text document. The ontology reuses the class foaf:Document to represent unstructured textual documents. We only consider one particular structured information published – the price agreed by both the authority and supplier. The agreed price should be the same as the price offered in the awarded tender but it can differ in some specific cases.

After the realization, the authority evaluates how the supplier fulfilled the requirements. This includes various sub-processes that we do not cover in our analysis. We are only interested in the actual end date and the actual final price of the contract. Moreover, the authority could cover the price of the contract or its part by subsidy from an external source (e.g., EU structural funds). Subsidies are usually provided in the form of one or more payments to the authority.

3   Procurement Data Extraction and Pre-processing

Although procurement data are published in a certain form in most countries in the world, we focused on three groups of sources:

1. The European TED (Tenders Electronic Daily) portal,[13] which contains data from a number of countries (thus allowing for cross-country comparisons, as shown in [9]), although only a subset of these (typically for contracts above a certain price level).
2. The Czech and Polish procurement data portals; the lead partners in the procurement linked data activity of the LOD2 project are based in these two countries, and therefore have both good contacts to the national publishing agencies, knowledge of the local regulations, and fluency in the languages in which the unstructured part of the data is written.
3. US and UK procurement data portals, as these are the countries where the open government publishing campaign started first and therefore even the procurement data sources are likely to be found sufficiently rich and well curated.

Regarding the source format of the data, the TED and Czech data were initially only available as HTML, and only at a later phase became also published in XML. In contrast, the Polish, US and UK data have been available in XML from the beginning. Data extraction (and RDFization) methods for both formats have therefore been investigated.

3.1   Data Extraction from HTML

TED and the Czech national portal ISZVUS (later renamed to Public Procurement Bulletin) had been the prime targets in the initial phase of the project. At that time, only the HTML pages were available for these resources. In Fig. 2, we can see two HTML fragments with information about one lot; we can demonstrate different flavors of HTML-based data extraction on them. Both contain red-labelled sections numbered 1 to 4 (the related properties are in Table 1).

The left side of Fig. 2 depicts a fragment of a TED HTML document. The data is stored in `div` elements combined with additional textual information. Section 1 of the document contains combined information about the lot ID and the lot name, so it is necessary to split these properties. Section 2 only contains

---

[13] http://ted.europa.eu/TED/

Table 1. PCO property mapping to HTML fragments

#	PCO property	#	PCO property
1	`dc:title` + `adms:identifier`	3	`pc:supplier`
2	`pc:numberOfTenders`	4	`pc:offeredPrice`

one property, with a textual label that has to be removed. In the Sects. 3 and 4 the fields are separated by `br` tags combined with additional labels.

In contrast, the data in ISVZUS is strictly structured using `input` elements with unique `id` attributes (see the right side of Fig. 2), which allows to access the data fields without any additional transformation.

Technologically, the extraction was based on CSS selectors, and (where the CSS selectors did not suffice) pseudo-selectors[14] allowing to search for elements containing a defined substring. In some cases the element content had to be modified or shortened, which led us to applying regular expressions.

The HTML-based ETL activities for both resources were later suspended when the future availability of full data in XML (rather than mere HTML) was announced. The processing was resumed in Spring 2014 based on XML dumps (and, for the Czech data, also an XML-based SOAP API), which are more reliable than data obtained via information extraction from semi-structured text embedded in HTML.

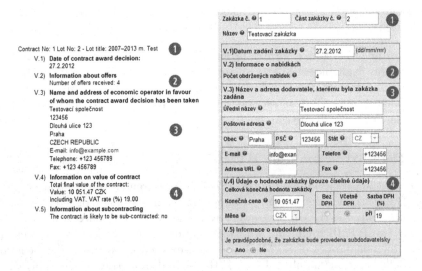

Fig. 2. TED fragment (left) and ISVZUS fragment (right)

---

[14] Provided by the JSoup library http://jsoup.org/.

3.2 Data Extraction from Structured Formats

The extraction from structured formats, namely, XML and CSV, started at different phases of the project and was carried out by different groups, therefore the used technology slightly varied. The first XML data addressed was the (British) Contracts Finder,[15] for which a standalone XSLT script for transforming all fields to RDF triples was developed in early 2012. Later, however, the main focus was on the European (TED), Czech, Polish, and also U.S. data (to have an extra-European source for comparison).

3.2.1 TED Data
In March 2014 the Publications Office of the EU opened access to the data from TED and ceased to charge licensing fees for data access. Current public notices for the past month are available to download for registered users of the TED portal and also via an FTP server. Archived notices dating back to 2010 can be obtained in monthly data exports. Data is published in 3 formats, including a plain-text one and 2 XML formats.

We created an XSL transformation script to convert the TED data into RDF. Using this XSLT script we performed a bulk extraction of the TED archival data via the Valiant tool[16]) from the LOD2 Stack. In parallel, using the UnifiedViews ETL framework,[17] we set up an automatic, continuously running extraction of the increments in TED data. In the further treatment of the extracted RDF data we focused on deduplication and fusion of business entities participating in the EU public procurement market, in order to provide a more integrated view on the dataset.

3.3 Czech Data

We developed an extractor data processing unit[18] for the UnifiedViews ETL framework, which is capable of incremental extraction of data from the *Czech public procurement register*[19] using its SOAP API. During the time we discussed the possibility of publishing raw open data in bulk with the company running the register. As a result of these discussions we were provided with an XML dump of historical data from the register to be used for research purposes. Combining the historical data dump with the access to current data via the SOAP API we were able to reconstruct the complete dataset of public contracts from the registry converted to RDF.

The second source of Czech public procurement data that we processed was a set of *profile feeds* of individual contracting authorities. As per the amendments in the Czech public procurement law, public sector bodies involved in public

---

[15] http://contractsfinder.businesslink.gov.uk
[16] https://github.com/bertvannuffelen/valiant
[17] https://github.com/UnifiedViews/Core
[18] https://github.com/opendatacz/VVZ_extractor
[19] http://vestnikverejnychzakazek.cz/

procurement are required to publish their own XML feed of data about public contracts they issue, including both public notices and award information. The set of public contracts that are published on profile feeds is a superset of what is available via the central Czech public procurement registry because the feeds also cover some lower price public contracts, which are not required to be published in the central register. The content of these feeds mostly mirrors the content of the central register, although for individual public contracts it is less comprehensive. While the data from the register is richer and more descriptive, the profile feeds contain information about *unsuccessful tenders*, which is missing from the register that only reveal information about winning tenders. We deem having data about both successful and unsuccessful tenders as vital in several analytical tasks over public procurement data, which is one of the reasons why we have invested effort into acquiring the data from feeds of contracting authorities. Since early autumn 2013 we have been scraping an HTML list of URLs of profile feeds and periodically convert each feed's XML into RDF using an ETL pipeline developed using the UnifiedViews framework. By using code-based URIs the data is linked to several external datasets. Company identifiers connect it to the Czech business register[20] that we also periodically convert to RDF. Common Procurement Vocabulary (CPV) codes[21] link it to the RDF version of CPV that we produced.

3.3.1 Polish Data

Public procurement data is published by The Public Procurement Office (Urzad Zamowien Publicznych[22]) in the Public Procurement Bulletin (Biuletyn Zamowien Publicznych – BZP[23]).

There are several means to access the data: browsing the BZP portal, subscription mechanism with some restricted number of criteria, and the download of XML files, which we employed in the RDFization. The structure of XML is basically flat: even though some attributes can be grouped that are put on the same level. This has implications for the parsing and conversion mechanisms. On the one hand, no subset of XML data can be selected for further processing. On the other hand, the extraction expressions as well as XML paths are shorter. Conversion of XML files containing notices about public contracts has been carried out by means of Tripliser.[24] The RDFization had to overcome some issues in the XML structure, such as the use of consecutive numbers for elements describing the individual suppliers (in Polish ''wykonawca') awarded

---

[20] http://www.czso.cz/eng/redakce.nsf/i/business_register

[21] By its definition from http://simap.europa.eu/codes-and-nomenclatures/codes-cpv/ codes-cpv_en.htm, "CPV establishes a single classification system for public procurement aimed at standardising the references used by contracting authorities and entities to describe the subject of procurement contracts."

[22] http://uzp.gov.pl

[23] http://uzp.gov.pl/BZP/

[24] A Java library and command-line tool for creating triple graphs from XML, https:// github.com/daverog/Tripliser.

the different lots of a contract: wykonawca_0, wykonawca_1, wykonawca_2 and so on. We also had to write our own extension functions for Tripliser allowing us to generate new identifiers for addresses, as data structures, from their parts: locality, postal code and street.

Automatic *linking*, using Silk[25] as one of the LOD2 stack[26] tools, was carried out for the problem of mapping the contact information of a given contracting authority or supplier to a classification of Polish territorial units called TERYT.[27]

3.3.2 U.S. Data

The dataset was created by combining data from two complementary sources: USASpending.gov[28] and Federal Business Opportunities (FBO).[29] USASpending.gov offers a database of government expenditures, including *awarded* public contracts, for which it records, e.g., the numbers of bidders. On the other hand, FBO publishes public notices for *ongoing* calls for tenders. USASpending.gov provides data downloads in several structured data formats. We used the CSV dumps, which we converted to RDF using SPARQL mapping[30] executed by tarql.[31] Data dump from FBO is available in XML as part of the Data.gov initiative.[32] To convert the data to RDF we created an XSLT stylesheet that outputs RDF/XML.[33] As an additional dataset used by both USASpending.gov and FBO, we converted the FAR Product and Service Codes[34] to RDF using LODRefine,[35] an extraction tool from the LOD2 Stack.

Data resulting from transformation to RDF was interlinked both internally and with external datasets. Internal linking was done in order to fuse equivalent instances of public contracts and business entities. Deduplication was performed using the data processing unit for UnifiedViews that wraps the Silk link discovery framework.[36] The output links were merged using the data fusion component of UnifiedViews.[37] Links to external resources were created either by using code-based URI templates in transformation to RDF or by instance matching based on converted data. The use of codes as strong identifiers enabled automatic generation of links to FAR codes and North American Industry Classification System 2012,[38] two controlled vocabularies used to express objects and kinds of public

[25] See Chap. 1 of this book.

[26] http://stack.linkeddata.org

[27] http://teryt.stat.gov.pl/

[28] http://usaspending.gov/

[29] https://www.fbo.gov/

[30] https://github.com/opendatacz/USASpending2RDF

[31] https://github.com/cygri/tarql

[32] ftp://ftp.fbo.gov/datagov/

[33] https://github.com/opendatacz/FBO2RDF

[34] http://www.acquisition.gov/

[35] http://code.zemanta.com/sparkica/

[36] http://wifo5-03.informatik.uni-mannheim.de/bizer/silk/

[37] Developed previously for ODCleanStore, the predecessor of UnifiedViews [6].

[38] http://www.census.gov/eos/www/naics/index.html

contracts. Instance matching was applied to discover links to DBpedia[39] and OpenCorporates.[40] Links to DBpedia were created for populated places referred to from postal addresses in the U.S. procurement dataset. Furthermore, Open-Corporates was used as target for linking the bidding companies. The task was carried out using the batch reconciliation API of OpenCorporates via interface in LODRefine.

4   LOD-Enabled Public Contract Matchmaking

4.1   Public Contracts Filing Application

Seeking the best possible match is an activity repeatedly undertaken by both sides of the procurement market: *buyers* (contracting authorities) and *suppliers* (bidders). Since most of the underlying computation, and even a considerable part of the GUI components, are similar for both cases, it makes sense to provide a single, web-based interface for them, which can be characterized as a *content-management system* for public contracts (and associated tenders). We denote the prototype developed[41] simply as *Public Contract Filing Application* (PCFA). Its features are (partly dynamically) derived from the Public Contracts Ontology.

4.1.1   Buyer's and Supplier's View

The *buyers* can use PCFA to create and manage their calls for tenders, publish them when they are ready, and wait for tenders from the candidate suppliers, as seen in Fig. 3. PCFA allows the buyer to compare the proposed call for tenders with other public contracts (published by the same buyer or by others) using the matchmaking functionality. The buyers can thus take into account, e.g., the cost or duration of similar contracts in the past, and adjust the proposed price or time schedule accordingly.

PCFA can help the buyers even further by allowing them to find suitable suppliers for their proposed call for tenders, as seen in Fig. 4. They can thus explicitly invite such potential suppliers via email and thus increase the competition for the given call. A published call for tenders can also be withdrawn; if the buyer later publishes a withdrawn call again, it is published as a new call, which ensures that the whole history of the procurement process is recorded properly. When the deadline for tenders passes, the buyers can easily reject the tenders that do not meet the criteria of the call, and they can also award the tender that offers the best conditions. Finally, when the public contract has been fulfilled, the buyer can briefly evaluate the progress and the outcome of the contract and record it in the application. This typically amounts to providing the actual price of the contract (which may be significantly higher than the price proposed in the awarded tender), the actual date when the contract was finished, and the

---

[39] http://dbpedia.org

[40] https://opencorporates.com/

[41] The code of the PCFA is maintained at https://github.com/opendatacz/ pc-filing-app.

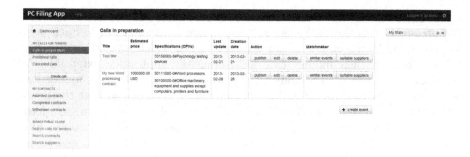

Fig. 3. Open calls for tenders from a buyer's perspective

overall experience of the buyer with this particular supplier. This information can later help the same buyer or other buyers in the future.

The interested *suppliers* can see the open calls for tenders suitable for them. This functionality is again provided by the matchmaking module. As mentioned above, a potential supplier can also be invited, by a contracting authority, to submit a tender to a certain call. The supplier can see and manage the received invitations in the PCFA as well. The invitations can be rejected or accepted; the latter automatically creates a tender. Alternatively, suppliers can find an open call for tenders on their own, and create a tender for it. The tender can be edited by the supplier and, when ready, submitted to the contracting authority. The suppliers are always informed by email when some update takes place for the call for tenders for which they submitted a tender.

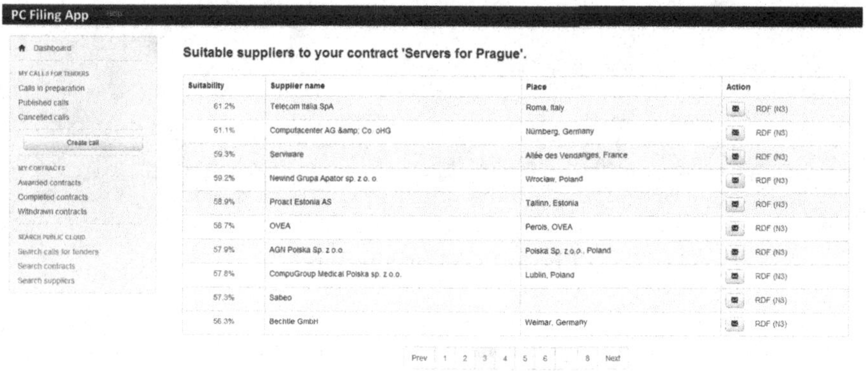

Fig. 4. Suitable suppliers for a call for tenders

4.1.2   Application Architecture

The *architecture* of the PCFA is modular, as can be seen in Fig. 5. Each module consists of both the client and the server side, which gives the developers freedom in what their module can do, making the application extensible. All the modules are based on a module template, which contains the code for user and context management as well as for *quad store*[42] access, so that the developer can focus on the added functionality. The modules use a shared relational database, which contains user information, user preferences and stored files, and can be used for caching of results of more complex SPARQL queries for faster response time when, for example, paging through a longer list of results. The public procurement data itself is stored in two instances of a quad store. The public quad store contains published data accessible to everyone (part of the LOD cloud). The private quad store contains unpublished data for each user of the application and for application management.

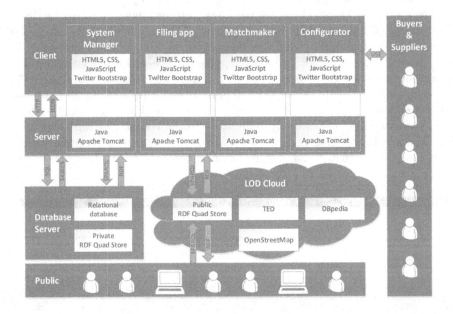

Fig. 5. PCFA architecture

The current implementation consists of the following modules. The system manager module handles registrations, logging in and out, and user preferences management. The filing module implements the lifecycles of calls for tenders, tenders and invitations to tenders. The matchmaking module implements the functionality behind the search for similar calls for tenders and suitable suppliers for contracting authorities (buyers) and suitable open calls for tenders for

---

[42] A database which stores RDF quads - subject, predicate, object and named graph, e.g., Openlink Virtuoso or Jena Fuseki.

suppliers. Finally, the configurations module allows the users to specify a more detailed configuration for individual types of public procurement (cars, IT, etc.).

There are two separate quad stores used in the application.[43] There is a *private* space for each user, where unpublished calls for tenders, tenders themselves and invitations for suppliers to submit a tender to a call are kept. This quad store is not accessible from the internet and is managed solely by the PCFA, which makes the private data secure. Additionally, there is the public space quad store, as part of the LOD cloud, where all the published information is kept and where also the calls for tenders to be compared by the matchmaker reside. This quad store is accessible to everyone on the internet for querying and downloading.

4.2 Matchmaking Functionality Internals

The core operation upon which others are based is the discovery of *contracts similar to a given contract*. To accomplish that, we first filter all contracts based on the similarity of CPV codes according to the hierarchical tree.

Then we refine these results by applying additional comparers, specialized, e.g., in:

1. Tender deadlines: the shorter the interval between the two tender deadlines, the higher the similarity
2. Publication dates: the shorter the interval between the two public contract publication dates, the higher the similarity
3. Geographical distance: we measure the distance between the places where the public contracts were (or are to be) executed. For this purpose, the addresses are automatically converted to geo-coordinates.
4. Textual similarity: we compare the titles of contracts using the SoftTFIDF [3] algorithm.

The overall match score is then a weighted sum of the scores returned by all comparers.

When looking for *suitable suppliers* for a given call for tenders, the above approach is used in order to filter suppliers that have been previously awarded a contract similar to the current one. Similarly, when looking for *suitable calls for tenders* from the point of view of a supplier, the information (including CPV codes) from the supplier's profile is assembled into a virtual tender, which is matched against the open calls for tenders.

5 Aggregated Analysis of Procurement Linked Data

5.1 Analysis Scenarios

The data on public contracts, in combination with external data retrieved from the linked data cloud, can be submitted to aggregated analysis. The beneficiaries of such analysis can be:

---

[43] They can be possibly replaced with two named graphs within a single quad store, each with a separate setting of access rights.

- *Journalists and NGOs*: the data may help them reveal corruption and clientelism in public sector.
- *Official government bodies*: both specific supervisory bodies that address the issues of transparency and fair competition and statistical offices that collect data as part of aggregated information on the national economy.
- *Bidders*: analysing the previous successful and unsuccessful tenders may be helpful when preparing a new one; in long term, the companies may also actively plan their bidding strategies based on procurement market trends (revealed by automated analysis).
- *Contracting authorities*: they want to understand the supply side in order to know how to formulate the contract conditions, in view of successful matchmaking. Good progress of a future contract may be derived from previous experience with certain bidders. An additional goal may be to attract an adequate number of bidders; excessively many bidders bring large overheads to the awarding process, while too low a number may reduce competition (and, under some circumstances, even lead to contract canceling by a supervisory body, due to an anti-monopoly action).

5.2   Analytical Methods

A straightforward approach to aggregated analysis is via *summary tables and charts* expressing the relationship between, e.g., the number of contracting authorities, contractors, contracts, tenders, lots, or geographical localities. The value of contracts can be calculated as a sum or average per authority, contractor, region, kind of delivery, classification of goods etc. Charts can be generated for presentation of these statistics split by various dimensions (e.g. bar charts) or showing the evolution (e.g. line charts, timeline). The geographical dimension is best presented on maps: detailed data can be shown as points on the map, e.g., pointers with shaded tooltips on OpenStreetMap. The data for such analysis are normally provided by SPARQL SELECT queries, which allow to both retrieve the data and perform basic aggregation operations.

More sophisticated analysis can be provided by *data mining tools*, which automatically interrelate multiple views on data, often based on contingency table. As an example, see a fragment of analysis of U.S. procurement data with respect to the impact various attributes of a contract notice may have on the subsequent number of tenders (Fig. 6).

The association rules listed in the table fragment regard both a CPV code of the contract object (mainObject attribute), originating from one of the core procurement dataset, and the population density attribute, originating from DBpedia. It indicates that contracts for 'Research and Development in the Physical, Engineering, and Life Sciences' in localities with higher population density tend to attract a high number of tenders (as higher interval values for the former mostly coincide with higher values for the latter, in the individual rules).

1	38	8.753	mainObject(*Research and Development in the Physical, Engineer*) & populationDensityPerKm2(>= 1700) >< Tenders(>=50)
2	39	7.562	mainObject(*Research and Development in the Physical, Engineer*) & populationDensityPerKm2(>= 1700) >< Tenders(>=30)
3	36	7.306	mainObject(*Research and Development in the Physical, Engineer*) & populationDensityPerKm2(>= 1600) >< Tenders(>=50)
4	32	7.190	mainObject(*Research and Development in the Physical, Engineer*) & populationDensityPerKm2(<1100; 1600) >< Tenders(>=50)
5	29	7.049	mainObject(*Research and Development in the Physical, Engineer*) & populationDensityPerKm2(<1000; 1500) >< Tenders(>=50)
6	37	6.490	mainObject(*Research and Development in the Physical, Engineer*) & populationDensityPerKm2(>= 1600) >< Tenders(>=30)
7	24	6.481	mainObject(*Research and Development in the Physical, Engineer*) & populationDensityPerKm2(<800; 1300) >< Tenders(>=50)
8	33	6.064	mainObject(*Research and Development in the Physical, Engineer*) & populationDensityPerKm2(<1100; 1600) >< Tenders(>=30)
9	1	6.022	mainObject(*Research and Development in the Physical, Engineer*) >< Tenders(N/A)
10	26	5.944	mainObject(*Research and Development in the Physical, Engineer*) & populationDensityPerKm2(<900; 1400) >< Tenders(>=50)
11	2	5.882	mainObject(*Research and Development in the Physical, Engineer*) >< Tenders(>= 100+)
12	31	5.866	mainObject(*Research and Development in the Physical, Engineer*) & populationDensityPerKm2(<1100; 1500) >< Tenders(>=30)
13	30	5.741	mainObject(*Research and Development in the Physical, Engineer*) & populationDensityPerKm2(<1000; 1500) >< Tenders(>=30)
14	28	5.695	mainObject(*Research and Development in the Physical, Engineer*) & populationDensityPerKm2(<1000; 1400) >< Tenders(>=30)
15	3	5.571	mainObject(*Research and Development in the Physical, Engineer*) >< Tenders(>=50)
16	18	5.494	mainObject(*Research and Development in the Physical, Engineer*) & populationDensityPerKm2(<400; 900) >< Tenders(>=50)
17	16	5.388	mainObject(*Research and Development in the Physical, Engineer*) & populationDensityPerKm2(<400; 700) >< Tenders(>=30)
18	17	5.235	mainObject(*Research and Development in the Physical, Engineer*) & populationDensityPerKm2(<400; 800) >< Tenders(>=30)
19	19	5.210	mainObject(*Research and Development in the Physical, Engineer*) & populationDensityPerKm2(<400; 900) >< Tenders(>=30)
20	20	5.080	mainObject(*Research and Development in the Physical, Engineer*) & populationDensityPerKm2(<500; 900) >< Tenders(>=30)
21	25	5.049	mainObject(*Research and Development in the Physical, Engineer*) & populationDensityPerKm2(<800; 1300) >< Tenders(>=30)
22	34	5.047	mainObject(*Research and Development in the Physical, Engineer*) & populationDensityPerKm2(<1200; 1700) >< Tenders(>=30)
23	35	4.965	mainObject(*Research and Development in the Physical, Engineer*) & populationDensityPerKm2(<1300; 2000) >< Tenders(>=30)
24	14	4.923	mainObject(*Research and Development in the Physical, Engineer*) & populationDensityPerKm2(<300; 800) >< Tenders(>=50)
25	4	4.916	mainObject(*Research and Development in the Physical, Engineer*) >< Tenders(>=30)

Fig. 6. Discovered factors correlated with number of tenders

5.3   Integration of Analytical Functionality into PCFA

Although the central role in the PCFA scenarios is reserved to matchmaking, there are also reserved slots for invocation of analytical features. Since this part of implementation has been ongoing till the final months of the project, it is not yet functional at the time of completing this chapter of the book. The analytical functionality will be at the disposal of the buyer (contracting authority), and will amount to:

- *Interactively exploring*, in graphical form, the linked data about
  - the current notice
  - a (matching) historical notice/contract
  - a relevant supplier, including its contracts.
- Viewing *suggested values* for the remaining pieces of contract notice information based on the already provided ones. The values will be provided by an inductively trained recommender.
- Getting an estimate of the *number of bidders* for (as complete as possible) contract notice information. For this, a predictive ordinal classifier will be developed.

When the integration of analytical functionality has been completed, usability testing by several contract authorities' representatives will take place.

6   Conclusions

The chapter outlined some of the promises and intricacies of using linked open data in the area of public procurement. It went through the different, yet interrelated partial tasks: data extraction and publishing (leveraging on Public Contracts Ontology as domain-specific, externally interlinked vocabulary), buyer/supplier matchmaking, and aggregated analytics.

Despite the numerous technical difficulties, especially as regards the coverage and quality of existing open data sources, it is clear that handling procurement data in RDF format and linking them to other (government, geographic, commercial, encyclopedic, etc.) data opens novel avenues for their matchmaking and aggregate analytics. The use of common data format (RDF), as well as common domain vocabulary (PCO) and classifications (such as CPV and TERYT) allow for integration of *external data*; furthermore, as the data are separated from their initial applications, they can be consumed by *third-party* applications originally developed for matchmaking over other procurement datasets. The often implicit model of legacy data can also be compared with a carefully crafted ontological domain model and *ambiguities* can be discovered. Finally, the data itself potentially becomes *cleaner* during the extraction and transformation process, so, even if some of the analytic tools require it to be downgraded back to simpler formats such as CSV, its value may be higher than the initial one.

Future work in this field will most likely concentrate on the last two tasks (matchmaking and analytics), however, with implication on extraction and publishing, too. Namely, precise matchmaking will require RDFization and publication of further information, some of which (such as detailed specifications of procured goods or services) will have to be extracted from *free text*. Exploitation of *product ontologies* such as those developed in the OPDM project[44] could then be beneficial. The analytic functionality should more systematically exploit external linked data as predictive/descriptive features [7]. Given the size and heterogeneity of the LOD cloud, smart methods of *incremental data crawling* rather than plain SPARQL queries should however be employed.

Finally, while the current research has been focused on the primary intended users of the PCFA, i.e. contract authorities and (to lesser extent) bidders, the remaining stakeholders should not be forgotten. While the generic features of contracts, products/services and bidders, captured by the *generalized* features (such as price intervals, geographic regions or broad categories of products) in data mining results, are important for these parties, directly participant in the matchmaking process, there are also *NGOs and supervisory bodies* that primarily seek *concrete* corruption cases. To assist them, graph data mining methods should be adapted to the current state of linked data cloud, so as to detect, in particular, instances of suspicious patterns over the (RDF) graph representing organizations (contract authorities, bidders and others), contracts and people engaged in them.

---

[44] http://www.ebusiness-unibw.org/ontologies/opdm/

References

1. Alvarez, J.M., Labra, J.E.: Semantic methods for reusing linking open data of the european public procurement notices. In: ESWC Ph.D. Symposium (2011)
2. Alvarez-Rodríguez, J.M., Labra-Gayo, J.E., Calmeau, R, Marín, A., Marín, J.L.: Innovative services to ease the access to the public procurement notices using linking open data and advanced methods based on semantics. In: 5th International Conference on Methodologies, Technologies and enabling eGovernment Tools (2011)
3. Cohen, W.M., Ravikumar, P., Fienberg, S.E.: A comparison of string distance metrics for name-matching tasks. In: Workshop on Information Integration on the Web, pp. 73–78 (2003)
4. d'Amato, C., Berka, P., Svátek, V., Wecel, K., (eds.): Proceedings of the International Workshop on Data Mining on Linked Data, with Linked Data Mining Challenge collocated with the European Conference on Machine Learning and Principles and Practice of Knowledge Discovery in Databases (ECMLPKDD 2013), Prague, Czech Republic, 23 September 2013, vol. 1082 of CEUR Workshop Proceedings, CEUR-WS.org (2013)
5. Distinto, I., d'Aquin, M., Motta, E.: LOTED2: an ontology of European public procurement notices. Semant. Web Interoper. Usability Appl. (2014) (Under review, IOS Press)
6. Michelfeit, J., Knap, T.: Linked data fusion in ODCleanStore. In: Glimm, B., Huynh, D. (eds.) International Semantic Web Conference (Posters and Demos), volume 914 of CEUR Workshop Proceedings (2012). http://CEUR-WS.org
7. Paulheim, H.: Exploiting linked open data as background knowledge in data mining. In: d'Amato, C. et al. [4]
8. Siemens: Study on the evaluation of the action plan for the implementation of the legal framework for electronic procurement (phase ii): analysis, assessment and recommendations. Technical report, July 2010
9. Valle, F., d'Aquin, M., Di Noia, T., Motta, E.: LOTED: exploiting linked data in analyzing European procurement notices. In: 1st Workshop on Knowledge Injection into and Extraction from Linked Data collocated with EKAW'10, Madrid, Spain (2010). http://CEUR-WS.org

Author Index

Printed in the United States
By Bookmasters